The Hands-On Home

"*The Hands-On Home* is the book that every household needs! It contains incredibly valuable wisdom that can help us minimize our consumerism and produce more of what we need, right in our own homes. Well organized with simple tips and recipes, Erica's engaging and witty tone will surely make the experience fun for anyone who wants to have a healthier and more abundant life!"

—JESSI BLOOM, author of *Free-Range Chicken Gardens*

"Get your hands on this detailed guide to turning your home into a center of production. Erica Strauss is one of the foremost practitioners of the new home economics."

—ERIK KNUTZEN, co-author of *The Urban Homestead* with Kelly Coyne

"Reading Strauss's handbook of modern homemaking is like having a very wise and funny friend at your elbow guiding the way towards a cleaner house, a healthier table, and a tastier pantry. With recipes for making everything from beeswax candles to divine homemade yogurt and tips on cleaning everything from soil-stained gardener hands to a greasy stove, Strauss proves that the road to a happy life is paved by taking pleasure in making and using simple things."

—WILLI GALLOWAY, author of *Grow Cook Eat*

The Hands-On Home

A Seasonal Guide to Cooking, Preserving & Natural Homekeeping

ERICA STRAUSS

Photographs by Charity Burggraaf
Illustrations and Lettering by Kate Bingaman-Burt

SASQUATCH BOOKS
SEATTLE

Printed in China

Published by Sasquatch Books
19 18 17 16 15   9 8 7 6 5 4 3 2 1

Editor: Susan Roxborough
Production editor: Em Gale
Design: Anna Goldstein
Illustrations and Lettering: Kate Bingaman-Burt
Photography: Charity Burrgraaf
Food styling: Julie Hopper
Copyeditor: Michelle Hope Anderson

Library of Congress Cataloging-in-Publication Data is available.

ISBN: 978-1-57061-991-5

Sasquatch Books
1904 Third Avenue, Suite 710
Seattle, WA 98101
(206) 467-4300
www.sasquatchbooks.com
custserv@sasquatchbooks.com

To Nick,

*I'd rather do nothing with you than everything
with anyone else, and everything with you most
of all. What something shall we do next?*

Contents

Recipe List

Year-Round

Spring

Summer

cooking

preserving

home care

personal care

Fall

cooking

preserving

home care

personal care

Winter

cooking

preserving

home care

personal care

Introduction

As we live and as we are, Simplicity—with a capital "S"—is difficult to comprehend nowadays. We are no longer truly simple. We no longer live in simple terms or places. Life is a more complex struggle now. It is now valiant to be simple: a courageous thing to even want to be simple. It is a spiritual thing to comprehend what simplicity means.

—FRANK LLOYD WRIGHT, *The Natural House*

How's your home life? If you are like most Americans, the honest answer to that question is, "What home life?"

Statistically, our homes are larger per person than they've ever been, and more crammed full of stuff than anyone a few generations ago could have dreamed possible. And yet, few of us spend much time at home. We sleep at home, and store things under our roof, and maybe, if we are very lucky, we have a job that lets us work from home once in awhile.

But we do not live in our homes, not really.

Our life is spent somewhere in the hours between the drive-through coffee we pick up in the morning on the way to work, the microwave meal eaten alone beneath the beige walls of our cubical, and the delivery pizza we order as we drive home.

We spend money to maintain and furnish our home, but we don't produce things there. The simple moments of being in our place, making a home, and rooting deep into the fabric of our community are now a rarity.

We trade our time and our skills for money, and then trade that money for the promise of things that will save us time. It's a vicious circle as we outsource the essentials of life: food, fuel, clothing, entertainment, and comfort, and then work to afford all that we've outsourced. We eat in our car, have a drink at a bar, and entertain ourselves by spending money we often don't have on stuff that will be in a landfill within a few years.

This is deeply unusual. For most of history, homes were where the essentials were handled. The small moments and daily rhythms of quietly cooking, preserving, cleaning, and caring for ourselves and our family have been an integral part of a well-lived life since the first Neanderthal felt compelled to sweep out a cave, make room for a hearth, and start boiling down mammoth fat for healing herb salves.

In our modern, connected economy, the temptation to outsource is always there, but more and more of us are rediscovering the joy and satisfaction in getting more hands-on in our own home, garden, and life. There is a renaissance of people who are turning their back on the recent logic of industrial meals, microwaved convenience, and daily drive-through. We have realized that jam, pickles, yogurt, beer, artisan bread, and delicious meals are far cheaper to make than to buy, and that they taste better because the ingredient list is simpler.

We've noticed those trendy eco-green methods for maintaining our home also happen to save a bunch of cash and keep our dollars out of the hands of companies that are basically in the toxic chemical business. Instead of stinky commercial cleaners, we use soap and sunlight to clean and freshen our homes. Instead of buying foods full of preservatives, we're preserving seasonal bounty from local farmers to enjoy all year round.

We are not radicals. We're just trying to find a new, more rewarding balance between the hands-on roots of our grandparents and great-grandparents and the consumption-driven convenience that screams at us from every street corner.

Many of these basic human skills have rural or homesteading roots, but even people who enjoy living in the highest density urban areas, in small apartments or shared housing, are proving every day that any home—no matter how small—can become a little more self-reliant, a little more deliberate, a little more hands on.

In focusing on what we can do, for ourselves, our family, and our community, instead of buying into a glitzy image of happiness dreamed up by some faraway marketing genius, we are re-embracing the temporarily abandoned notion of home economics.

The modern hands-on home and DIY movement is the latest effort in a long line of similar efforts. Every generation that has lived isolated from the rhythms of the land has grown out some wild-eyed component determined to reclaim an earlier, more honest, more agrarian influence for themselves. From Thoreau to the Back-to-the-Landers of the 1970s, claiming the good life through the sweat of your brow and the practice of the old skills has a noble, if occasionally kooky, pedigree.

What is unique about the modern productive-home movement is that my generation—people currently in their twenties to forties—are not necessarily interested in abandoning their careers, community, or that really good Thai restaurant down the street to live off-grid and off the land. We don't want to be isolated or drop out of society. We want to do what we can, where we are, with what we have, to build a more satisfying life for ourselves.

If a movement as diverse as the hands-on-home trend can be said to have any universal philosophy, it's that as our time and space allow, we nudge our home from consumption to production, from a mentality of "just buy it!" to "let's try to DIY it!"

This latest generation of hands-on homekeepers are aggressive consumers of information before anything else, and the unprecedented availability of knowledge makes it easier than ever for us to each find our own best path toward a life that balances our limited time and money with health, personal reward, and ecological and societal concerns.

Need to learn how to do something—anything? YouTube. Want to find a community of pickling freaks in your neighborhood to swap jars with? Meetup. Got a great idea for a new fermentation product? Kickstarter.

So instead of waiting for someone else—someone bigger and more powerful and more important—to tackle environmental, economic, or health issues at the painfully partisan macro level, we are using the power of our purse and our decision-making at the super-micro level to advocate for our values. We may not be able to directly influence national farm policies, but we sure as hell can influence the success of one particular small farmer or dairyman with our support.

While the scale of our consumption dependency and the resource use that accompanies it can seem daunting, the truth is that this system imbues us, the consumer, the end user of all those consumables, with the ultimate power. *If* we buy, *what* we buy, and *from whom* we buy can make or break giants of industry, local farmers, and every business in between. How and where we spend (or don't spend) our dollars allows us to nudge the whole system ever so slightly toward the things we value. That dollar in your wallet is power.

For this reason, hands-on homekeepers have come to view cooking dinner for oneself and one's family, from ingredients that either grew in the dirt or rolled in it, as a kind of delicious activism. When it is entirely possible to let huge corporations assemble all your meals from a profitable mix of corn syrup, soy protein isolate, and pink slime beef, opting to sit down with friends and family for a plate of home cookin' is a line in the sand.

This is a quiet advocacy, and it looks an awful lot like really great food on the table at night. It is disguised as kids picking blackberries and the scent of line-dried sheets on the bed. It feels like rhythm, both the rise and fall of the seasons and the shorter, sometimes monotonous, daily routines that make keeping a productive home really work.

Once you embark on your hands-on-homekeeping journey, you may well find, as I have, that it is a bit addictive. You may be having such great fun cooking for yourself and you may find such pride in that jar of jam that you are eager to take that next step into gardening or beekeeping or sewing or homemade herbal medicinals. Wonderful! There are so many amazing skills out there just waiting to be rediscovered!

But don't be afraid to take it slow at first. Like everything worth having, the feeling of accomplishment that comes with this homemade life takes some effort. It isn't given out freely—it's earned. Hours in front of a canning kettle can seem silly when your feet ache—after all, you could just buy strawberry jam from the store—but somehow when you spoon your own unique, perfect strawberry creation over a little homemade yogurt in the morning, the work is forgotten in the satisfaction of the moment.

The hands-on skills needed to keep a home humming are not hard to learn or implement. Make yogurt once and you've got the idea; make it twice and you're a master. Remember, people have been doing this kind of stuff for thousands of years without the benefit of electricity, active dry yeast, or food processors. You can totally do this.

The cooking, the organization, the homemade bread, the pantry full of healthy home-canned fruits and vegetable—that's all simple. It may not always be easy—ask anyone on their fiftieth quart of canned tomatoes in late August if hands-on homekeeping is easy and you may get a scowl as an answer—but it is simple.

The complicated part of this life is finding balance. How do we live in an information-age society without abandoning our claim to the simple joys of slower, more self-reliant days? How do we prioritize our time and our money so that our hands-on home enhances our freedom instead of diminishing it? How do we live an actively simpler life while surrounded by messages of ever-greater consumption? This is our great challenge.

In this book I lay out many of the techniques and tips I've used to get more hands-on and sustainable in my own home. Nudging my own home toward greater production has been a crooked path. Some efforts—like cooking from scratch most nights and eliminating nearly all commercial cleaners from my home—have been a huge success. Others, like getting all plastic out of my kitchen, have proved too much for where I am now.

But this is not an all-or-nothing thing. The ultimate goal of a hands-on homekeeper is to be proactive about shaping your own healthy domestic life. So take what works for you, what gives you the most bang for your literal or proverbial buck, and do that. As your life changes—and it inevitably will—what makes sense for you to do may change as well.

The key is to step back every once in awhile and ask yourself honestly if you are living the right life for you. What do you really value? Is your time and money being directed toward those things? Do your daily decisions encourage a healthy, engaged home or an exhausted, stressed-out home? Are you surrounded with things you cherish and use, or are you just drowning in a visual ocean of useless clutter?

If you can ask yourself some hard questions and answer honestly—just for yourself—then your own priorities and your own path become more clear.

All you have to do is take that first step.

Basics & Techniques

Simple Cooking

The routines I use in my kitchen are strongly influenced by my time working in professional kitchens. These systems allow me to keep my family fed, day in and day out, without turning to a bunch of industrial convenience food or going crazy.

YOU ARE MORE LIKE A PROFESSIONAL CHEF THAN YOU KNOW

The dedication and skill set required by the hands-on homekeeper has quite a bit in common with the professional chef. Both the productive home cook and the professional chef need to be aware of their food costs and should strive to minimize waste in food preparation. Both must consider their audience and prepare meals that nurture and comfort those who dine with them. Both must balance cooking with countless other tasks essential to running their kitchen or their home. Both must assess which food items should be made from scratch and which should be outsourced when time, quality, and money are taken into consideration.

In other ways, the challenges of the productive homekeeper in the kitchen are unique. After all, it's rare that a famous celebrity chef has to meet her obligations with a toddler hanging off her leg or a dog running through her kitchen. The responsibilities of cleaning, cooking, baking, and being nice to other people (professional chefs generally leave this task to waitstaff) rarely fall to one person in a professional kitchen, but they often do at home. In short, the productive homekeeper has to wear many hats.

Professional cooking is not, despite what TV shows depict, particularly glamorous. The hours are long and physical, the work can be monotonous, the kitchen is hot, and the pay is meager. And yet for all that, when I did that work, I loved it. It was excellent practice for productive homekeeping and an excellent source of inspiration for ways to make my own cooking more efficient and satisfying.

Every family has slightly different pressures, perspectives, and constraints when it comes to meals. Some operate under very tight budgets, while others have more income to allocate toward their food choices. Some people refrain from meat, others from gluten or grains or dairy. Some families eat a lot, others much less.

Organic, local, GMO-free, or otherwise sustainable food is of very high importance to some people but less critical to others. Sometimes a productive homekeeper is able to dedicate hours of his day to cooking, but, more frequently, cooking, food preservation, and home care must find space where they can in between careers, family, and other responsibilities.

And yet, for all the differences in our situations and values, a few tricks borrowed from old-school farm grandmas and professional chefs can help every modern-day hands-on homekeeper.

PROFESSIONAL CHEF TIPS FOR THE HANDS-ON HOME COOK

1. HAVE A MENU BUT BE FLEXIBLE

A good chef knows what she will be serving but can adapt to take advantage of a specialty item, a great deal on seasonal produce, or a loss leader from a vendor. The busy productive homekeeper will have a general menu plan but will also be willing to adapt when a friend hands her a few zucchini or the market has a great deal on grass-fed beef short ribs. This flexibility allows you to take advantage of good deals and seasonal bounty.

2. WASTE NOT, GET FIRED NOT

The profit margins in a restaurant are thin. There is simply no room in the budget to waste food. Every tub of salad dressing gets scraped clean; every part of the animal is utilized. Food is repurposed into new creations and no one complains about leftovers. The average American family of four throws out more than two thousand dollars of food every year. Pretty expensive trash or compost—that's money not available for college savings, retirement accounts, charitable giving, or travel. Keep your food waste tight and watch your savings account grow.

3. INGREDIENTS DO DOUBLE OR TRIPLE DUTY

The first restaurant I cooked in was a little pub with a heavy-drinking clientele and a cigarette smoke–stained ceiling. We sliced tomatoes for sandwiches and burgers, but the stem and blossom end of the tomato didn't make nice slices. Those bits got diced for salads. The amount of truly unusable tomato was about the size of a small marble. At home, tending to the bits and scraps of food means your food dollar goes further. The picked remains of a roast chicken aren't thrown out but made into broth. Fruit peels and trimmings can find a new life as a homemade vinegar. Stale bread becomes croutons or bread crumbs or a crowd-pleasing bread pudding.

4. OUTSOURCE WHERE IT MAKES SENSE

Sure, really good restaurants cook most of their food from raw ingredients—bread, sauces, soups, and entrées are all typically made from scratch. But even great restaurants rely on trusted suppliers for specialty items. You should too. For example, unless you keep dairy animals, all but the most dedicated DIYer will probably find that it just makes more sense to buy aged cheese than to make it. And while we can take it upon ourselves to make soy sauce, maybe the bottle of Kikkoman in the refrigerator will do the job just fine.

The line between DIY productivity and BUY outsourcing isn't clean—it's a messy moving target that shifts as life and other demands ebb and flow, but the job of the hands-on homekeeper is to remain thoughtful of why and how and when we outsource. Be conscious of your decisions.

5. EMBRACE SIMPLICITY

True foodies love to find the most obscure ingredients and spend hours perfecting a single meal. That's great, but it's not practical for the bulk of our cooking. If we are going to commit to doing it daily, most of our cooking has to be fast, simple, and delicious. There is nothing wrong with simple. In France, the vast majority of the bread is stunningly delicious and has exactly four ingredients: flour, water, salt, and yeast. Sure, you can make bread with lots more than these essential components, but is more really necessary?

Simple, productive kitchen craft is a lot like making a loaf of bread—think about the ingredients you need and how one component can be used in lots of different ways to suit the unique needs of your home and family. More is not always better. Often, more options, sauces, and boutique oils do little more than clutter up your space. Be very honest about how you live and cook when determining how to stock your larder. If you are gluten-free, wheat flour doesn't have a place in your kitchen. If your family is full of unabashed seafood haters, stocking your pantry with cheap, healthy sardines is hardly going to help streamline your nightly cooking. Learn how to substitute one ingredient for another and do not be afraid—ever—to adjust a recipe to the needs of your family and your taste.

6. IT'S EASIER TO COOK EVERY DAY

When I ran a small catering business, I didn't have employees. I rented space in a commercial kitchen and only took on two or three events a month. Every event had a massive ramp up and ramp down phase that was just exhausting. It was terrible! In contrast, I've worked for large-scale caterers who had three or four events—or more—every day. There is no ramp up or ramp down phase—just a steady hum of productivity that got channeled toward whatever event was needed. It's similar in a hands-on home kitchen: it's actually easier to just get in the rhythm of cooking daily, or very near to it. A natural routine establishes and you build up the basic components of easy, fast meals. The feeling that you are dragging yourself through the process of cooking every night as a separate and exhausting event fades as you build skills and a functional larder. Eventually, it really does become easier to cook at home than to run out for burgers—I promise!

7. THOSE AREN'T LEFTOVERS; THEY'RE PREP

I always laugh when I hear someone say, "I just don't like leftovers," or, more commonly, "but my spouse refuses to eat leftovers!" I think a disdain for leftovers comes from boredom—and I'm not too keen on reheating the same food three days in a row, either. But if you've eaten in a restaurant, or off a buffet line, or at someone's wedding, then you've eaten leftovers and probably paid good money for the privilege. No restaurant makes everything from scratch at the time the customer places an order—most food is preprepared up to a point to streamline service times without compromising quality. This is called "prep" and is essential for timely service in a busy restaurant.

At home, we can utilize the idea of prep to turn our refrigerators into fast meal-making helpers. For example, if you set aside a half hour or so after returning from the market to prepare all your produce—wash and dry lettuce, peel carrots, chop up kale, trim green beans and blanch them, etc.—then your refrigerator turns into a salad bar, only without the eleven-dollar-a-pound price tag. Go a bit further and turn some of those ingredients into long-lasting salads or pre-grill some meat. Now your refrigerator is a grab-and-go deli case. Go even a step further and set aside two hours every Sunday to precook several meals or the components to throw meals together and now weeknight dinners are a snap.

8. USE YOUR FREEZER

It's only trivially more time and effort to make a big batch of something than to make a small portion. Use this to your advantage by making double batches of basic dinners and freezing enough for those nights when you need heat-it-and-eat-it convenience. Unless it's a salad, there's a decent chance you can freeze it successfully. Cheese, baked goods, breakfast items like waffles and pancakes, meatballs, soups, stews, casseroles of all kinds, uncooked pizza, cooked rice, grains, and beans—all these items and more freeze beautifully. I even freeze raw scrambled eggs during the summer when my chickens are laying like crazy, for those slower production days in winter. Some folks go a step further, cooking an entire month's worth of meals in a day and stashing them in the freezer. While once-a-month cooking doesn't fit my family's style of eating, it can be a real lifesaver for some families.

9. ARGGGH, YE RECIPES BE MORE LIKE "GUIDELINES"

There's a scene in the movie *Pirates of the Caribbean* where old Pirate Captain Barbossa is explaining that the pirate's code is more like a "guideline." That's how recipes are. Read through a recipe carefully and make sure you understand what ingredients are needed and what kind of time commitment the recipe is going to take, but understand that a million variables—from the humidity in the air to the age of dry beans to the calibration of your oven—all effect the final outcome of your dish.

Truly great cooks must trust their senses more than rigid steps in a recipe, because, no matter how well tested a recipe is, your humble cookbook author cannot predict how all those variables will come together in your home. In the recipes in this book, I try to give descriptions of how the food will look and feel at various stages to help beginning cooks still developing their own culinary senses.

10. GO SEASONAL

Seasonal cooking is just better—better tasting, better for your pocketbook, and better for the local farmers you can support. This book is organized seasonally because so many of the rhythms of the hands-on homekeeper follow the natural rise and fall of the seasons. What grows near us and can be used in the kitchen or preserved for later changes. But cooking seasonally doesn't mean a brand-new plan every few weeks—sensible seasonal cooking is adaptive. The same basic recipe concept, like a simple flatbread or a fruit crisp, gets reimagined over and over in countless ways just by tweaking a component or two.

ESSENTIAL EQUIPMENT

It doesn't take a lot of gadgets to cook well. Your great-grandma probably put amazing food on the table with just knives, a cutting board, a big pot, and a couple of cast-iron skillets. And truthfully, day in and day out, those old classics are still the best and will handle all the essential tasks and allow you to feed yourself and your family extremely well.

Because of my background in professional cooking, I've tried a lot of kitchen gear. Some of it helps make time in the kitchen far nicer, and some of it just takes up precious cabinet space. Here are the tools I recommend.

CAST-IRON SKILLETS: Once you go cast iron you never go back. My nested collection of cast-iron skillets stays on the stove all the time. The best way to keep cast iron in great shape is to use it! Cook with it often, scrub it without soap to clean it, dry it well, and rub it with a little oil before you store it. At a minimum, get a ten-inch skillet for searing, sautéing, and pan-roasting. Once the cast-iron bug hits you, you'll probably start scouring thrift stores for vintage pieces in unusual sizes. My six-inch skillet is perfect for fried eggs, and I even have a giant seventeen-inch skillet for really big meals and campouts.

CUTTING BOARDS: Because I often put my cutting boards in the dishwasher, I prefer professional-style plastic boards. There is an argument about which type of board is more sanitary, plastic or wood. Once plastic has been used for a while, it is very hard to thoroughly clean by hand without a chemical sanitizer like bleach, because the microscopic chopping marks in the board will harbor bacteria. Wood cutting boards should never be put in the dishwasher, and so they cannot be heat sanitized. They, too, can build up grooves over time that make truly thorough cleaning difficult. However, most hardwood used for cutting boards contains natural tannins that have antimicrobial properties. Whichever board you prefer, I recommend owning at least two, so that you can always keep raw meats and other potentially contaminating foods well away from ready-to-eat food.

TIP: If your cutting boards tend to move around on you, wet a dish towel and wring it out. Lay the damp towel between the counter and the cutting board. No more slip!

DUTCH OVEN: Invest in a cast-iron or an enameled cast-iron Dutch oven. Look for one between eight and twelve quarts, depending on the size of your family. Pure cast iron is cheaper and heavier than its enameled equivalent, such as those made by Le Creuset. Heavier can be good, in that more metal holds and retains more heat, but many people will find a large cast-iron Dutch oven too heavy and ungainly to comfortably pick up, particularly once it's filled with something hot and bubbly. Enameled cast iron, while still very substantial, will be somewhat lighter in weight. It is also lower maintenance and can even be run through the dishwasher. Enameled cast iron is also better for cooking items containing tomato, wine, or vinegar, because it will not react to the acid in food the way cast iron can. Its drawback is primarily price. The best-known brands of enameled cast iron are quite expensive.

FOOD PROCESSOR: Where would I be without my food processor? I honestly can't think of a more valuable kitchen helper. I use mine nearly daily. From quick pie crusts to shredded carrots to pesto, a good, heavy food processor like those made by Cuisinart help with so many kitchen tasks. It's my number one pick for most versatile small appliance.

IMMERSION BLENDER: I adore my immersion blender. I use it to make everything from carrot soup to apricot jam to mayonnaise. Immersion blenders aren't too expensive—I've had a thirty-dollar model I got at a drugstore for about ten years now and it's still going strong. Look for one with an included chopper attachment for maximum versatility.

INSTANT-READ THERMOMETER AND KITCHEN SCALE: An instant-read thermometer takes the guess work out of meat doneness, ensures your milk is at the right temperature before you culture it into yogurt, and gives you confidence when making pectin-free jams. Measuring ingredients by weight is more accurate than measuring by volume, and a kitchen scale is priceless when you need to work with precision. These two tools will help you get greater control over your cooking, food preservation, and even your home and personal care products.

KNIVES: Buy a chef's knife, a bread knife, a paring knife, in that order. You should buy high-quality knives that are comfortable in your hand. There is really no substitute for feel; look for one with a handle that fits your hand. Small-handed people may feel more comfortable with a seven-inch santoku-style knife than an eight- or ten-inch chef's knife. Heavier is better, up to point, but never buy a knife so heavy that it might fatigue you to use it. Signs of quality on a chef's knife include a full tang, multiple rivets in the handle, a well-balanced bolster, and a perfectly straight edge. Most knives are high-carbon stainless steel. This metal can be sharpened to a long-lasting, durable edge, and it's easy to clean. Like any tool, knives require frequent maintenance. I am not a fan of any of the moderately priced roller-type knife sharpeners on the market. These leave ragged edges and remove far too much metal for my liking. I recommend learning how to sharpen your knives on an oilstone or taking them in every six to twelve months for professional sharpening. This service is provided for only a few dollars per knife at many grocery stores, butcher shops, and specialty knife stores. Serrated (bread) knives are a pain to resharpen. Generally, I would only have my serrated knife resharpened if I noticed a loss in its effectiveness.

LARGE POT: If you are planning on doing any water-bath canning (see page 25), you're going to need a large pot anyway. Save your money and your storage space and skip those thin-walled, bumpy-bottomed, speckled-enamel canning kettles and get a big multipurpose pot instead. I have several large pots. The most used is a twelve-quart pot, about ten inches in diameter and ten inches tall. This is plenty big for cooking pasta, blanching vegetables, simmering beans, or making big batches of sauce. If you tend to cook in smaller quantities, this might be more than you need. Stainless is better than aluminum so you can cook acidic sauces without worry of off flavors.

PORTION SCOOPS: A good friend of mine once told me about how she'd made a big batch of meatballs for freezing. "They turned out so great, but it took forever to roll them!" she told me. "Don't you have a portion scoop?" I asked, incredulous. "You gotta get a portion scoop."

Portion scoops look like ice-cream scoops with a little wire sweeper on the inside of the scoop. Don't use them for ice cream—the wire sweeper isn't rugged enough to dig through hard frozen ice cream without bending. Instead, use them for cookie dough, muffin or pancake batter, meatballs, hamburger patties, crab cakes—anything where creating a consistent-size product gives you a better, more uniform outcome. Pro tip: Skip the overpriced and weak portion scoops available at fancy kitchen stores and go straight for the industrial versions available at restaurant supply stores. They will have color-coded plastic handles and a number that indicates the scoop size, based on how many level portions of the scoop will fill a one-quart container. A #60 scoop creates a one-tablespoon portion, a #8 creates a four-ounce portion. Get the sizes that make sense for the items you scoop.

Basics & Techniques

The next time I saw my friend, she had taken my advice and stopped by the restaurant supply store for her very own portion scoops. "It's changed my meatball-lovin' life!" she enthused, no longer bound to unnecessary meatball-maker tedium. Get a portion scoop or four.

SHEET PANS AND PARCHMENT PAPER: You really can't have too many sheet pans. In the restaurant industry, most everything is size standardized. I use the same heavy-duty, eighteen-by-thirteen-inch aluminum sheet pans called "half sheet pans" that are used in restaurants all over the country. These nest politely together, last basically forever, and are inexpensive at restaurant supply stores. I also highly recommend parchment paper. I buy a thousand-sheet case of parchment pan liners at a restaurant supply store for about forty dollars every five or six years. Flat sheets of parchment are far easier to work with than rolls of the stuff.

STAND MIXER: A stand mixer—KitchenAid is the most well-known brand—is a great tool if you do a lot of baking, bread kneading, egg-white whipping, or similar. I love my twelve-year-old stand mixer and use it often, but it's an expensive and bulky purchase. Folks who bake only occasionally may find it's not worth the investment. Optional attachments for stand mixers expand the versatility of this appliance but are also quite spendy. I've had mixed luck with the attachments I've purchased for my KitchenAid. The meat grinder and pasta roller are quite good; the ice cream maker and sausage stuffer didn't impress me. Proceed with caution.

WHISKS, SPOONS, AND OTHER HAND TOOLS: I keep a variety of simple wire whisks, spring-loaded stainless tongs, sturdy wooden spoons, and high-heat silicone spatulas in a crock near my stove. These are the basic tools I turn to every day. I highly recommend investing in a heavy-duty, high-heat spatula. I once grabbed a cheap rubber spatula to stir a simmering pot of tomato sauce and melted my spatula right into the sauce! What a waste!

I also recommend the very thin, wide stainless steel spatulas called fish spatulas. They are ideal for manipulating and turning delicate food on a pan or a grill. I use my fish spatula for fish, burgers, pancakes, fritters, hash browns, and more. Anything that needs to be flipped for even cooking needs a fish spatula.

BASIC TECHNIQUES

Here are a few common techniques you'll see repeated throughout this book because they are the techniques I use, over and over, to get dinner on the table in my own home.

BRAISING: Low and slow cooking with a bit of flavorful liquid, this is the technique that turns tough, inexpensive cuts of meat into fork-tender yumminess. It's ideal for meat, but also a great technique for sturdy root vegetables, cabbage, or onions.

Here are the basic steps to any braise: If it's meat, season and sear the heck out of it. If it's a vegetable, don't. Put it in a pan in a single layer. Pour some very flavorful sauce-type liquid in, enough to come about halfway up the side of what you're braising. Cover and cook over low heat for as long as it takes to make your ingredient super tender. Braised meats keep well for several days in the refrigerator and taste better when reheated. They also freeze well, so braises are a great choice for batch cooking.

PUREED SOUPS: An immersion blender makes these a snap. Simmer just about any vegetable in broth until it's very tender—add a bit of seasoning and a few drops of something acidic and perhaps something creamy—and blitz until smooth. I love pureed soups because they are so forgiving, and yet give a pleasing, elegant result. If you have young kids who have issues with texture, or who only eat "hidden" vegetables, pureed soups can be your best friend.

Here are the basic steps to any pureed soup: To build flavor with aromatics, heat some fat in a big pot and add garlic, onion, or spices. Cook gently until fragrant, then add in broth or water—whatever the liquid base of your soup will be—and a generous dash of salt. Add in dry herbs like bay leaf, and anything that takes a fairly long time to cook—soaked beans, potato, carrot, or winter squash—and simmer everything together gently until it's falling apart. At this point, pull out anything you don't want in the finished soup, like old herb twigs, and add in anything that doesn't take long to cook, like fresh green herbs. Puree everything until smooth, adjust seasoning with a bit of salt or vinegar, and voilà—soup.

ROASTING MEAT: Roasting a big piece of meat—anything from a chicken to a prime rib to a pork butt—tends to be a special occasion technique, which is why I think it intimidates people. You spend a lot of money on a big hunk of meat and you don't want to mess it up. But really, roasting is simple if you understand how hot to cook the meat and how long to cook it.

To determine cooking temperature, assess the shape and density of the meat. The bigger and denser the meat, the lower the temperature you want to use. The smaller and more tender the meat, the higher the temp you can use. Roasts that are shaped like basketballs should be cooked low and slow; roasts that look more like baseball bats can be cooked at higher temps. If you're not sure, 300 degrees F for large beef or pork roasts is a good rule of thumb. I go much hotter for my roast chicken, because it's not very dense—the cavity of the bird allows the meat to cook evenly even at high temperatures.

Either way, the perfect roast has a delicious caramelized crust on it. Moisture inhibits the formation of this crust, and fat helps, so make sure your roasts are dry when you pop them in the oven and, if your roast isn't naturally covered with a fat layer, give it a rub with oil.

The lower the cooking temp, the longer the cooking time. Get an instant-read thermometer, and pull your meat when it's a few degrees below your ideal doneness. Then let it rest in a warm place for one to two minutes per pound of meat. While the meat is resting, the doneness coasts up the final few degrees (this is called "carryover cooking") and the juices of the meat become more uniformly distributed, so your roast doesn't leak all its juices onto the cutting board as soon as you slice into it. This resting step really makes a difference—please don't skip it.

meat doneness

All meat doneness temperatures listed here are in the degrees Fahrenheit at which to pull the meats from the heat source; carryover cooking will take the final temperature up a few degrees. Ground beef or pork should be cooked to 160 degrees F; ground poultry should be cooked to 165 degrees F. Use an instant-read thermometer and you can't go wrong.

	RARE	MEDIUM-RARE	MEDIUM	MEDIUM-WELL	WELL
BEEF	120	128	135	145	155
LAMB	120	128	135	140	155
PORK	130	140	150	155	160
CHICKEN	←		165		→

ROASTING VEGETABLES: To roast vegetables, heat and fat are your friends. Set the oven somewhere between 400 and 475 degrees F. Denser foods, like potatoes, can be cooked a bit lower; tender vegetables like asparagus should be cooked as hot as you can brave it.

Put a piece of parchment on a sheet pan—this makes cleanup so much easier. Try to cut all your vegetables about the same size so the pieces cook in the same amount of time. The more flat surface you can give your vegetables, the more tasty caramelization you'll get.

Coat everything with oil. Don't get squeamish about using a generous glug of olive oil here—you want every piece to be lightly coated. Season with salt, pepper, and any herbs or spices you like. Put the vegetables on the sheet pan in a single layer—if you crowd your veggies, they will steam instead of roasting.

Cook as long as it takes to get them tender, with nice dark caramelized patches where they sat on the pan. This takes about ten minutes for small, tender vegetables like asparagus or broccoli, and up to forty minutes for larger pieces of dense carrot or potato. Stir occasionally if your veggies will be roasting for longer than about fifteen minutes to get more uniform caramelization. When the vegetables are fully roasted, serve as is or sprinkle a bit of cheese over the top.

SAUTÉING: Sautéing is quickly cooking small pieces of food over high heat with a little bit of fat. The food is stirred or shaken frequently. Stir-frying is a variation of sautéing. This is a great technique for fast weeknight dinners because you can build an entire meal—protein, vegetable, sauce—in one pan.

Here are the basic steps to sautéing: Get everything ready before you start since you'll move fast. Heat the pan, then add enough oil or other fat to thinly coat. When the oil shimmers, add any ingredients that you want to season the oil—like garlic, onion, or spices. When these aromatics are fragrant, add the ingredient that will take longest to cook first, then add ingredients in reverse-cooking-time order so everything finishes up at the proper doneness. Finish up, if needed, with seasoning or a sauce.

SEARING: Deeply browning the outside of a piece of meat, fish, vegetable, or fruit by exposing it to very high temperatures, searing caramelizes surfaces and adds a bunch of really delicious flavors to your food. It doesn't "lock in juices" or anything silly like that—but it does make food golden-brown, crusty, and extra delicious. There is a saying in professional cooking: if we can make food crispy on the outside and tender on the inside, people will eat it. There is something deeply ingrained that makes caramelized, crispy, and seared food delicious to most people.

One of the most reliable ways to make a food crispy on the outside is to deep-fry it, which is why deep-fried items are so often "comfort foods." Deep-frying is a pain in the home kitchen—I do it only very rarely—but roasting, sautéing, and grilling all provide opportunities to get that perfect sear. Any time we expose the dry surface of food to high temperatures, the proteins undergo a process called the Maillard reaction while the sugars in the food undergo caramelization. Both of these processes brown the surface of the food and create a cascade of yummy new flavors. Food cannot sear until the surface reaches around 300 degrees F, and generally hotter is better. Any moisture on the food surface will keep the food in steam mode, not sear mode. A bit of fat on the food or in the pan greatly increases heat transfer and helps food sear well.

SEASONING: This might refer to the addition of any seasoning or spice, but it more commonly means salting. How you use salt critically impacts the quality of your food. One of the reasons restaurant food tends to taste good is because professional chefs are not shy with the salt. (The other reason is butter, which we also use with happy abandon.) So consider seasoning a critical cooking technique, just like searing or roasting.

A few tips: Get good salt. This doesn't mean some exotic pink sea salt from Himalaya. I, along with nearly all professional chefs I've ever worked with, prefer Diamond Crystal kosher salt. It's a widely available flaky salt that's easy to measure "by feel" once you get used to it. Salt throughout the cooking process, not just at the end. For example, heavily salt cooking water for anything starchy like pasta or potatoes, or for green vegetables you want to blanch. When the food cooks, that salt will be pulled into the food along with moisture, helping to create an evenly seasoned product. Seasoning vegetables you are cooking in a pan will tend to help the veggies release moisture. This is good if you want to evaporate that moisture, but bad if you want the veggies to sear.

Simple Preserving

I made my first jar of jam many years ago, from a Costa Rican pineapple I bought at Costco. There was nothing local or organic about it. I remember that week very well. I was cooking on a 1950s Hotpoint stove. It was smooth white enamel with thick electric coils that curled like an extruded sausage. Built long before anyone thought to moderate the energy use of appliances, those burners glowed like campfire coals just hit with a gust of wind.

I started with the pineapple, and in the next twenty-four hours went on to make peach jam and strawberry jam too, in full defiance of seasonality. I lost my enthusiasm for the process just as it was time to scrub all the burned sugar and fruit from that lovely vintage stove.

I didn't grow up around canning, and this was long, long before the current revival of food preservation swept the nation. So maybe it was strange that I felt a sudden compulsion to put food in jars. Or maybe not: several days later I found out I was pregnant with my first child.

Storing food away has always had a sort of domestic, nesting, hunker-down-and-get-ready-for-winter vibe. Perhaps the instincts of hundreds of generations of farm grandmas—"Be prepared! Build a pantry!" they would whisper through the ages—were kindled in me right alongside that sparkle that would grow to be my daughter.

I have a hard time now imagining not preserving my own food. I have become spoiled by a larder full of the foods I need to build fast and easy meals, and by the confidence of knowing what all these prepared foods contain and where they came from.

Food preservation can be very intimidating to the beginner, and unfamiliar equipment and techniques can make things like pressure canning or fermentation seem pretty scary. But remember that food preservation takes many, many forms—even just refrigerating milk is a form of short-term food preservation, and you do that all the time, right? From the wild-yeast Lambic beers of the Belgians to the sour-milk yogurt of the Mongols to the sun-dried fruit of the Romans, as long as there have been people, we've practiced methods to extend the life of seasonal and highly perishable foods. You can totally do this.

But why should you—hip modern human that you are, with access to well-stocked grocery stores—preserve your own food? Here's why I get steamy with my canning kettle.

THE FIVE C'S OF HOME PRESERVING

1. COST—ARTISAN RESULTS FOR MASS-MARKET PRICES

Sure, I can get blackberry jam at the store on sale. Unless I go for the very high-end artisan jam, it'll be mostly high fructose corn syrup and added pectin and not much fruit, but it'll be cheap. Or, I can grow or glean or buy fruit in season at rock-bottom prices from farmers I know and spend an afternoon making all the jam I'll need for the whole year. My ingredient cost will probably be less than the crappy jam at the store, and the quality will be better than the best stuff available for sale.

2. CONVENIENCE—FAST FOOD YOUR WAY

We all have nights where we just want dinner handled fifteen minutes ago. I'm no exception, so I build that convenience right into my food preservation. A little work up front stocks my pantry with easy basics that make meals fast and simple. Canned garbanzo beans, shelf-stable soups and chili, heat-and-eat meats, long-lasting fermented fresh salsa, rows of crushed tomatoes, and little jars of sauces take much of the work out of dinner on those nights when I need it to be easy. When you only have to go to the pantry, pop open jars, and assemble your dinner components, home cooking really is fast food.

3. CUSTOMIZATION—MAKE IT HOW YOU LIKE IT

Good luck buying peach jam spiked with ginger and bourbon or finding fermented pickled carrots with just the right amount of spice. When you preserve your own food you can—within the confines of what is necessary for a safe and wholesome product—adjust spices and flavorings to your taste. For those folks with food allergies or sensitivities, DIY food preservation can be the best option for avoiding food additives common in commercially processed products.

4. CONTROL—OF YOUR MONEY, FOOD WASTE, AND MORE

If you go far enough up the chain, nearly all commercially available, mass-market prepared foods are owned by huge (and I mean really giant!) international food processors. Even if the packaging looks like something from Farmer Joe's Happy Family Farm, chances are the profits of that box are going to a company that doesn't give one fig about Farmer Joe, or his family farm, or you—as long as commodities like corn and soy stay as cheap as possible and you keep buying.

This is something that, as thoughtful consumers, we need to consider. The money we spend is supporting someone's business practices. By putting in some of the effort of preserving food myself, I can afford to support the folks I want to more of the time. Besides, it's nice to know the orchardist who grew the peaches you made into peach butter.

When you take on some of these actions yourself, you also radically reduce your waste. Some of my canning jars are older than me and still going strong. I use my standard glass canning jars for everything from jam to yogurt, infusions to ferments. There is very little to no packaging waste associated with most home-preserved food. Even if the bulk of your preserving is freezing in a heavy-duty ziplock bag, you're still able to reuse that bag several times before it wears down—something you could never do with commercial plastic packaging.

5. CRAZY FUN—PRODUCTIVE HOBBIES ARE A BLAST

There's a reason so many people have taken up canning, fermenting, and other forms of DIY food preservation: it's fun! I love the process and I love stocking my pantry with home-canned (and mostly homegrown) foods. I love experimenting with the delicious, powerful, pungent flavors of ferments and capturing bright, ripe, seasonal fruit in a sauce or jam or compote. I love knowing I can enjoy preserved produce from my garden and from the farms of my local growers even when there is snow on the ground. I love giving my kids snacks of home-dried fruit or cracking open a jar of homemade chicken broth to make soup on a cold day. I love not being dependent on a supermarket for every little thing, and I love the feeling of confidence and pride, knowing that my efforts have helped my family achieve food security for the upcoming year.

Basics & Techniques

TOP TIPS FOR FOOD PRESERVATION

1. FOCUS ON CONVENIENT, VERSATILE MEAL COMPONENTS

Specialty jams have that fun Pinterest appeal, but if you have enough space and resources to tackle pressure canning, heat-and-eat meals and staples like beans, broth, soups, stews, chili, and more will make your life easier and are good to have on hand in a power outage.

2. DON'T THROW GOOD FOOD AFTER BAD

One year, in an effort to use up a bumper crop of green tomatoes, I made eight pints of green tomato mincemeat. I took those free tomatoes that I didn't want to waste and I added sugar, spices, raisins, vinegar, apples, and more to the mix. Well, we had no idea what to do with the mincemeat and didn't like it all that much anyhow. After two years of guilt, I composted the contents to get my jars back. I hate food waste, but in a misguided attempt to not waste my green tomatoes, I ended up wasting even more food.

3. FREEZE FOR EASE

Canning is trendy and canned food is very convenient, but freezing is the easiest way to put food by. If you have the space and budget, a separate chest or upright freezer makes it far easier to stock up on farm-raised meat, seasonal seafood, produce from your garden, and homemade freezer meals. The upfront costs of a separate freezer and the ongoing cost to maintain items at 0 degrees F should be assessed against the savings of bulk purchasing to see if that kind of investment makes sense for your family.

4. . . . OR FREEZE TO BUY TIME

If canning is the end goal, you can still lean on your freezer in the short-term. Berries, fruits, and tomatoes that will be cooked down for jam or sauce can be popped whole into the freezer and held for a few months until you have more time to can them. This is also a great way to shift some of summer's preserving to fall or winter when the weather is cooler.

5. IF YOUR TIME IS LIMITED, THINK SMALL BATCH

Small batches of jam, pickles, tomatoes, and sauce can be managed in an evening after work. Large processing jobs of a hundred pounds of tomatoes or a whole bushel of corn can take the better part of a day and may not be worth it depending on your goals and circumstances.

6. BIG-BATCH CANNING IS MORE FUN WITH A FRIEND OR TWO

If you do go in for a big can-o-rama, why not make a party of it? Pick the kitchen with the biggest stove and the most counter space; have everyone bring their produce, jars, and the biggest pots they own; and make a work party of it. Cold beer is typically appreciated after a few hours in front of the kettle.

7. BRINE FERMENTING IS FASTER AND SIMPLER THAN VINEGAR PICKLING, ESPECIALLY FOR SMALL BATCHES OF VEGETABLES

Select fermented foods for small batches, traditional flavor, and health benefits, and go with vinegar pickling and canning when you want a big batch of one flavor of pickle that will last for a full year.

8. CONSIDER STORAGE FOR FERMENTED PRODUCTS

Unless you have a traditional root cellar (and if you do I'm jealous!), your fridge will probably be the best place for your fermented vegetables. Keep this in mind when deciding what to ferment, and in what quantities.

9. MAKE HAY WHILE THE SUN SHINES AND MAKE SAUERKRAUT WHENEVER

Some items, such as apples or beets or cabbage, have a fresh eating season of four or five months or more, and some items, like dry beans, can be dealt with at any time of the year. Preserve these things during the slower days of late fall or winter, and leave high summer and early fall for the bounty of fresh fruits and tender vegetables that won't keep.

BASIC FOOD PRESERVATION TECHNIQUES

In this book, we talk about water-bath canning (instructions follow), pressure canning (see page 32), and lacto-fermentation (see page 41). This is not even close to the full range of ways people preserve food, but my editors tell me that this book is too long already, so I had to draw the line somewhere. If you like this kind of thing, I encourage you to explore other methods of food storage, including drying, root cellaring, salting, curing, or smoking; brewing, winemaking, and other forms of alcoholic fermentation; sugaring, candying, and preservation in honey; and many more.

water-bath canning

Water-bath canning is what most folks think of as canning. When you see a photo of an adorable woman with a great manicure and a cute apron, carefully placing jewel-toned jars into a steaming, speckled kettle—that's water-bath canning.

Here's how it works: High-acid foods like fruits are turned into strawberry jam or applesauce or peach slices to prepare them for canning. Or low-acid foods like vegetables are tuned into high-acid pickles or relishes through the addition of sufficient vinegar, citric acid, lemon juice, or other high-acid ingredients. Once the high-acid food is prepared, it's measured into a spotlessly clean canning jar, sealed, and then placed into a pot of boiling water to be processed for a specific amount of time.

At sea level, the food inside the jar reaches 212 degrees F, which is hot enough to kill most—but not all—pathogens and spoilage organisms. High-altitude canners have to make adjustments to their processing time to compensate for the lower temperature of boiling water at higher altitudes.

The combination of heat-treating the food and removing all the oxygen from the jar puts water-bath-canned food in a kind of stasis. The quality of the food deteriorates only very slowly. Properly home-canned foods are safe to eat for several years but should be consumed within a year for best quality.

essential equipment

You don't need much for water-bath canning, but a few tools will make the job much more pleasant.

CANNING JARS AND THEIR LIDS: Most popular and widely available are standard-size threaded jars with two-piece lids, such as Ball and Kerr jars, both made by Jardin Home Brands. Other jars, such as Weck, are made from all glass in the European tradition, with a rubber gasket for sealing. These type of jars are gaining in popularity but are more expensive and less common in the United States.

LARGE POT TO USE AS A CANNING KETTLE: This doesn't have to be one of those speckled-enamel beasts, it just needs to be wide enough to accommodate your preferred number of jars and deep enough for boiling water to cover those jars by two inches. I recommend a pot at least four inches taller that the jar you're using, to give some headroom for a rolling boil.

RACK: You'll need a rack that will fit inside your canning kettle and allow free circulation of the water all around your jars. Anything that keeps the jars off the bottom of the kettle will do. Round cake cooling racks are great, and in a pinch I just zip-tie old rusted, narrow-mouthed rings together and use those.

JAR LIFTER: This is a special type of tongs designed to grip securely around the neck of a canning jar and lift it out of boiling or very hot water so you never experience a slipped jar and the terrible combination of boiling hot strawberry jam and shattered glass all over your feet.

JAR BUBBLER: This is a long, pokey tool that helps you remove the bubbles from jars after you fill them but before you process them. Wooden chopsticks do the job well if you don't want to buy a dedicated bubbler tool. Never use something metal—like a butter knife—as a jar bubbler; the metal utensil may leave microscopic scratches on the inside of the jar and make the jar more likely to crack in processing.

CANNING FUNNEL: Designed to fit in canning jars, this will help you get your food in the jars instead of all over the counter. A friend of mine gave me a canning funnel with measurements on the edge that confirm accurate headspace. I love it!

basic steps

1. Read the recipe all the way through and make sure you understand what you'll be doing and have everything you will need to proceed.

2. Take care of any advance processing in the recipe before proceeding. For example, a recipe may call for an overnight maceration of fruit with sugar.

3. Inspect your jars and lids. Make sure the jars are spotlessly clean, and check each one for hairline cracks or defects in the jar lip. If you see any kind of damage, even an itty-bitty nick on the edge of the jar, don't use that jar for canning. It might still be okay for dry storage, but not for food processing. Assemble as many new, unused lids and bands in good condition as you will need. Wash these well, then set aside.

4. Boil your jars to sanitize and pre-warm the glass. Set the rack on the bottom of the boiling water-bath canner or pot and arrange your empty, inspected jars in the kettle. Fill the jars and kettle with fresh, potable water to just over the top of the jars (just push the jars back down if they attempt to float up in the water) and set the kettle on a back burner over high heat. It can take quite awhile for a full kettle to come up to a boil, so get this started first. Let the water boil for ten minutes, then, if you are still preparing your recipe, keep the canner covered to prevent excessive evaporation and turn the heat down to maintain a bare simmer. As you near the canning step, just turn the burner back up to return the water to a boil.

5. Set out the tools you'll need for canning. I recommend a jar bubbler, jar lifter, ladle, and canning funnel at a minimum. You'll also need a clean, lint-free towel or paper towels for wiping the rims of the jars. I set out a sheet pan to serve as a staging area when I'm filling my jars.

6. Prepare your recipe. This is just like cooking—you chop, simmer, and stir—but there's not really room for playing around. Because the acid levels of water-bath-canned preserves must be aggressively accurate to prevent the potential growth of botulism (see page 36), you should stick to the quantities and ingredients given. You must be particularly careful never to increase the quantity of low-acid ingredients in a recipe.

7. When your recipe is ready to transfer into jars, turn the heat down under the recipe so nothing scorches while you fiddle with your jars. Then, use the jar lifter to carefully remove the jars from the canning kettle, tipping the hot water back into the kettle as you go, and move the jars to the filling area. Ladle a bit of the boiling water from the kettle into a small bowl or glass measuring cup; you will use this later to wipe the rims of your jars. Working calmly but quickly, set the canning funnel in your first jar and ladle your recipe in, up to the specified headspace. Really try to be accurate with headspace to ensure all the air is exhausted from the jar during the water-bath processing.

8. Use your jar bubbler to remove any air pockets from the jar and, if necessary, top up the jar with additional product to get to the stated headspace.

9. Transfer the funnel to the next jar and repeat the filling and bubbling step until all jars are full.

10. Carefully dip a lint-free towel or paper towel into the hot, clean water you ladled from the kettle. Wipe the rims of each jar completely and thoroughly. Set the flat lids centered on the jars, then hold the lids steady while screwing on the bands. Screw the bands just fingertip tight; do not overtighten.

11. Using your jar lifter, carefully lift the jars into the boiling water-bath canning kettle and double check that the water is at least two inches over the tops of the jars. When the kettle returns to a full rolling boil, put the lid on the kettle and start the timer.

12. Process the jars for the full time specified in the recipe, keeping the canning kettle at a full boil for the entire processing time. Consult the chart with time adjustments for altitude (see page 31) as appropriate.

13. When the processing time is complete, turn off the heat and let the jars sit for 5 minutes. Then carefully remove the jars from the canning kettle with the jar lifter. Lift jars straight up and set them straight down as you remove them from the canning kettle; tilting the jars at this stage could prevent strong seals. Set the jars on a clean kitchen towel with a bit of space between each jar. Avoid cool or drafty spots—these can lead to overly quick cooling and an increased chance of siphoning and poor seals. Don't push down on the tops of any jars, tighten rings, or in any other way fiddle with the jars. Resist the temptation!

14. Soon you'll start to hear the satisfying PING! of sealing jars. Small jars tend to seal more quickly than large jars. Let the jars sit undisturbed for eight to twenty-four hours before checking to see if any seals failed to form. Press the center of the lid gently; it shouldn't move or pop up and down when you press it. If the lid does spring back when you press it, the jar has not sealed. Place jars with failed seals in the refrigerator for consumption within the next few days.

15. Remove canning lid rings and wash, dry, and label your successfully sealed jars. Store them in a cool, dark place until ready to consume. Properly processed home-canned foods are best consumed within a year.

gelling point

There are two easy ways to determine if a fruit preserve has reached the gelling point, at which the final texture of the jam will be nicely firm.

temperature

The most reliable way is simply to take the jam's temperature with an instant-read thermometer. At sea level, the jam will gel at 220 degrees F.

Like processing time, the gelling point should be adjusted for your altitude. For every 1,000-foot gain in elevation above sea level, subtract 2 degrees from the gelling point to find the right gelling temperature for you.

sheeting

Dip a metal spoon into your preserve and hold it up vertically, so the preserve drips down off the side of the spoon. When the preserve stops dripping and instead falls from the spoon in a wide "sheet," the jam has reached the gelling point.

With a little experience, you'll be able to recognize this sheeting texture of a jam at the gelling point reliably.

Sanitize jars.

Fill hot jars.

Wipe jar rims carefully.

Lid jars.

Carefully lower jars into water bath.

Bring water up to a boil.

After processing, remove jars.

Let jars sit undisturbed to set seals.

stuff to remember

1. Be very, very cautious about making any changes to a canning recipe, and never increase the quantity of low-acid foods in a water-bath-canned recipe. **Why?** Because we rely on high acidity levels to stop the germination of botulism spores and development of the botulism toxin. Changing the type or quantity of ingredients in a water-bath-canned recipe can change the total acidity and potentially lead to an extremely unsafe product.

2. Pull out however many jars the recipe calls for, plus one more. **Why?** Even the best-tested canning recipe can vary from the yield given in the recipe based on the moisture content of ingredients and how long the recipe is cooked down. It's a pain to realize you are one jar short as you are filling jars, so just get in the habit of grabbing an extra as you set up to can.

3. Start timing the processing only when the canner has returned to a full rolling boil. **Why?** Because cutting down on processing time or temperature could lead to a potentially unsafe product.

4. Make adjustments for altitude. **Why?** At higher altitudes, water boils at lower temperatures. If adjustments are not made, the processing temperature could be too low, leading to an unsafe product.

altitude adjustments for water-bath canners

All the water-bath processing times given in this book are appropriate for canners at 0 to 1000 feet above sea level. Canners at higher altitudes must adjust their processing time to compensate.

0–1000 FT ALT:	As directed
1001–3000 FT ALT:	+5 min
3001–6000 FT ALT:	+10 min
6001–8000 FT ALT:	+15 min
8001–10000 FT ALT:	+20 min
10,001+ FT ALT:	Contact your local university extension service for information on the feasibility of safe canning at superhigh altitude, or drive your canner down the mountain to a friend's house for a canning party.

pressure canning

Pressure canning is the only safe way to can low-acid foods like vegetables, meat, broth, or soups. It's a step up in food preservation commitment in terms of equipment, so typically it's not the first kind of canning people try. But if you have a pressure canner, a whole world of DIY convenience food opens up to you.

essential equipment

You'll need the same jars, lids, jar lifter, bubbler tool, and canning funnel that you use with water-bath canning (see page 26). You'll also need a pressure canner.

PRESSURE CANNER: Pressure canners are designed to be sealed, so that the atmospheric pressure inside the canner can get higher than the atmospheric pressure in your kitchen. This higher pressure raises the temperature at which water will boil and allows the home canner to get her food hot enough to kill botulism spores. A pressure canner is not the same as a pressure cooker, and you cannot substitute a pressure cooker for a pressure canner.

Maintaining an accurate calibration of the pressure canner is important—I recommend a weighted-gauge pressure canner if you can afford one, because they don't require yearly calibration. Less expensive dial-gauge pressure canners work just as well, but should be checked annually by your local university extension office or the manufacturer to ensure they are maintaining a safe and accurate pressure.

Modern pressure canners are built with all kinds of redundant safety features, and, as long as you follow some simple safety guidelines when using your pressure canner, you won't blow up your house or endanger your family or end up with exploded corn on your ceiling. However, because of the advancement in pressure canner safety features and because of the risk of miscalibration, I discourage folks from using vintage pressure canners picked up from a local thrift store or tag sale.

Your pressure canner will come with a rack—depending on the size, maybe even two. It's perfectly acceptable to stack one layer of jars atop another in a pressure canner, as long as there is a rack separating the layers and the equipment is sized to accommodate such stacking.

I'm not going to lie: the first time you use a pressure canner, you'll probably be in minor terror the whole time. I know I was. But once you get a few sessions of pressure canning under your belt, the whole process will become second nature.

Before your first pressure-canning session, or if using a new pressure canner for the first time, get familiar with your equipment. Do an inexpensive "test run" of your canner by filling mason jars with water tinted with food coloring. Seal the jars and step through the entire process of pressure canning with those tinted-water jars. This way you can figure out the specific operation of your canner before you put your hard-earned food in jars for the first time.

If the temperature control of your pressure canner is erratic, the tinted water from the jars will be pulled out of the jars and into the canner. This is called siphoning, and you'll know it's a problem if the water in your canner is colored at the end of your canning test run. Practice maintaining a smooth, consistent temperature and pressure level in the canner until you can minimize siphoning.

basic steps

1. Read the recipe all the way through and make sure you understand what you'll be doing and have everything you will need to proceed.

2. Take care of any advance processing in the recipe before proceeding. For example, a recipe may call for soaking dry beans overnight.

3. Inspect your jars and lids. Make sure the jars are spotlessly clean, and check each one for hairline cracks or defects in the jar lip. If you see any kind of damage, even an itty-bitty nick on the edge of the jar, don't use that jar for canning. It might still be okay for dry storage, but not for food processing. Assemble as many new, unused lids and bands in good condition as you will need. Wash these well, then set aside.

4. Place the rack in your pressure canner and fill your canner with about three inches of water. Set your jars on the canner rack, set the lid on your canner (but don't seal) and heat the water to a bare simmer. This preheats the canner and jars, reducing the chance of a jar breaking during processing. While your jars should be spotlessly clean, there's no need to sanitize them before pressure canning—the processing takes care of this. Adjust the temperature as necessary to keep the jars warm, and maintain the water level in the canner by adding a bit more water as needed.

5. Prepare your pressure-canning recipe. This is just like cooking—chop, simmer, and stir.

6. When your recipe is ready to transfer into jars, use the jar lifter to carefully remove the jars from the pressure canner to your work area, tipping any hot water in the jars back into the pressure canner as you go. Ladle a bit of the simmering water from the canner into a small bowl or glass measuring cup; you will use this later to wipe the rims of your jars. Working calmly but quickly, set the canning funnel in your first jar and ladle or arrange your prepared food into the jars up to the specified headspace. Try to be accurate with headspace to minimize siphoning during processing.

7. If appropriate to the recipe, use a jar bubbler to remove any air pockets from the jar and, if necessary, top up the jar with additional product to get to the stated headspace.

8. Transfer the funnel to the next jar and repeat the filling and bubbling step until all jars are full.

9. Carefully dip a lint-free towel or paper towel into the hot, clean water you ladled from the pressure canner. Wipe the rims of each jar completely and thoroughly. Set the flat lids centered on the jars, then hold the lids steady while screwing on the bands. Screw the bands just fingertip tight; do not overtighten.

10. Place your jars in the pressure canner with the jar lifter. Be sure to keep the jars level so the seal area stays clean. If you have a multi-level pressure canner, once the bottom level is full, place the "second story" rack in and begin loading jars into the upper rack.

11. Once fully loaded, put the lid on your pressure canner and fasten it securely according to the manufacturer's instructions. Turn the heat on to the highest position and wait until the water in the pressure canner begins boiling. At this point, the weight should remain off the vent pipe or the vent petcock should be open, depending on your model of pressure canner. When the water in the pressure canner begins boiling, steam will shoot from the open vent pipe. Once you can see a visible line of steam coming from the vent, set a timer for ten minutes and let the steam keep flowing to exhaust any remaining air from the pressure canner.

12. After ten minutes of venting, put the proper weight on the vent pipe, close the petcock, or take whatever steps are required for your particular model of pressure canner. Each model is slightly different but what is most important is that you get the canner up to the pressure called for in the recipe. Consult the chart with pressure adjustments for altitude (see page 39) as appropriate.

13. In three to ten minutes, the pressure will rise to the desired level. You'll hear the weight start to jiggle if you have a weighted pressure canner. If not, keep a close eye on the gauge! Verify that the pressure is in the range desired and start your timer for the processing time specified in the recipe.

14. Keep an eye and ear on the pressure canner to make sure it isn't running too hot or, even more critically, doesn't cool down. Most manufacturers will include tips on how to judge this. For a typical weighted pressure canner, listen for a venting jiggle a few times a minute. A dial-gauge canner calls for eagle-eyed attention. Adjust the heat down as necessary to stop the pressure from getting too high or the valve from venting too often. Make small adjustments and wait a minute or two to see what happens before adjusting again. **IMPORTANT:** If your canner's PSI dips below the required level, you have to start your processing time all over from the beginning.

15. After the processing time is complete, turn off the heat and allow the pressure canner to cool naturally. Do not try to speed up the cool-down process by prematurely venting the pressure canner or cooling it with cold water. This can cause siphoning and loss of seals. Keep an eye on the pressure gauge and wait for it to reach the zero mark. If your canner doesn't have a gauge, follow the manufacturer's instructions for how long to wait to ensure the pressure has fully dropped.

16. Once the pressure canner has cooled and the pressure inside has dropped to ambient, carefully remove the weight from your canner or open the petcock. A little residual pressure may still vent out, so be careful (I use a towel to grasp the weight on my pressure canner). Don't let the cooling process go too long that the gauge is below zero or you may experience siphoning of the product in your jars.

17. Let the pressure canner sit for at least ten minutes with the vent open or weight off. Carefully remove the pressure canner's lid away from you, and in accordance with the manufacturer's instructions.

18. Carefully remove the jars from the canning kettle with the jar lifter. Lift jars straight up and set them straight down as you remove them from the canner; tilting the jars at this stage could prevent strong seals. Set the jars on a clean kitchen towel with a bit of space between each jar. Avoid cool or drafty spots—these can lead to overly quick cooling and an increased chance of siphoning and poor seals. Don't push down on the tops of any jars, tighten rings, or in any other way fiddle with the jars. Resist the temptation!

19. Let the jars sit undisturbed for twelve to twenty-four hours before checking to see if any seals failed to form. Press the center of the lid gently; it shouldn't move or pop up and down when you press it. If the lid does spring back when you press it, the jar has not sealed. Place jars with failed seals in the refrigerator for consumption within the next few days. Remove the rings from the jars, then clean, dry, and label your successfully sealed jars and store them in a cool, dark place.

how not to die of botulism

Botulism toxin is the most powerful neurotoxin in the world, and its association with home-canned foods has probably scared more people away from home canning than any other thing. I don't want to downplay this: botulism poisoning is very bad. The botulism toxin paralyzes muscles, and without medical intervention, it's often fatal.

That's the bad news. The good news is food-borne botulism is exceedingly rare, and modern canning practices have been established to ensure all your home-canned foods are, without question, impeccably safe.

Here's what you need to know about botulism, why certain canning rules exist, and how to can safely with confidence.

The bacterium that causes botulism is called *Clostridium Botulinum*. *C. Botulinum* is a bacterium that really hates oxygen—he's what is called an obligate anaerobe, meaning he can only grow and thrive and reproduce in oxygen-free environments. If *C. Botulinum* senses that oxygen is showing up to his party, he goes hyper-introvert and turns himself into a dormant spore.

Spore *C. Botulinum* is kinda like Iron Man—he's wearing this impenetrable supersuit that makes him practically unkillable. Boiling water, bleach, freezing, rapid-fire insults about his mother—none of these have any effect on Spore *C. Botulinum*.

C. Botulinum spores are everywhere in the environment and can stay dormant for years—some research suggests the spores can stay viable for thousands of years. For the most part we don't have to worry about them, because as long *C. Botulinum* stays a spore, he's totally inactive and can't hurt us.

If Spore *C. Botulinum* finds himself back in a hospitable environment—low in acid, moderate in temperature, and oxygen-free—he will "reanimate" into his vegetative, bacterial form. In this form, he can cause all kinds of trouble, rapidly multiplying and producing the toxin that causes botulism poisoning.

All properly canned foods are anaerobic and are typically stored at room temperature, which means they have the potential to be the perfect environment for Spore *C. Botulinum* to unpack and set up his house of toxic horrors. Home canners have two ways to ensure that this never happens:

1. **CONTROL THE ACIDITY:** *C. Botulinum* remains dormant in high-acid environments. If a food has a pH of 4.6 or lower, the spore will never germinate into the active bacterial form, and so no botulism toxin will be produced. High-acid foods—most fruits—are safe to can in a boiling-water-bath canner (see page 25). Other foods, like vegetables, can be pickled to sufficient acidity to be safely water-bath canned.

2. **CONTROL THE TEMPERATURE:** Even Spore *C. Botulinum* will die eventually—but only at temperatures higher than the boiling point of water (212 degrees F). Using a pressure canner, we can raise the processing temperature of canned foods to 240 degrees F, which is hot enough to kill even the spore form of *C. Botulinum*. Low-acid foods—including meats and non-pickled vegetables—must be processed in a properly tested pressure canner for the full time specified to ensure a safely canned product.

Remove pre-warmed jars.

Fill jars, leaving appropriate headspace.

Wipe jar rims carefully.

Lid jars.

Carefully lower jars into pressure canner.

Vent canner for 10 minutes.

Bring pressure canner up to pressure specified.

Ensure pressure doesn't drop during processing.

After processing, allow canner to drop to 0 PSI, then carefully remove jars.

stuff to remember

Vent the pressure canner for ten minutes before timing. **Why?** Because trapped air in the canner can lower the processing temperature, leading to a potentially unsafe product.

Check the dial gauges yearly. **Why?** Because if the pressure readings are off, the pressure canner can operate at lower-than-safe temperatures, leading to a potentially unsafe product.

Make adjustments for altitude. **Why?** At the same PSI, the temperature inside the canner is lower at higher altitudes. If adjustments are not made, the processing temperature could be too low, leading to a potentially unsafe product.

All the processing pressures and times given in this book are appropriate for canners at 0 to 1000 feet above sea level. Those at higher altitude must adjust the processing PSI of their canner.

altitude adjustments for pressure canning

DIAL-GAUGE PRESSURE CANNERS

0–1000 FT ALT:	11 PSI
1001–2000 FT ALT:	11 PSI
2001–4000 FT ALT:	12 PSI
4001–6000 FT ALT:	13 PSI
6001–8000 FT ALT:	14 PSI
8001–10000 FT ALT:	15 PSI
10,001+ FT ALT:	Contact your local university extension service for information on the feasibility of safe canning at super high altitude, or drive your canner down the mountain to a friend's house for a canning party.

WEIGHTED-GAUGE PRESSURE CANNERS

0–1000 FT ALT:	10 PSI
1001–10,000 FT ALT:	15 PSI

lacto-fermentation

Lacto-fermentation is one of the cheapest, easiest forms of food preservation. This process is what turns cabbage into sauerkraut and milk into yogurt. Various beneficial bacteria eat sugars and give off lactic acid. This lactic acid lowers the pH of the food, effectively pickling it without any added acid such as vinegar. The process described here will generally work with vegetables and even many fruits, such as lemons (see page 347), but the specifics for yogurt are a bit different and are described on page 132.

essential equipment

GLASS JAR OR NONREACTIVE, FOOD-SAFE CERAMIC CROCK: I advise against fermenting fruits and vegetables in plastic because its porosity makes it prone to absorbing odors (your tub will forever smell vaguely of sauerkraut), and there is a reasonable potential for some chemicals in the plastic to leech into the ferment, particularly as it becomes increasingly acidic. When I ferment in larger quantities than quart-size mason jars, I typically use five-liter bail-top glass jars with a rubber gasket seal.

WEIGHT: A weight is necessary to hold your fermenting vegetables under the brine. The lacto-fermentation process is anaerobic, and if your vegetables float up to the top of the brine, yeasts, molds, and other spoilage organisms can take hold.

Any nonreactive weight that will hold the vegetables under the brine can be used. One classic way to weight vegetables is to use a piece of cabbage, or other large, sturdy leaf, as a kind of lid, tucked in to hold any floating bits down into the brine. My favorite way to weight ferments is with a handful of ceramic pie weights bundled inside a mesh produce bag. The pie weights spread out over the ferment, keeping everything under the brine.

Other options include rocks (scrubbed perfectly clean, of course), glass weights, or heavy-duty plastic ziplock bags filled with excess brine. A brine-filled plastic bag as a weight is very effective at excluding oxygen from a ferment, but concerns about pesky chemical leaching put me off.

If you want to get fancy, you can make or buy various devices that will guarantee a more reliable ferment. All these devices, which include specialty crocks with air-locks, water-filled moats, spring presses, and more work by more effectively excluding oxygen access to your ferment. If you find yourself fermentation obsessed, you'll find plenty of products to tempt you, but nothing beyond a food-safe vessel and a weight is truly necessary to ferment vegetables.

Add salt to prepared ferment.

Pack into scrupulously clean jars.

Press to remove any air from the ferment.

Top off brine as needed.

Prepare fermentation weight.

Check headspace.

Ensure ferment is fully submerged under brine.

Lid jar loosely so carbon dioxide can escape.

Wait patiently and watch as fermentation happens!

basic steps

When you lacto-ferment, you're just setting up an environment that's more hospitable to certain strains of bacteria than others, so those good bacteria do the fermenting for you. You need to do four important things to make your ferments good-bacteria friendly.

1. Start out with scrupulously clean equipment. Jars should be perfectly clean and well rinsed. I like to flip jars upside down onto a clean towel after rinsing them to cut down a bit on random bacteria falling in. Starting with a very clean jar or crock ensures the desired bacteria don't have to compete as much with other microbes.

2. Control the salinity (salt levels) in the ferment by adding salt directly to the vegetables or by making a salt and water brine. The lactic acid bacteria we want are more salt tolerant than most bacteria, so by adding the right amount of salt, we inhibit the growth of the undesirable bacteria and give the good bacteria an advantage.

A 3 to 5 percent brine solution will work well for most vegetables that you ferment whole or in large pieces, like jalapeño peppers, green beans, or carrot sticks. This works out to two to three tablespoons of fine sea salt per quart of water. For vegetables that are shredded and mixed with salt to form their own brine, like cabbage for sauerkraut, add eleven grams salt per pound of prepared vegetable. This is three tablespoons of fine sea salt for every five pounds of prepared vegetable, or two teaspoons of fine sea salt per pound.

3. Control the oxygen. Most spoilage bacteria, molds, and yeasts require oxygen to thrive. Keep ferments firmly under brine and out of reach of those guys. The top of the brine will be in contact with oxygen even if the ferment is weighted (unless some kind of airlock is used in the ferment) so as you ferment, carefully skim off any scum that form on the surface of the brine. The most common scum is a white film of wild yeasts. While this isn't harmful, if left to grow it will taint the flavor and color of your ferment and can disturb the acidity. Very occasionally, ferments can be contaminated by colonies of mold. If you see mold colonies, particularly black, red, or pink molds growing in your ferment, compost it. It's just not worth the risk.

4. Control the temperature. Vegetables ferment best at cool room temperature: 60 to 68 degrees F is excellent. Cooler temps inhibit microbial activity, and your ferment may take longer to finish, but this does not typically compromise the flavor. Warmer temps encourage a fast ferment and favor the growth of molds and microbes that can make fermented foods slimy. If your fermented product is unpleasantly slimy, compost it.

RHYTHMS AND ROUTINES

My first jars of pineapple and strawberry jam not withstanding, the rhythms of food preservation shadow the harvest, and so are strongly seasonal. Traditionally, late summer was a busy times for putting food by, as fruits and vegetables were being picked far faster than they could be eaten. These days, it's fun and wise to spread your food preservation out throughout the year to even out the peaks and valleys of the harvest, but I still find myself doing much of my food preservation in late summer and early fall.

my food preservation calendar

early spring

+ Take an inventory of your larder before the preserving season comes on strong. Decide what must-haves are on this year's list, and be honest about what items weren't so popular. Make a list of what to tackle in the upcoming year. Eat exclusively from the larder for several weeks or a month, in order to save money and eat down the inventory from last year while making room for the upcoming harvest.

+ Make room in the freezer—pull out chicken and beef bones, make broth (see page 112), and pressure can (see page 192).

late spring

+ Make Rhubarb Syrup (page 187) for shrubs and cocktails.

+ Make Pickled Asparagus (page 189).

+ Ferment cauliflower (see page 195), spring turnips (see page 196), and radishes.

+ Make pectin from apple thinnings.

+ Make Apricot Barbecue Sauce (page 183) and apricot jam.

+ Make Strawberry Preserves in Balsamic–Black Pepper Syrup (page 184) and freeze strawberries.

early summer

+ Dry cherries for snacks and baking.

+ Freeze cherries and can whole in syrup.

+ Pickle the first tiny cucumbers for cornichons.

+ Cut herbs like mint, lemon balm, lemon verbena, sage, chamomile, thyme, and oregano, and dry for teas and cooking.

late summer

+ Make butter, jams, preserves, sauces, and infused vinegars from summer berries and fruit.

+ Make relishes, salsas, and chutneys from summer berries and fruit.

+ Cure garlic and onions.

+ Make Lacto-Fermented Pico de Gallo (page 239).

+ Freeze Romano green beans.

+ Ferment dilly beans (see page 240).

+ Make and freeze pesto (see page 243).

+ Make summer squash, cucumber pickles, and relish.

+ Make and freeze big batches of zucchini bread.

+ Make soups from summer vegetables and pressure can for easy meals throughout the year.

early fall

+ Make jams, preserves, sauces, and infused vinegars (see page 139) from fall stone fruit.

+ Make relishes, salsas, and chutneys from fall stone fruit.

+ Ferment hot pepper sauce (see page 303).

+ Lift potatoes, cure for storage, and pressure can.

+ Make fennel agrodolce.

+ Cure winter squash and store.

late fall

+ Make and can applesauce and pearsauce.

+ Make quince paste.

+ Infuse vodka with pear and ginger.

+ Buy a half beef from a local farmer, and pressure can beef chuck and short ribs (see page 301).

+ Pickle beets (see page 291).

+ Freeze fall greens.

+ Make Sauerkraut with Apples and Caraway (page 305) and kimchi.

early winter

+ Dry citrus peels for spices.

+ Make Cranberry-Pear-Walnut Conserve (page 341).

+ Make Persimmon-Apple Chutney (page 339).

+ Make salt and spice blends for gifts.

+ Buy a pig from a local farmer, pressure can pork shoulder (see page 297), cure bacon, and render lard.

+ Ferment carrots (see page 345).

+ Cook Caramelized Onions (page 354) and freeze.

late winter

+ Make Meyer Lemon Curd (page 356) and freeze.

+ Ferment salt-cured lemons (see page 347).

+ Make Citrus Vinegar Concentrate (page 362) for cleaning.

+ Make whole grain mustard (see page 343).

+ Pressure can beans (see page 350).

Simple Home Care

My mudroom used to look like a janitorial closet, jammed full of industrial-size plastic containers of brightly colored, toxic, artificially scented cleaners. Wandering the cleaning aisles of big-box stores, I was sure that, if only I found the right cleaner, my home would, like magic, become shiny and spotless.

The logic can only have been, "Maybe if I get this flimsy mop thing with the disposable pads that look disturbingly like panty liners, mopping will be so fun and easy that my floors will never get dirty again!" Uh-huh, right. Just guess how that worked out for me.

One day, I realized that all those cleaners I had paid good money for were actually making my home a less wholesome place to be. Every product was marketed as a way to make toilets, showers, kitchen cabinets, grout, or laundry sparkly and pure. But these products weren't pure, they were filling up the space where my kids played with harmful fumes. When I saw this for what it really was, the whole thing was just so silly.

I went through my cabinets and threw out, gave away, or donated four grocery bags full of cleaners, housekeeping tools, lotions, potions, and all manner of snake oil. This greatly simplified my personal and home care routine, and I discovered that it didn't take much time or money to DIY the products I really needed.

It seemed like the more I got those industrial products and artificial fragrances out of my life, the better the organization and calm in my home grew. It was rather amazing—when I gave up the consumerist crutch of perpetually searching for the right product to be successful in caring for my own home and body, I was finally able to embrace that it's the little actions done every day—the routines and the habits—that make all the difference.

That's the ethic behind DIY home care. You figure out what you can let go of and then you build up what you still need from stuff that won't slowly poison you. Sensible, really.

HOME CARE BASICS

Have you ever thought about what cleaning really is? Let's say you have a stain on your cotton shirt or dirt on your tile floor or a greasy film on your stainless steel pot. In all these cases, the process of cleaning is the same: get the grime off your stuff and into suspension so it can be rinsed away with clean water or absorbed by a clean rag.

Effective cleaning means selecting the right cleaner to get that grime into suspension and hold it there. Thankfully, you don't need to clutter your cabinets and closets with toxic commercial cleaners to get the job done. It's time to put on your geektastic science hat and learn why you can clean nearly everything in your home with just a few household basics.

Professional cleaning chemists call the different types of grime you're likely to encounter "soil," as in "soiled baby diaper" not "rich garden soil." There are four different types of soil, and each calls for a different type of cleaner.

INORGANIC SOIL: Grime that originates from stuff that was never alive. Think mineral buildups, lime deposits, rust rings, and hard-water marks. In typical homes, inorganic soil is most likely to build up in bathrooms. Inorganic soils are cleaned with acidic cleansers.

ORGANIC SOIL: Grime that originates from stuff that was—at some point—alive or part of something alive. Most household dirt, dust, food grease, cooking oil, proteins, yeasts, and molds fall into this category. Organic soil is cleaned with alkaline cleaners.

PETROLEUM SOIL: Heavy-duty grime derived, as you'd expect, from petroleum. Machine and engine oil, gear grease, and many waxes, paints, and varnishes fall into this category. Petroleum soil can typically only be cleaned with solvents, many of which are also derived from petroleum. Sneaky, sneaky petroleum.

COMBINATION SOIL: A grimy mix! Should you crawl under a car to look for leaks, afterward you would probably find your clothing stained with combination soil—motor oil would be a petroleum soil, while the mud on the tires is an organic soil. Combination soils require cleaning with combination cleaners—either more than one cleaner in succession, or a blended cleanser designed to tackle multiple types of gunk at once.

DIY HOME CARE ESSENTIALS

The good news is, getting your home clean in a safe way isn't hard, time-consuming, or expensive. In fact, you'll probably end up saving a bunch of money. So ditch that giant mess of toxic commercial cleansers cluttering up your cabinets and closets. You can clean nearly everything in your home with four things: an alkaline cleaner for organic soils, an acidic cleaner for inorganic soils, a solvent for cutting through light grease and for increasing the cleaning power of acid and alkaline cleaners, and a mild abrasive to scrub out tough stains and cut through built up layers of grime.

As the level of soil that needs to be tackled goes up, or as you ask your cleaner to do more of the cleaning work so you don't have to, the strength of the cleaner you need goes up. This is why laundry detergent and automatic dishwashing detergent is formulated with a strong alkali like washing soda, and toilet cleaners are often strong acids—the cleaner must be stronger anytime you're not scrubbing.

PH isn't the only thing that determines the safety of cleaners, but as products get more extreme in either direction—base or acid—the more careful you need to be while using them. Extreme alkalies, for example, can cause devastating chemical burns on skin.

alkaline cleaners

Good ol' fashioned soap is still the best all-purpose household cleanser. All true soap is made from fat and a strong alkali, typically lye. When lye and water are added to a fat, a process called saponification converts the harsh alkali and fatty acids into an effective cleanser—soap—and glycerin.

Soap works because it can bond at the molecular level to both oil and water. Oils like to stick to other oils, and water likes to bond to itself. And, as every kid who's ever attended a third-grade science fair knows, oil and water don't mix. Soap is like the gregarious party host who can get strangers mingling, and in its presence water is able to get under and around oil and rinse it away. Since dirt typically comes packaged with grease—food grease, body oils, and the like—soap is an essential cleaner.

In areas with hard water, using pure soap can be a problem—ions from the dissolved minerals in the hard water bind to the part of the soap that should bind to water, like an oblivious party guest who totally monopolizes the host's time. The soap still binds to dirt and oil, but now can't be washed off in water. This creates soap scum and buildup.

The solution in this sticky situation is to add a water softener to your alkaline cleaners. A water softener is an alkali that acts like soap's wingman, keeping the problematic

the problem with commercial cleaners

Many commercial cleaning products are "all-in-one" combo cleaners. Because they are trying to be all things to all soils, they take a brute-force approach, using chemical cleaners that are often far stronger and more caustic than are necessary. Common household cleaners are frequently a grab bag of powerful solvents, petroleum-derived surfactants, and caustic detergents. Artificial colors and scents are added, and clever plastic packaging is developed to differentiate these products from all the other irritating chemical cleaners already on the market. This gives the advertising folks a unique hook to sell you on yet another unnecessary cleaner.

Even task-specific cleaners tend to use far stronger components than are necessary to sell the idea that you can get your house clean without any work. Back in my toxic-cleaner days, I bought those automatic toilet bowl–cleaner pucks to save me the fourteen seconds it takes to run a toilet brush around the water line of my commode a few times a week. Well, the toilet bowl puck people didn't lie—their product had superstrength! It was so strong, the oxidizers quickly ate through every rubber toilet flapper valve and gasket in my house. One toilet leaked from the tank onto the floor; all needed their flapper valves replaced.

While those slow-release toilet pucks are probably the worst, many of the harshest "low-work" chemical cleaners will damage the parts and finishes around your home over time. This can lead to expensive repairs and surfaces that are microscopically pitted and actually harder to keep clean in the long run.

ions in the hard water occupied so the soap can do its job. Borax, a natural mineral water softener, boosts the effectiveness of soap.

For everyday household cleaning, I mostly use liquid castile soap, which is made from plant oils and is very mild, and borax. You can make your own liquid castile soap, or buy it in bulk. Dr. Bronner's is a widely available brand. A dilute castile soap–water spray is totally sufficient for many regular cleaning tasks.

Many of the cleansers loosely marketed as "soap" are in fact petroleum-derived detergents. I try to stay away from these because I give enough of my money to the oil-processing industry when I drive my car; I don't need to send them funds every time I wipe down my counters too.

common alkaline pH cleaners, in pH order

The pH of anything changes with the concentration. So think of this chart, and the corresponding acid chart (see page 56), as indicative of the relative strength of these cleaners to each other.

MORE ALKALINE   NEUTRAL   MORE ACIDIC

14 ←——————— 7 ——————→ 0

DISTILLED WATER: pH 7.0. Totally neutral.

BAKING SODA: pH 8.4 in solution. Very gentle. No special precautions needed.

LIQUID CASTILE SOAP: pH 8. Very gentle. No special precautions needed.

BORAX (SODIUM BORATE): Up to pH 9.3 in solution. Slightly irritating to the skin, moderately irritating to eyes, mucus membranes, and respiratory tract. Avoid breathing dust. While borax is a mild, naturally occurring mineral with low irritation potential when used sensibly, it can be toxic if ingested in large quantities. Particular care must be taken to keep borax and borax-containing products away from children. Overuse may contribute indirectly, through applications of municipal sewage sludge to farmland, to excessive boron buildup in the soil. Avoid releasing directly into the environment.

POWDERED OXYGEN BLEACH (SODIUM PERCARBONATE): Up to pH 11 in solution. Gloves should be worn with high concentrations. Moderately irritating to skin. Irritating to eyes, mucus membranes, and respiratory tract. Don't inhale dust. Harmful but typically not toxic if ingested. Breaks down into hydrogen peroxide and washing soda when combined with water. Not toxic to aquatic life if properly treated through wastewater treatment. Avoid releasing directly into the environment.

WASHING SODA (SODIUM CARBONATE): Up to pH 11 in solution. Gloves should be worn with high concentrations. Moderately irritating to skin. Highly irritating to eyes, mucus membranes, and respiratory tract. Don't inhale dust. Harmful but typically not toxic if ingested. Not toxic to aquatic life if properly treated through wastewater treatment. Avoid releasing directly into the environment.

LIQUID AMMONIA: pH 11. Highly irritating and corrosive to skin, eyes, mucus membranes, and respiratory tract. Don't inhale fumes. Very harmful to toxic if ingested. Highly toxic to aquatic life. Highly toxic fumes are produced if ammonia is mixed with household bleach or strong acids. Use only with an abundance of caution, or avoid.

HOUSEHOLD CHLORINE BLEACH (SODIUM HYPOCHLORITE): pH 12. Highly irritating and corrosive to skin, eyes, mucus membranes, and respiratory tract. Don't inhale fumes. Very harmful to toxic if ingested. Bleach breaks down rapidly in freshwater, or when exposed to sunlight, into harmless oxygen and table salt. However, in salt water, the breakdown of bleach creates hypobromite, which is acutely toxic to aquatic life. Highly toxic fumes are produced if bleach is mixed with liquid ammonia or strong acids. Use only with an abundance of caution, or avoid.

LYE OR CAUSTIC SODA (SODIUM HYDROXIDE): Up to pH 13.5 in solution. Eye protection, skin protection, and heavy-duty gloves are essential if working with lye. Exceptionally irritating and corrosive to skin, eyes, mucus membranes, and respiratory tract. Permanent blindness can occur from eye contact. Do not inhale fumes. Exceptionally harmful to toxic if ingested due to extreme corrosion of esophageal tissue. Not toxic to aquatic life if pH is properly buffered through wastewater treatment. Do not release directly into the environment. The only reason to have lye in the home is for powerful drain-clearing or soapmaking. Unless you can commit to using and storing this chemical safely at all times, avoid.

acid cleaners

No surprise here—plain distilled white vinegar is a very effective cleaner. Most household distilled white vinegar is 5 percent acetic acid, which is more than strong enough to handle typical inorganic soil deposits around the house when used regularly, but not so strong as to be generally corrosive. Acid cleaners are excellent at stripping off mineral buildup that occurs in bathrooms and can help cut through the dreaded soap scum you might be prone to if you live in a hard-water area.

Plain distilled white vinegar can be used at various dilutions depending on how strong a cleaner you need. A cup of vinegar diluted in a thirty-two-ounce spray bottle is a good general purpose bathroom cleaner. At full strength, vinegar greatly reduces bacterial loads on surfaces. If you need a stronger acidic solution, granulated citric acid is your best bet. It can be added to water to achieve powerful acid levels while still being safe to use in the home. See page 56 for more information on types of acid cleaners.

Be careful not to use acidic cleaners, even natural ones like vinegar, around natural stone. Many stones, particularly marble and limestone, can be permanently etched by acidic cleaners.

TIP: Many natural homekeeping recipes call for both soap and vinegar. The problem with this is that soap (an alkali) and vinegar (an acid) both become less effective when mixed together because they tend to neutralize each other's pH. When using natural soaps, as opposed to synthetic detergents, it's particularly important to resist the temptation to add vinegar to your alkaline cleaners. If you add enough acid to a liquid castile soap, for example, you will undo the saponification process that converted natural plant oils to soap, and be left with a messy, gloppy, ineffective cleaner.

solvents

I once lived in a house half a block from Interstate 5, and the exterior window ledges were perpetually covered with a film of black grime. Soap didn't clean it and straight vinegar just rolled off. It took me over a year to realize that the black film was the fine dust from aerosolized car tires, millions of which slowly wore down as they rolled past our home every day. Unless you live in a machine shop, this degree of petroleum soil is unlikely to be a big component of the grime in your home, but that doesn't mean solvents don't have an important role in cleaning.

A solvent is a cleaner that works by dissolving something to form a solution. By the strictest definition, water is an awesome solvent! But in cleaning, water has one fatal flaw: it's useless by itself against greasy, sticky, gummy, or oily things. The most useful solvents for the DIY homekeeper are plain alcohol and citrus oils.

Isopropyl alcohol, sold as rubbing alcohol, and ethanol, sold as the cheapest rotgut vodka you can find, are both excellent solvents. Isopropyl alcohol can be dangerous if inhaled, and is definitely not good for you, so it's firmly in the dark-gray zone when it comes to nontoxic cleaners. I used to use rubbing alcohol in some of my DIY cleaners, because it's reliable, cheap, and effective, but I switched to vodka because I wasn't comfortable spraying (and therefore aerosolizing) rubbing alcohol near my kids and their adorable developing brains.

Another excellent solvent is d-Limonene, a volatile essential oil extracted from citrus. Sweet orange essential oil is about 90 percent d-Limonene and is powerful enough to eat through paint if used undiluted. All those "orange cleaners" and "citrus-dissolve" type cleaners you can buy are based on the solvent power of d-Limonene. Add sweet orange essential oil to give a grease-cutting boost to cleaners. I use leftover peels from winter citrus to make my own d-Limonene-based cleaner (see Citrus Vinegar Concentrate, page 362).

abrasives

Sometimes elbow grease is the best cleaner, and that's where abrasives come in. Abrasives wear away at dirt, grease, stains, and discoloration. Their scouring ability is their greatest asset but also their greatest drawback, as anyone who's ever scratched the heck out of an appliance by using the wrong type of scouring pad will understand.

Scratching up the natural surface of your stuff is unsightly, of course, but it also makes it harder to clean in the future. Scratches give dirt and pathogens more surface area to colonize and more nooks to hide in. So the aggressiveness of the abrasive you use should always be matched to the durability of the surface you are cleaning. Enameled cast iron can take a more vigorous scouring than your plastic toilet seat or your wooden furniture.

My starting abrasive is baking soda, a powder so gentle on surfaces that I use it to brush my teeth. In addition to its versatility in polishing surfaces, buffing out stains, and taking scuff marks off walls, baking soda absorbs odors and is slightly basic, so it freshens carpets and upholstery, stops garbage can stink, and more. When I need a stronger cleaning abrasive, I mix kosher salt and borax in with the baking soda.

common acidic pH cleaners, in pH order

In general, common household acids pose less concern to safety than common household bases. The reason is simple: While many bases are sold in a pure powdered form, most strong acids aren't sold in such concentrated forms. Take acetic acid. In its pure form, it's highly corrosive to the skin, eyes, and mucous membranes. Inhalation of concentrated acetic acid requires immediate medical attention. Household vinegar is typically 5 percent acetic acid but is perfectly safe to pour on your lettuce as a salad dressing. The poison is in the dose, as the saying goes.

When it comes to contact irritation, our skin is naturally acidic, with a pH of 4.5 to 5.5 depending on the person. So acids like cream of tartar don't irritate our skin in the same way bases like washing soda will.

```
        MORE ALKALINE      NEUTRAL      MORE ACIDIC
          14 ←——————————— 7 ———————————→ 0
```

DISTILLED WATER: pH 7.0. Totally neutral.

ASCORBIC ACID (VITAMIN C): pH 5.8 in solution. A mild acid naturally produced from glucose by both plants and animals. Water soluble, safe, and edible at naturally occurring levels and reasonable supplementation, ascorbic acid is found in many fruits and vegetables. High levels occur in citrus fruits, tomatoes, and berries. As a cleaner, ascorbic acid is good at cleaning iron and rust deposits. No special precautions are needed.

BLACK COFFEE: pH 5.0. I'm from Seattle, where coffee is like religion, so I never brew coffee just to clean. But if a pot gets cold, this mildly acidic cold brew can be put to good use in a few ways. You can use it to wipe down hard surfaces or spray it very lightly on dark wood floors and wipe clean. Moderate consumption of coffee may result in increased awesomeness. No other precautions needed.

CITRIC ACID: pH 3.9 in solution. Also called sour salt or lemon salt, citric acid is versatile. I use granulated citric acid in cleaners, personal care products, foods and beverages, and canning. In nature, citric acid is especially abundant in citrus fruits (no surprise there). In cleaning, it removes limescale and mineral buildup and helps to soften water. Pure citric acid is a skin, eye, and mucous membrane irritant—avoid breathing in the dust, exercise reasonable care, and wear gloves when cleaning with concentrated solutions of citric acids. If you splash a concentrated citric acid solution on your skin and notice any kind of burning or tingling feeling, dilution is the solution. Running cold water over the area will typically take care of any irritation. The only environmental concern is that citric acid is industrially produced through a rather weird process that starts by feeding cheap sugars to a particular fungal strain. The cheap sugars are often derived from genetically modified corn, so if GMOs concern you, consider seeking out certified non-GMO citric acid.

CREAM OF TARTAR (POTASSIUM BITARTRATE): pH 3.6 in solution. Cream of tartar precipitates naturally in some wines and is sold as a powder for baking. It's often used in meringues because it stabilizes and strengthens foams. It's sold as a fine powder, and, while it's a bit expensive to use as a pure acid cleaner, I add it to my homemade deodorant to lower the pH to a more skin-friendly range. Exercise reasonable care: Avoid getting it in your eyes and inhaling dust, and wear gloves if using concentrated cream of tartar solutions for cleaning.

DISTILLED WHITE VINEGAR, 5 PERCENT ACETIC ACID: pH 2. The king of acid cleaners, distilled white vinegar is cheap, readily available, and highly effective at cleaning non-greasy stains, deodorizing, and polishing stainless steel. It's great for tackling hard-water stains and soap film in the bathroom and also makes an excellent rinse agent in the dishwasher or washing machine because it will dissolve residual alkalies from soap or detergent. At typical household concentrations, vinegar is quite mild. Exercise reasonable care and you'll be fine. Often sold as an organic herbicide, 20 percent acetic acid vinegar is far, far stronger and is a severe eye and skin irritant. Use extreme caution and follow safety warnings if using 20 percent vinegar.

LEMON JUICE, FRESH OR BOTTLED: pH 2. Lemon juice works in much the same way as vinegar. It's slightly stronger but far more expensive, so I tend not to use lemon juice as a cleaner. Forty-six grams of granulated or powdered citric acid (about 3 tablespoons) can be mixed with 1 quart of water to economically create an acid cleaner with the same cleaning power as bottled or fresh lemon juice.

HOME CARE RHYTHMS AND ROUTINES

There is no daily chore so trivial that it cannot be made important by skipping it two days running.

—Robert Brault

Re-embracing our home as a place where we truly live, make, and do means freeing ourselves from those images of showpiece homes marketed to us by design catalogs and furniture stores.

This does not mean slumping toward filth or allowing piles of clutter to overtake us. Just the opposite, in fact: maintaining a pleasant, calm, and healthy home environment is essential if we want to take care of more of our own domestic needs. A messy kitchen is hard to cook in; piles of dishes in the sink just beg you to groan, look the other way, and order takeout.

At the same time, a home where people really live and cook and play will show signs of that vitality. A productive home is not full of museum pieces, and setting our standards as reliably functional instead of flawless is essential to both our productivity and our sanity.

Attending to the basics of life—feeding, cooking, bathing, dressing, bill-paying, and movement in and out of the home—creates teeny domestic disorders. Pots get used, plates get dirtied, dust settles, mud gets tracked in, jeans and socks and washcloths and bed linens are made dirty. If we attend to these small disorders frequently, they never get to the point of overwhelming us. But, if we allow the little things to pile up, soon the domestic resources of the home—clean dishes, fresh clothes, clear counter spaces—are exhausted and we are forced to confront a mountain of laundry, a flotilla of dishes, and a wobbly tower of bills.

I am not what you'd call a naturally tidy person. I don't really like cleaning. For years, I frequently put off basic maintenance as long as I could and thoroughly exhausted the resources of my home. It was only when my surroundings became intolerable that I finally dived in and tackled basic household chores. I didn't homekeep so much as I home-panicked. And if company was coming—forget it. Everything else was dropped to make time for full-on crisis cleaning.

It took a deliberate effort for me to learn the skills of basic homekeeping, and time for new habits to take firm root in my life. As I've cultivated routines of care that are customized and effective for my home, I've been rewarded with a domestic environment of relative calm. So while I still don't really love doing the dishes and laundry, I suck it up because the reward—a calm and well-functioning home—is worth the discipline.

The feeling of being calm and empowered in your own home instead of stressed and thwarted by it—that is the real reason to keep a home well. It's not about fancy decor or spotless, impossible standards. It's not about keeping up with how the magazines say you should be living or buying what they tell you to buy—it's about maintaining a home that allows you the space to relax and engage in your interests.

ROUTINES = CALM HOME

> We dream of having a clean house—but who dreams of actually doing the cleaning? We don't have to dream about doing the work, because doing the work is always within our grasp; the dream, in this sense, is to attain the goal without the work.
>
> —MARCUS BUCKINGHAM

The trick to creating a peaceful home that works for you is to create routines that are designed around your life, to give you the outcome you want. You already have a routine of some kind, even if it doesn't look like it from the outside.

Your dishwashing routine might be to pile everything in the sink and do dishes when the smell becomes unbearable. Your bill-paying routine might be to just ignore it until somebody shuts off a utility. Your laundry routine might be to buy new underwear at a discount store when you run out of clean ones.

My own home care routines have been so dysfunctional in the past that I've done all those things. A routine is really nothing more than a habit applied to some aspect of your life. Just because the outcome sucks doesn't mean you aren't practicing a routine in your home care. So the question isn't, "Do you have a routine?"—because you assuredly do—but, "Does the routine you have work? Does it give you the result you want?"

You can build a home care routine that will turn your home into a place of calm, or creativity, or socializing and fun—whatever you value—but it's as much of a hands-on DIY task as making sauerkraut or hand scrub. You have to be the designer of your own system.

THE HOME CARE TRIANGLE

Effective home care has three levels: daily routines, regular maintenance cleaning, and seasonal or special project cleaning. You can think of these as the things you do every day, the things you do weekly or biweekly, and the things that happen just a few times a year at most. These tiers build on each other, like a pyramid.

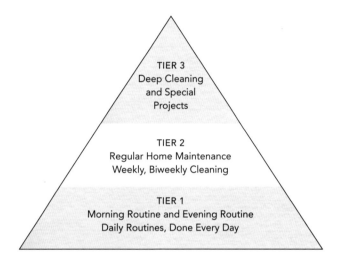

TIER 3
Deep Cleaning
and Special
Projects

TIER 2
Regular Home Maintenance
Weekly, Biweekly Cleaning

TIER 1
Morning Routine and Evening Routine
Daily Routines, Done Every Day

tier one: daily routines

Daily routines are done, as you'd expect, daily. They return your home to a base level of tidiness and stop the slide into domestic dysfunction. If you are a family with children, have pets, or like to engage in lots of hands-on projects around the house (which I imagine describes the majority of readers of this book), then a good daily routine is the most important thing you can do to maintain a general sense of order in your home.

You can go a long way with just your daily routines. Even if you rarely actually clean beyond what's necessary to make it through your daily routine, these basics will keep your domestic world manageable.

If necessary, prioritize your daily routine over maintenance cleaning. If you keep up on your daily routines, your actual maintenance cleaning is faster and easier because all you have to do is clean away actual dirt—the time-consuming tidying and basics like dishes are already out of the way. However, if you let your daily maintenance go, and the garbage and dishes pile up, and no one has any clean pants, and every surface is covered in paperwork, then it really doesn't matter how clean your shower door is, because your domestic scene will feel chaotic.

tier two: regular maintenance

This is your basic weekly or biweekly cleaning, and these acts are the ones that take your home from tidy to actually clean by removing dirt, grime, and deposits from your home's surfaces. Health, safety, and the preservation of your home's value should be prioritized in your time and efforts. Any languishing food, bacteria breeding grounds, trip hazards, or things that might encourage mold, mildew, or insects are must-tackle activities.

Regular, weekly dusting, vacuuming, and changing of bed linens is a good idea for everyone but particularly important for folks with dust or dust mite allergies, asthma, or a generally sensitive respiratory system.

It's nice to take care of smudgy fingerprints on the wall, dog nose imprints on the sliding glass door, and water spots on the shower door, but letting these things slide isn't going to kill anyone or make your indoor air quality atrocious. So prioritize depending on your time, energy, and baseline need for clean. As you work your regular home care and maintenance routine, these things will trend toward clean too.

tier three: seasonal and special project cleaning

Spring cleaning, deep cleaning, seasonal cleaning—call it what you will, these tasks have to get done, but they don't have to get done very often. These are the things you might do once or twice a year.

Deep-cleaning tasks can take some time, but if you do your maintenance cleaning regularly, much of it'll keep until you have the motivation. If seven years go by and you never actually wash your walls, who really cares? Give it another year and you'll probably need to repaint anyway. So prioritize the tasks that will result in damage to your health or home if left undone. For example, windows can get microscopic pitting and scratching on the glass surface if not cleaned regularly and dirty air filters fill your home with dust and allergens.

Then, tackle the projects that make your life easier in the long run, like culling clutter and organizing closets. I've seen home care lists that call for polishing of all your cooking pots every four months. Many of us struggle to find the time to simply boil water in the pot to make dinner. Give yourself permission to discard the ridiculous. Make dinner, wash your pot, and get on with your life.

A PLAN AND A SPRAY-BOTTLE
CAN TAKE YOU FAR

I make no secret of the fact that I would rather lie on a sofa than sweep beneath it. But you have to be efficient if you're going to be lazy.

—Shirley Conran

If you've tried—and failed—to stick to someone else's cleaning routine before, you're not alone. Take it from me, a mostly reformed slob—anyone can create a home where they love to be. But your family and your home is unique, and you need a home care routine made for you, not someone else. In this book, I'm going to give you great recipes for DIY cleaners, but if your home currently overwhelms you, first you need to DIY your home care routine and figure out what's important to you.

picture it

Look around your space and think about what the physical characteristics of a comforting home really are to you. Forget the images from magazines and Pinterest boards—you don't live in those homes and your kid or dog or party guests would ruin those white linen couches in ten minutes anyway. What state would your home have to be in for you to be able to grab a cup of tea and a favorite book and relax on your couch, or play with your kids, or spend an entire evening with your partner, without the nagging feeling that you maybe should, *should*, *SHOULD* be doing something else?

What would your home smell like? How clear would the surfaces be? Would there be flowers on the table? Would the bills be paid weekly? Monthly? Would your refrigerator be well stocked with food? What would be in there? How much decor would there be—do those little collections on the shelves add to your feeling of being happy at home, or are they just something that needs periodic dusting? Is your bed made, or rumpled? What does the front entry look like when people walk in the door?

Your idea of a peaceful home might be a restrained away space of Zen-like minimalism and quietude, or it might be a bustling, boisterous hub of activity, full of bright colors, lots of music, and laughter. There is no right or wrong here, because this isn't about some image of a home, it's about the deep way you and your family connect with your space, and how that connection makes you feel.

Now, take a minute and think about what tends to make your home a less peaceful place to be. Does anything stop you from walking in your door after a day at work and thinking, "Wow, I am so happy to be here!" Is it a toilet that keeps backing up? Tripping over shoes and toys? The dread of having to figure out what's for dinner at 5:45 . . . again?

Is getting everyone out the door in the mornings fairly calm, or more like herding cats, or just a frantic whirlwind of forgotten papers, missing homework, and unmade lunches?

Are there home care concerns you and a spouse, partner, or roommate argue about? If arguing about home care is really about the home care (and not, say, a proxy for some other issue), then perhaps managing the issues that lead to that relationship stress is your biggest priority.

write it

With your vision of your home clear in your head—both the calm ideal and the regular frustrations—write it down. If you are struggling with a sense of domestic chaos, please really do this. I know it seems silly, but what you write down here will guide you to create a homekeeping routine that can transform your home (or hey, maybe even your life).

Write down five to seven physical home care things that define your specific vision for a calm, comforting home. From a clear counter to a clean toilet to fresh flowers to a nicely stocked wine rack to music in the background—this is whatever makes your space wonderful to live in to you.

1. ....

2. ....

3. ....

4. ....

5. ....

6. ....

7. ....

Now write down three to five things that seem to get in the way of your calm-home vision.

Basics & Techniques

1. ....

2. ....

3. ....

4. ....

5. ....

Write down three specific things that make your mornings hectic.

1. ....

2. ....

3. ....

Write down three specific things that make your evenings hectic.

1. ....

2. ....

3. ....

Good. Now keep this with you—you'll need it for the next step.

make it: your custom daily routine

routines in the morning

The goal of a morning routine is to make your home a pleasant place to return after a day spent at work or school, or to create a calm environment in which to spend the day working or relaxing. If you work or raise children from home, "calm" is a relative term here.

The two areas of the home most likely to suffer minor upheaval in the morning are the bathroom (or bathrooms, depending on the size of your family and home) as we handle basic hygiene needs, and the kitchen as we break our nighttime fast. The morning routine puts those areas back in order.

Truly washing the bathroom is a pain, so I try to "make the clean last" as long as possible. I recommend keeping a squeegee in your shower and developing the simple habit of squeegeeing the hard surfaces of the shower after every use. This does so much to cut down on water spots and mineral buildup, and that means less frequent scrubbing and cleaning.

I also make it easy to wipe down my bathroom every morning by keeping a basket of inexpensive washcloths in a basket on the counter. Typical daily grime just wipes away onto a washcloth—it doesn't even need a spray down. After I'm done getting ready for the day and put away any toiletries I've used, I just spot wipe the mirror of any toothpaste splatters, then wipe the faucet, sink, and counter dry. I wipe the outside of the toilet and sprinkle a little Potty Powder (page 150) inside the toilet bowl on my way out. The washcloth gets tossed in the laundry, and I'm done. This takes about two minutes but resets the bathroom to cleanliness every morning.

In the kitchen, the same kind of reboot takes place after breakfast. Every morning, one of my kids unloads the dishwasher while the other feeds and waters our flock of chickens and ducks, and I make everyone a simple breakfast. After breakfast is over, dishes get loaded, counters get wiped down, and we head out the door. Our morning routine used to be far more frantic—trying to get lunches packed, finding paperwork or keys, etc.—but a good evening routine (see page 67) put a stop to that stress.

Your morning routine might also include time for yourself to exercise, meditate, pray, read, deal with paperwork, or just have quiet time before the rest of the family gets up. I know many, many people who enjoy taking half an hour a day to exercise, but if that self-care doesn't happen before the rest of the day's demands tumble into their laps, it's just not going to happen at all.

Sometimes carving out time at the beginning of the day means shifting your awake hours a bit. I'm a natural night owl. When I had the ability to set my own schedule, I tended to go to bed at about two a.m. and sleep until ten or eleven. I used to swear up and down that the only thing that would get me out of bed before eight a.m. was an international flight I was in danger of not catching.

Oh, how times have changed. I get up around five-thirty a.m. most mornings these days, and I'm pretty much toast and ready for bed by nine p.m. And you know what? I've actually come to like it. When you get up early, you own your time. By nine a.m. the rest of the world has reasonable expectations that they can jump in, dictate, interrupt, or otherwise steal bits of your time. Before dawn, your time is your own.

If you find you never have enough time in the day, or you just wish you could make a bit of time for yourself, consider the advantages of shifting your sleep patterns a bit. For me, both psychologically and practically, having a chunk of time in the day that's just mine has been incredibly rewarding.

Okay, now turn back to the list you made on page 64. Look at the three items you said make your evenings hectic. I'd place money on the odds that at least one of those items has to do with getting dinner ready. Even people who enjoy cooking don't like coming home at six-thirty and trying to figure out how to MacGyver dinner. So don't play that game. Work dinner prep into your morning routine. Pull out a freezer meal to thaw, marinate meat, or chop vegetables. Or, toss something in the Crock-Pot and program your rice cooker so that dinner is ready when you walk in the door in the evening. My mom calls this "getting your machines working for you" and, when time is tight, having a little robot food army to help you put dinner on the table can be a real stress buster.

Whatever bits of domestica are stealing the calm from your day or making evenings overfull, there is probably a way to get out ahead of them. Figure out what you can do in the morning to make your day smoother and more streamlined.

COMMON MORNING TASKS:

+ Squeegee shower
+ Wipe down bathroom surfaces
+ Open window curtains or blinds
+ Make bed
+ Turn off any exterior lights
+ Start a load of laundry

- Make breakfast
- Feed pets
- Clean up kitchen from breakfast
- Make coffee
- Prep for dinner

routines in the evening

The goal of your evening routine is to set yourself up with a pleasant home the next day. Your evening routine is a gift that Today You gives Tomorrow You—the gift of a house that isn't a train wreck. When wrangling a family, in particular, the stress of trying to get out the door for assorted school, day care, work, and other appointments can make mornings hair-rippingly painful. Your evening routine is the key to getting ahead of all that stress.

Look at the three things you identified on page 64 as making your mornings more frantic. Packing lunches; finding your car keys, bus pass, or parking permit; getting kids dressed; packing your computer case or diaper bag; getting an IV drip of coffee plugged directly into a major vein as soon as possible—whatever. What of those things can be eliminated from your morning to-do list or made simpler by actions taken the night before?

Those items should be the nonnegotiable heart of your evening routine. Do not let yourself whinge about these few basic things—Tomorrow You will thank Today You for your efforts.

COMMON EVENING TASKS THAT WILL STOP TOMORROW MORNING FROM SUCKING:

- Pack lunches
- Set out clothes
- Pack backpacks, suitcases, gym bags, laptop cases, purses, or diaper bags
- Set keys, wallet, phone, etc. someplace consistent (I'm terrible at this)
- Set up and preprogram the coffeemaker
- Premake breakfast (muffins, waffles, granola, frittatas, hard-boiled eggs, breakfast burritos, soaked oatmeal, etc.) or set out a "breakfast kit" to make it easier for older kids to handle their own breakfast prep
- Check tomorrow's schedule and prepare paperwork, etc., as needed

+ Check kids' homework, school papers, field trip permission slips, etc.

+ Gather anything needed for errands the next day, like library books to return, mail to post, or donations to drop off

Once you have established solid habits that stop tomorrow morning from being a sucky stress-fest, think about those peaceful-home priorities you set on page 63. What can you do every night to wake up to a home that gets you a little closer to those priorities? Those actions should form the second part of your evening routine, and you can work into these a bit at a time, building habits slowly as you go.

COMMON EVENING TASKS TO WAKE UP TO A CALMER HOME:

+ Do dishes and put away or load dishwasher and run, if needed

+ Clear and wipe down counters and sinks

+ Take out garbage, recycling, and compost

+ Set out clean kitchen towels

+ Sweep and quickly mop the kitchen floor

+ Put out-of-place stuff around the house back where it belongs

+ Check menu plan and take out items to thaw, marinate ahead, etc.

+ Fold and put away laundry

+ Spend a few minutes organizing a drawer, shelf, or area of your home to stay ahead of clutter

Finally, what can you do for you in the evening to increase your personal level of calm, boost your own resiliency to stress, and become a more productive person? A tidy house at the cost of a frantic mind is a poor trade-off. A few minutes of self-care every night can make a huge difference.

COMMON EVENING TASKS TO HELP BODY AND MIND WAKE UP REFRESHED THE NEXT DAY:

+ Meditate, pray, journal, read, or reflect to unburden yourself from the mental and emotional stressors of the day

+ Exercise, stretch, or take a bath to unburden yourself from the physical stressors of the day

+ Write down or say aloud one or two specific goals you'd like to achieve the next day

- Write down or say aloud some issue or problem, then relax and let your brain work on it while you sleep

- Get some sleep!

Look at your own calm-morning tasks and peaceful-home priorities on page 63 and develop an evening routine customized for your needs that will set you up for a great tomorrow.

implement it!

Making a list is the easy part; implementing is the tricky part. Write down your morning and evening routines and tape them someplace obvious while you are building these habits. I kept my morning routines taped to my bathroom mirror for about three years until I was sure I had them down. If you prefer, set alerts on your phone to remind you about your routines. That extra reminder can make all the difference.

Pick a week to start implementing your routines that's relatively calm, when you can take a few extra minutes in the morning and the evening to work through your list. Acknowledge that building new habits is a bit of an effort at first, but know that the payoff of a better-running home is worth it.

It's good to go slow, and, if your morning or evening routine list seems intimidatingly long, don't try to implement the whole thing at once. Start with those key evening things that will give you a calmer morning, and work from there.

Above all, don't worry if it takes you a few tries to build up your discipline muscle and stick to your routines. If you let it all go for awhile, just start back up when you can, with a set of routines that are designed for and realistic to your life.

YOUR CUSTOM REGULAR MAINTENANCE PLAN

Sticking to morning and evening routines will get you about 70 percent of the way to keeping your home a place you love to be. Most of the remainder is regular maintenance. This is the routine cleaning that marks the difference between a tidy home and a clean home.

There are four basic methods used for routine cleaning of a home. They all work, so pick the method or combination that works best for your schedule, personality, home, and family and customize away.

by day

"Before anyone does anything on Saturday, this house gets picked up."

A designated housecleaning day, where all deep-cleaning tasks are tackled in one big push, is a common and traditional way to keep house. This method has the advantage of giving you that glorious moment where everything is sparkling clean, all at the same time. For folks who work Monday through Friday, Saturday is the most common day to clean house. This method is typically excellent for singles or working couples with a modest-size home, because all the regular cleaning tasks can be tackled efficiently, leaving the rest of the weekend free for other activities.

For families with children, pets, and other sources of regular messes, waiting seven days between routine cleaning may result in more work, not less, and carving out several hours or more every week just to clean may be totally impractical. For families with larger homes, leaving all the cleaning for one big housekeeping session often means sacrificing an entire precious weekend day. When a housekeeping routine entails that much drudgery, for that long, it will almost certainly be abandoned.

by time

"I'm going to set a timer for twenty-five minutes. How much of the house we can clean in that time?"

Cleaning by time assigns a certain number of minutes beyond the daily pickup and tidying to actual cleaning. As much of the house is cleaned as possible during that time frame, and then cleaning time is over. The next day's cleaning takes up where the prior's left off.

This is a very effective way to get a lot done in a little amount of time, and the use of a timer can be very helpful in incentivizing children and other family members to participate in the daily clean. In fact, this method is really at its best when great music is put on and everyone pitches in until the timer goes off. It's also ideal for people who get distracted easily when cleaning and tend to wander off to other activities (I'm raising my hand here).

If you set a timer for five minutes a day this week, seven minutes a day next week, ten minutes a day the week after, and so on, you can build up your mental, emotional, and even physical stamina for cleaning without getting overwhelmed. Cleaning by time can also be excellent for naturally tidy folks who want to challenge themselves to get the housework done as quickly as possible.

This method can be more challenging for people who do not yet instinctively know what to do to clean a space or how long certain tasks, once started, will take to complete. The "stopping to figure it out" aspect of cleaning can eat up a lot of time. Without a little experience and "cleaning sense," a time-based method can require more setup and strike cost compared to other cleaning methods. Let's say the timer goes off halfway through vacuuming the living room. Well, tomorrow you'll be getting out and putting away the vacuum cleaner to fully finish the task of vacuuming that carpet. These issues can tend to cause "timer creep," because most people realize that it's less efficient to vacuum half a room twice than a full room once. For cleaning by time to be it's most psychologically effective, you have to know there is a defined stopping point.

by zone

"Today we clean the kitchen, tomorrow the dining room, the day after the front entry."

Cleaning by zone has many of the same benefits of cleaning by time. There is a defined end, and you can push yourself to accomplish the day's goal faster. While I am a big advocate of everyone in a family pitching in to help maintain the family home, in many homes most cleaning is still done primarily by one adult. Cleaning by zone is a great option in situations like these, where many bodies in the same space can lead to more chaos than help anyway.

When well planned, cleaning by zone can accommodate regular activities better than cleaning by time. You simply assign more labor and time-intensive tasks, like deep-cleaning the kitchen, to days with a bit more unscheduled time, and light tasks, like sweeping the front entry, to days that are more full.

For homekeepers who don't know where to begin, I believe cleaning by zone can be the best way to tackle a home maintenance routine. When you are first starting, it's easy to develop a checklist for each zone and keep it with you as you clean that area. Over time, your checklist will migrate mostly to your head and you will get more efficient with your motions. Home maintenance guru FlyLady advocates cleaning by zone, and her system has helped countless beginning homekeepers get their routines in order.

by task

"Today we clean all the mirrors in the house, tomorrow we wipe and scrub all the toilets, the day after we sweep or vacuum the floors."

Cleaning by task minimizes the setup and strike time of each job. You might only get your glass cleaner or your vacuum cleaner out a few times a month, instead of nearly every day, as with many other methods. This method is ideal for singles or couples who don't make their house particularly dirty through day-to-day living, and for folks living in modest homes where it won't take a discouraging amount of time to, say, vacuum all the carpet in the house.

A well-implemented cleaning routine based on task will leave the impression that nothing is ever that dirty, but a poorly implemented one can leave the impression that nothing is ever really clean, either. In larger families, or for homes with young children or pets, if cleaning by task isn't very well planned, tasks can be too spaced out for the daily mess created. Imagine spending the time to mop the bathroom floor, but leaving the mirror and toilet untouched for several more days or a week. If this scenario would work fine in your home, cleaning by task can be a great way to hit all the major areas of cleaning in a minimum of daily cleaning time. If all you can picture is dried little boy pee on the toilet ruining your impression of a clean bathroom, cleaning by task probably isn't right for you right now.

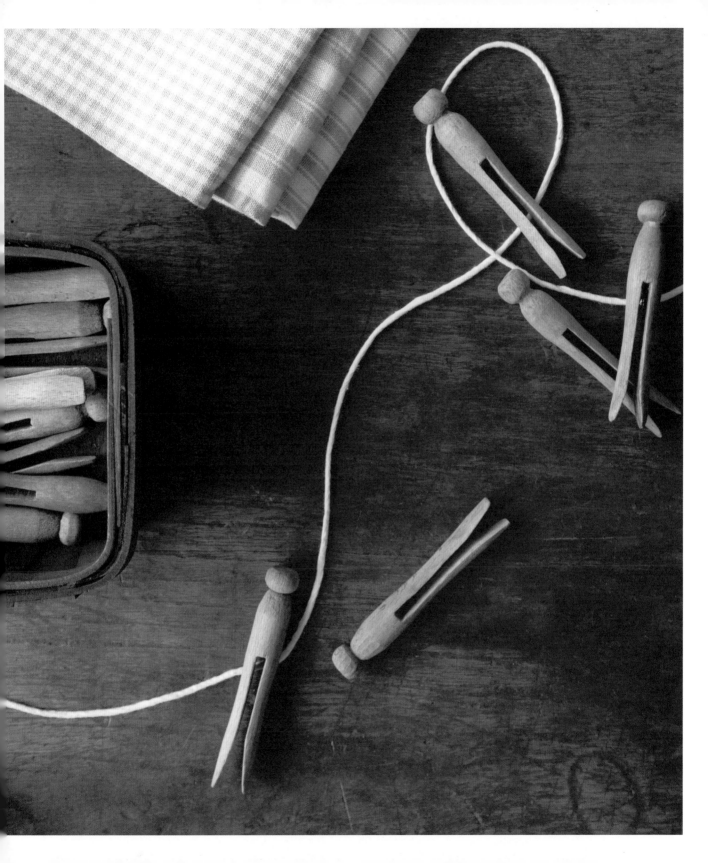

Before you even worry about this, get your daily routines down. Tackle dirty dishes before worrying about your dusty knickknacks. Got it? Good.

Think about which of the cleaning methods make the most sense for your family, home, and lifestyle. How can you best fit routine cleaning into your week? I like to plan my routine maintenance on a biweekly basis. Some people prefer a weekly routine.

If your routine is day-based, write down what day the main cleaning will take place and a checklist of tasks to complete. If your routine is task- or zone-based, make a weekly or biweekly chart of what gets done when. If your routine is time-based, schedule a regular appointment for cleaning on your calendar.

Here's my home care routine as an example. It's based on cleaning by zones, and is designed so that the main powder room and the kitchen are cleaned weekly (because they need it!), but everything else is spread out over two weeks so no single day's cleaning takes too long. It's simple and straightforward.

	WEEK ONE	WEEK TWO
MONDAY	Kitchen + Deep Clean One Appliance	Kitchen + Deep Clean One Appliance
TUESDAY	Master Bathroom	Dining Room
WEDNESDAY	Master Bedroom	Living Room
THURSDAY	Laundry Room, Hallway, Stairs	Desk + Bill Pay
FRIDAY	Kids' Bedroom + Bathroom	Front Hall + Home Entrance
SATURDAY	Powder Room + Catch-up	Powder Room + Catch-up
SUNDAY	Rest	Rest

SIX TIPS FOR A PERFECT HOMEKEEPING ROUTINE

1. KEEP IT SIMPLE—If you make this more complicated than it needs to be, you won't do it.

2. MAKE IT YOURS—Design your homekeeping routine around your life, schedule, and needs, not some magical plan from a magazine.

3. BE CONSISTENT—A little bit done every day will keep your house from falling into disaster. If you fall off the home maintenance wagon, just jump back on as soon as you can.

4. COME HELL OR HIGH WATER, DO YOUR EVENING ROUTINE—A completed evening routine is the gift Today You gives Tomorrow You. More than anything else, this sets you up for homekeeping success.

5. MAKE A LIST—I'm sure many people get so good at maintaining their home that they'd never forget to sweep the kitchen before bed. Me? I still like the reminder.

6. BE FOCUSED—When you are cleaning something, just clean it. Don't get distracted into a tizzy of other tasks. You can get cleaning done really fast if you just suck it up and do it.

HOW TO SET UP A CLEANING TOTE

I set aside time every day to get my maintenance cleaning done—not time to wander all around my house trying to find a toilet brush and the cleaning spray. My cleaning tote is where all my routine cleaning sprays and tools live. You can fit everything you need to clean your house in one tote, except a mop, a long-handled duster, and a vacuum. If you can't, you've probably fallen prey to the siren marketing song of the chemical companies who want you to think you need a separate foam, spray, wipe, or gel for everything in your home.

Totes themselves are inexpensive and widely available. Substitute a medium-size bucket if you prefer. With tote in hand, everything you need to efficiently get a space clean fast is right there and ready. Stock your cleaning tote with the following:

+ Glass Cleaner (page 143)
+ All-Purpose Cleaner (page 144)
+ Acidic Bathroom Cleaner (page 146)
+ Greasy Grime Spray (page 148)
+ Basic Scrubbing Powder (page 149)
+ Potty Powder (page 150)
+ Several lint-free rags or microfiber cloths
+ Scratch-free scrubbing pad
+ Squeegee
+ Cleaning toothbrush
+ Rubber gloves
+ One disposable bag for garbage
+ One reusable market bag, for returnables

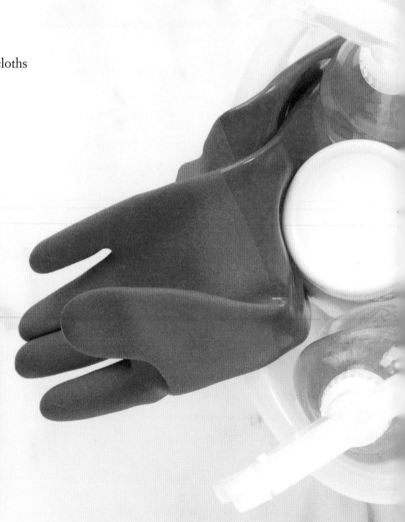

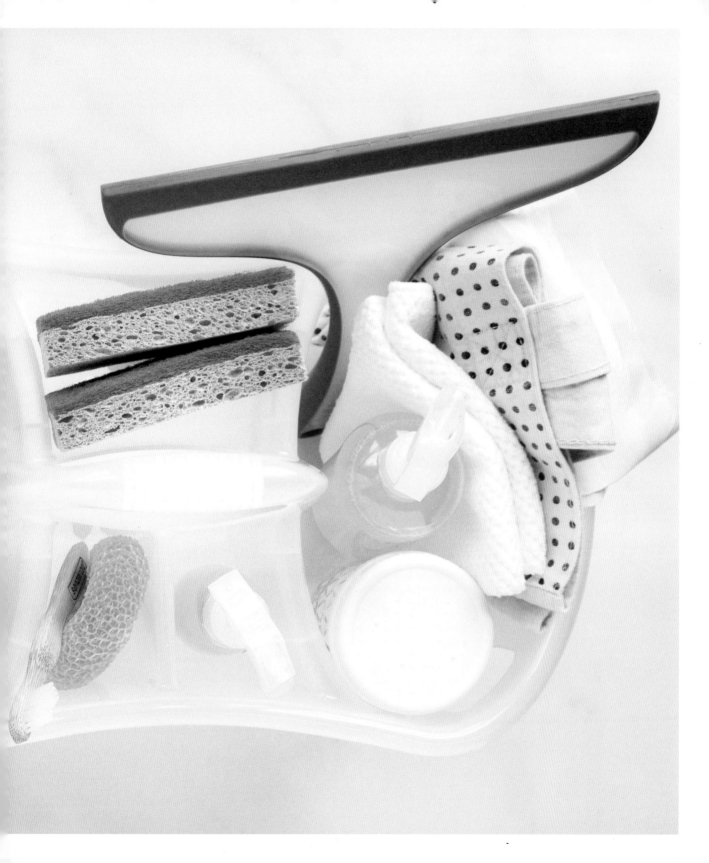

HOW TO CLEAN A ROOM

It's worth learning how to clean a room efficiently, so you can spend less time cleaning! I only learned how to clean really efficiently when I had to teach my oldest child (not a naturally tidy child—she takes after her mama) how to clean her room. I thought about cleaning from first principles, did some research on how professional housekeepers clean efficiently, and developed this method to help her. In the process, I honed my own cleaning.

When cleaning, the golden rules are (1) work top to bottom, (2) no backtracking, and (3) clean by circling a room, not going back and forth across it.

For most rooms, start your cleaning action at the door, work around the room in a loop (I generally work to the right), and end at the door. This way you know you haven't missed a spot. I repeat this circle a few times, focusing on the task I'm doing during that "loop" and, even if I end up circling a room three times, the total time spent cleaning is minimized. Working in a loop allows me to keep my cleaning supplies at the door as a sort of "home base" of cleaning.

1. STEP ONE: THE TRASH AND TIDY LOOP

Circle the room with a disposable garbage bag and a reusable cloth market bag. All garbage goes in the garbage bag and anything that needs to be returned to some other room ("returnables") goes into the reusable bag. As you make this circle, straighten items within the room that are out of place. End the tidy loop by dropping garbage and returnables at the door and start another circle.

2. STEP TWO: THE DUSTING LOOP

Grab the long-handled duster and dust anything tall: light fixtures, ceilings, walls, trim, etc. Work in a loop around the room, ending at the door. Drop off your duster.

3. STEP THREE: THE CLEANING LOOP

Grab the cleaning tote from the door. Spray one rag with all-purpose cleaner and one with glass cleaner. Work around the room, wiping hard surfaces with the all-purpose cleaner rag and glass surfaces with the glass cleaner rag. Remember to work top to bottom—and use both hands to make the work go faster. End at the door.

4. **STEP FOUR: THE MIDDLE**

With three quick circles of a room, everything is straightened, dusted, and wiped down. After this, I deal with anything like making beds or vacuuming furniture, then vacuum, sweep, or mop the floor, working back out toward the door.

5. **STEP FIVE: THE PUT AWAY**

An oft-forgotten part of cleaning! Throw out the trash, return "returnables" to their home, put away the vacuum and your cleaning tote. You're done!

In "wet rooms," like the kitchen and bathrooms, the same basic principles apply, but things like stoves, refrigerators, bathtubs, and showers are deep-cleaned between dusting and general wipe-down.

SEASONAL CLEANING AND SPECIAL PROJECTS

> *I hate housework. You make the beds, you wash the dishes, and six months later you have to start all over again.*
>
> —JOAN RIVERS

Spring cleaning, deep cleaning, seasonal cleaning—call it what you will, these tasks have to get done, but they don't have to get done very often. These are the things you might do once, twice—up to maybe four times a year if you're very ambitious. (I'm not.)

Some people set aside a long weekend every year to clean the house top to bottom. For the right person, there is something very fulfilling about giving your space a thorough going-over. Personally, I am of the philosophy that, if you are regularly doing the maintenance cleaning of your home, you will notice when things should be attended to at a deeper level. In other words, I think it's perfectly fine to spring clean as the mood strikes.

If the mood never strikes, well then you may have to force the issue. Twice yearly, in spring and again in fall, attend to those things that are brought out and brought in seasonally, like outdoor furniture and clothing. Check around the house for any evidence of water or pest damage and attend to anything that might damage your home promptly. Water—either from internal leaks or from exterior intrusion—will mess your space up fast, so any sign of water damage, leaking, drips, mold, or mildew should be dealt with ASAP.

Here are a dozen deep-cleaning tasks you should tackle even if spring cleaning doesn't put the bounce in your bungee.

1. Wash windows and their screens, inside and out—once a year in the spring, or every six months if you can manage. If you never clean your windows, airborne pollution can actually damage the glass over time, leading to microscopic pits and etching of any surface coatings on your windows.

2. Deep clean carpets—once a year or once every other year, if you are very tidy. A good, annual deep-extraction cleaning will help your carpets last far longer, saving money in the long run.

3. Test all your fail-safe devices: smoke alarms, sump pumps, carbon monoxide detectors, fire extinguishers, etc. Repair or replace anything that's not working. A fire or flood in your home is bad enough; the thought that you could have prevented it with a four-dollar battery will make it even worse. Do this twice a year.

4. Vacuum the condenser coils on your refrigerator annually. This will help your refrigerator run more efficiently, saving you money.

5. Go through each closet and pull out clothes you or family members will never wear again. Donate them and make someone else's life better, or, if they are too worn to donate, tear them up for cleaning rags or discard. Do this once a year if you don't swap out warm weather and cool weather wardrobes, or twice a year, on the switch, if you do. Only store things you'll really wear in the future.

6. Go through each bathroom and utility space and throw out expired or unwanted medicines, cosmetics, cleaning supplies, etc. Less is more.

7. Clean out the lint from your dryer exhaust vent to keep your dryer operating efficiently and cut down on the risk of a lint fire. Save the lint if you want and mix it with old candle wax to make homemade fire starters (that's ironic, huh?).

8. Change or wash the air filters on heaters and air conditioners, so that you aren't breathing gross dusty air. You should do this about every three months, but check with your particular model of heater and/or air conditioner.

9. Move beds or mattresses and vacuum underneath because there might be a monster there made of old socks, books, and rubber bands. Do this once a year, or more often if your under-the-bed monster might be made of discarded pizza crusts and stinky gym shoes.

10. Air out mattresses and box springs by opening all the bedroom windows on a pleasant day and tipping up the mattress and box spring for maximum airflow, or hauling the mattress outside if you are certain the day will be sunny and dry. Give An Old-Fashioned Mattress Airing for a Sunny Day (page 252) a try.

11. Take down and wash light fixtures once a year to cut down on that overhead "bug mausoleum" vibe in your bedroom.

12. Open up any drawers that have been colonized by crumbs, clutter, or mystery stickiness and give them a good organization and scrub.

There are a million checklists for seasonal cleaning you can download, but if you keep in mind that spring cleaning is mostly about throwing open the windows and letting the fresh air in, and fall cleaning is mostly about buttoning everything up for winter, you won't go wrong.

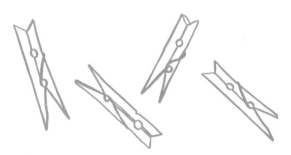

Simple Personal Care

Your skin, as I'm sure you've heard, is your body's largest organ. So really, does it make sense to wash, moisturize, scrub, and spritz with a bunch of chemicals, petroleum byproducts, and fragrances, all bound up in various harsh alcohol-based solvents? You wouldn't do that to your heart or your liver, so why put your poor epidermis through it?

Your body is a finely crafted organism that makes minute adjustments at the cellular level every moment of every day to keep things in balance. Sure, during times of sickness, hormonal flux, or stress, things can get funky, but generally speaking a healthy human body does a pretty great job at self-regulating everything from the pH and sugar levels in your blood to the temperature of your body. Even things like the oil and sebum content of your skin are subject to minute adjustments as your body tries to balance everything out.

The vast majority of the most effective, nonprescription personal care products out there work on a few simple properties.

1. CLEAN
They remove oils, dirt, and odor-causing bacteria from the face, body, or hair.

2. MOISTURIZE
They add oils or other moisture-enhancing substances to the face, body, or hair.

3. EXFOLIATE
They remove dead skin cells and break up sebum in clogged pores through scrubbing or the topical application of acids to the skin.

Unfortunately, the products used to achieve these simple ends often do more harm than good. When the skin is stripped of all its natural oils with harsh detergents or alcohols, it freaks out at losing this natural moisture layer and responds by increasing oil production to make up for what has been lost.

This is a vicious skin care cycle. When strong chemical exfoliants are over-applied, they strip the protective outer layer of the skin, and side effects are increased susceptibility to damage from the sun, redness, and inflammation. In this way what we do to look healthy and glowing often backfires, leaving our body less able to naturally repair itself and actually be healthy and glowing.

As I've moved away from commercial body care products, I've been rewarded. My skin and hair appreciate a DIY, lighter-touch approach to personal care. The less I fuss, the happier I am with how I look. So many of the personal care products we buy are designed to mimic the look of health: clear skin, shiny hair. I'm no supermodel, but my skin cleared up when I stopped coating it with chemical goos every day, and my hair became softer and shinier when I stopped stripping it of its natural oils. Sometimes, less really is more.

PERSONAL CARE BASICS

I believe the best body care solutions are usually cheap and simple: common, natural products that gently achieve your cleaning, moisturizing, and exfoliating needs while letting your body self-regulate. Putting these products together is very simple, and with a little experimentation you can customize your own personal care products with your preferred textures, cleaning or moisturizing properties, and fragrances—all while saving money and knowing exactly what went into every cleanser, cream, and scrub.

If DIY personal care is so easy, why are there thousands and thousands of commercial products out there, all trying to convince us that they—and they alone—have the solution to our body care needs? Well, it's big business! The personal care industry in the United States is worth about $80 billion annually, with new products released nearly every day. That's a lot of face goo.

The first step in moving toward a healthier personal care routine is asking yourself what's really necessary. Some people have transitioned off shampoo and conditioner entirely—and their hair is better for it. Still others have discovered that skipping soap and washing their face with oil actually prevents their skin from getting greasy. Look at your personal care routines as a skeptic, unbiased by the powerful marketing images in magazines and online, and question what you consider essential. It might be possible to radically simplify your personal care routine without turning yourself into a stinky mess of a person.

Once you've simplified, you'll probably find that with just a few ingredients, you can make nearly everything that meets your personal care needs yourself. Heck, you can even make stuff you just want because it's fun or nurturing. More good news: many of the components for these items are probably in your kitchen already.

PERSONAL CARE ESSENTIALS

APPLE CIDER VINEGAR, LEMON JUICE, AND CITRIC ACID: Diluted, these acids are used to pH-balance the skin or hair after cleaning with alkalies like soap, provide a light chemical exfoliation, and adjust the pH of body care products.

ARROWROOT POWDER, CORNSTARCH, MAGNESIUM CARBONATE POWDER, AND CREAM OF TARTAR POWDER: These absorbent powders can be used in deodorant powders and stick deodorants to blot up moisture, and in bath soaks or bath bombs.

BAKING SODA: What can't baking soda do? A very gentle exfoliant, baking soda can be mixed with oil to create a scrub that won't irritate skin (see page 203). It's a key ingredient in Peppermint Tooth Powder (page 153) and Creamy Bar Deodorant (page 160). Baking soda is often added to bath soak mixtures and can be blended with water, castile soap, or shampoo to strip excess styling product buildup from hair.

BEESWAX: Beeswax is mixed with oils when a natural hardener is needed to keep personal care products solid. It's used in moisturizing bars, lip balms, hair styling products, and stick deodorant. Pure small beeswax disks (called pastilles) are the easiest to work with. Seller claims of organic or cosmetic-grade beeswax should be approached with caution. Read online reviews to find a reliable source for high-quality wax.

COCONUT OIL, SHEA BUTTER, AND COCOA BUTTER: Soft-solid at cool room temperature, these fats are common ingredients in balms, moisturizers, scrubs, and thicker oil-based cleansers.

EPSOM SALTS: Pure magnesium sulfate, Epsom salts are the primary ingredient in many bath crystals. Used as a bath soak, the magnesium is absorbable through the skin and soothes sore, tired muscles. Epsom salts can also be used as an exfoliating body scrub, though the chunky crystals are too rough to use on delicate facial skin. Less drying to skin and hair than regular salt, Epsom salts are used in salt-based hair sprays.

LIQUID CASTILE SOAP: Useful for cleaning nearly every part of the body, this gentle but concentrated soap can be diluted to the appropriate strength required for different cleaning needs.

OAT FLOUR AND MILK POWDER: These soothing ingredients can be added to bath soaks and facial blends. Oat flour is rich in beta-glucan, which helps calm itchy or irritated skin. Milk powder is also soothing, and contains small amounts of lactic acid, a mild chemical exfoliant that helps minimize pigmentation spots and roughness on the skin. For an even bigger dose of lactic acid, yogurt powder can be used in place of milk powder.

OLIVE, AVOCADO, GRAPESEED, SWEET ALMOND, AND CASTOR OILS: Liquid at room temperature, these oils are widely available, gentle, and effective at cleaning facial skin. They are also blended with other oils and natural waxes as an ingredient in balms, moisturizers, scrubs, and oil-based cleansers.

ORGANIC SUGAR: An excellent exfoliant, the gritty texture of organic sugar (often sold as evaporated cane juice) makes an ideal hand or body scrub when mixed with oil, for moisture, or soap, for cleansing.

VEGETABLE GLYCERIN AND HONEY: Glycerin is a byproduct of soapmaking. Both glycerin and honey are hydroscopic, which means they draw moisture to them, and emollient, which means they soothe the skin. You'll find both glycerin and honey used as ingredients in skin and hair care products. Honey is well known as a natural sweetener. While I don't recommend chowing down on glycerin, it is also edible and is used as a sweetener in processed and low-carbohydrate foods. Synthetic glycerin is petroleum-based, so stick with vegetable glycerin, which can be made from coconut, palm, soy, or other vegetable oils. If you have concerns about specific oils, look for glycerin derived from an oil you can support.

FUN WITH FRAGRANCE: ESSENTIAL OILS

You know when you squeeze an orange wedge and a bunch of oil squirts out of the peel and all over your counter and then everything smells like an orange juice factory for awhile? Well, those teeny drops that puffed out of the orange peel are the orange's essential oils.

Essential oils are the volatile aroma compounds of a plant. All plants have minuscule amounts of essential oil and through various methods (some more earth-friendly than others), these volatiles are extracted, then bottled. In the case of oils, "essential" refers to the aroma essence of a plant, flower, or whatnot; it doesn't mean that these oils are essential to human health or well-being.

Many essential oils—tea tree chief among them, but also cinnamon, clove, rosemary, and thyme oil—have proven antibacterial properties in lab settings. The essential oils of eucalyptus seem to relieve symptoms of colds and common respiratory ailments. There's even one study that suggests a blend of several essential oils can help regrow hair in balding men.

But most studies of essential oils are quite limited, and unfortunately the proven efficacy of these oils does not generally match the enthusiastic claims of those selling them. As with anything that seems too good to be true, it's wise to approach broad-spectrum claims about the therapeutic aspects of essential oil therapy with some skepticism.

Undiluted essential oils can irritate skin, trigger rashes or allergic reaction, and increase the skin's sensitivity to sunlight. If consumed, some essential oils are toxic in even small amounts. Use good judgment: don't use essential oils on children, if you are pregnant, or internally. If you have concerns, consult a doctor, qualified naturopath, or herbalist who can guide you in their safe and appropriate use.

I love how the concentrated, potent smells of essential oils can make my home and personal care products smell wonderful. I don't always love cleaning my kitchen, but the fresh smell of mint and rosemary in my DIY cleaning spray sure makes the process more pleasant. I use my favorite oils to achieve fragrances I love and to help inspire certain moods. As used in this book—in tiny amounts, well diluted for home care and topical uses—essential oils are safe and fun.

top essential oils

Just starting out? Interested in exploring the yummy-smelling world of essential oils without spending an arm and a leg on little bottles? You can buy "starter" or "sampler" kits of essential oils online, and these can be cost effective.

However, I think it's better to find someplace where you can actually smell the testers of various scents. Large health-food-oriented supermarkets, co-ops, wellness stores, and large drugstores are good places to find racks of essential oils. Sniff around and have fun. You may find, as I have, that one brand's version of an essential oil can smell very different from another, and you might have a distinct preference.

The top five most versatile essential oils for home and personal care are:

+ Tea tree   + Sweet orange

+ Lavender   + Rosemary

+ Peppermint

If you have a bit more money to spend, the following round out my top ten:

+ Lemongrass   + Cedarwood

+ Eucalyptus   + Cinnamon

+ Bergamot

Note that pets, and cats in particular, don't always metabolize essential oils the same way people do. Many of our most popular and most used essential oils, including peppermint, lavender, and citrus can be harmful to our fluffy little friends. Some authorities just warn against using these essential oils directly on pets or diffusing them into the air, while others recommend avoiding them in household products as well. If you have pets in the house, do a little research to determine which essential oils can be used safely in your home.

favorite essential oil blends

These blends make twenty to thirty drops of essential oil, enough to scent most of the recipes in this book. Scale up or down as you desire and play around with your own favorite scents.

Most essential oils are sold in very small bottles with a built-in restrictor insert at the mouth of the bottle. To measure out drops, unlid the bottle and flip it upside down. Hold the bottle still—don't shake—and individual drops will fall from the insert. Just count them as they fall from the bottle.

If your essential oil bottle comes with a suction dropper or pipette, squeeze the bulb at the top of the dropper, then suck up your essential oil by releasing pressure on the bulb. Gently squeeze the dropper bulb so that individual drops of essential oil can be counted out. Return any unused essential oil to the bottle.

There is some variation in the size of "drops" you'll get from different brand's restrictor inserts and droppers but generally, twenty to twenty-five drops of essential oil equal a milliliter, or just under a quarter teaspoon. For the purposes of the recipes in this book, small variations in the size of drops don't matter.

fresh and cleansing

My personal favorite essential oil blend, this gender-neutral scent is clean, fresh, and just a little medicinal. Use with spray cleaners, hair rinses and hair styling creams, and body and room sprays. The tea tree oil makes it especially appropriate for deodorant sticks and powders where a little boost of antibacterial power is appreciated.

+ 12 drops tea tree essential oil
+ 8 drops peppermint essential oil
+ 8 drops rosemary essential oil

calming

Excellent in bath-soak applications and for body moisturizers and powders, this has a floral, feminine scent for relaxing applications.

+ 10 drops lavender essential oil
+ 5 drops chamomile essential oil
+ 3 drops lemon essential oil
+ 2 drops ylang-ylang essential oil

spa treatment

A clean, wide-awake scent great for home care products and in bath crystals, oils, and soaks. I also like this blend in leather and wood polishes.

+ 10 drops eucalyptus essential oil

+ 8 drops lemongrass essential oil

+ 5 drops peppermint essential oil

+ 4 drops rosemary essential oil

woods and spice

This is a warm, masculine scent good for hair-styling creams, body sprays, deodorant sticks, and powders, and any home care products or room sprays when you want a "Cabin at Christmastime" kind of vibe.

+ 10 drops cedarwood essential oil

+ 5 drops fir essential oil

+ 5 drops clove essential oil

+ 5 drops sweet orange essential oil

citrus and spice

Another warm, wintertime scent, this manages to smell both comforting and spice-road exotic at the same time. A great choice for potpourri, seasonal soaps, and hand creams, and for adding to a revitalizing leather furniture or shoe polish cream.

+ 7 drops clove essential oil

+ 7 drops lemon essential oil

+ 5 drops cinnamon bark essential oil

+ 3 drops eucalyptus essential oil

+ 2 drops rosemary essential oil

+ 2 drops sweet orange essential oil

buzz-off insect-repelling blend

The oils in this blend have insect-repelling qualities. Although this isn't a substitute for commercial insect repellents in areas at high-risk for insect-spread diseases like lyme disease, it can help make a summer picnic a little more pleasant. Use very diluted as a body spray, or make a more concentrated version for applying to picnic blankets and beach towels. Do not apply a concentrated essential oil blend directly to the skin.

+ 8 drops citronella essential oil
+ 5 drops tea tree essential oil
+ 5 drops eucalyptus essential oil
+ 5 drops rosemary essential oil
+ 3 drops lemongrass essential oil

fresh grapefruit

Another personal favorite, this is mostly that pure, refreshing grapefruit smell, just slightly warmed up with a little bergamot, mint, and cinnamon. To me, this combo just smells happy! A great all-purpose, gender-neutral blend for home and personal care. I am particularly fond of this blend when added to carpet fresheners, glass cleaners, and when diluted as a body spray in the summer.

+ 15 drops grapefruit essential oil
+ 5 drops bergamot essential oil
+ 5 drop peppermint essential oil
+ 2 drops cinnamon essential oil

tea, earl grey, hot

Dominated by bergamot oil, the same oil that gives Earl Grey tea its characteristic taste and aroma, this gender-neutral blend is a great choice when you want a very relaxing scent that's not floral-forward. Ideal for bath and body care products, this wouldn't be out of place as a room or linen spray.

+ 15 drops bergamot essential oil
+ 8 drops lavender essential oil
+ 4 drops lemon essential oil

COLD-PROCESS SOAP

When I first tried soap-making, I didn't know that I would become moderately obsessed with this creative, fun, productive hobby. I love the scientific alchemy of soap, and the skin-friendly, natural cleaning bars that result. Traditional cold-process soap is better for your skin than most commercial bars because all the naturally occurring glycerin remains in the bar. Glycerin is moisturizing, so it makes for a more skin-friendly bar of soap, and is an essential ingredient in many moisturizers. In most commercial soaps, the valuable glycerin is separated from the soap itself and sold off as a separate product.

what is soap?

Bar soap is made through a specific chemical reaction between fats and a strong alkali called sodium hydroxide, or lye. This process is called saponification, and when it's complete, no lye and only very small amounts of fat remain—everything gets converted to this amazing new thing we call soap. It's essential that the lye and fat quantities be weighed precisely because any residual lye in a bar of soap would be a very bad thing.

Different oils require different amounts of lye to fully saponify, so this is one of these things where you can't substitute whatever oils you have on hand. If you make adjustments to any soap-making recipe, check your recipe with an online lye calculator (there are several—just search) to ensure all your quantities will result in a safe and fully saponified soap. The recipes for bar soap in this book are all designed to leave between 5 and 7 percent of the oils in the soap unsaponified. This allows for a little safety margin with the lye and makes for a more moisturizing bar of soap.

soap safety—read this first!

Making soap is a little like swimming with sharks. If you don't want to end up in the hospital, you need to protect yourself and pay attention the whole time. You must be very precise because making soap means working with lye. Never forget that lye is a highly corrosive alkali that will happily eat through your skin or eyeballs if it splashes on you. Always wear eye protection, gloves, and long sleeves, and weigh everything carefully, and you'll be totally fine.

packaging and containers

One of the tremendous advantages of more DIY in your home is getting away from excess packaging and the disposable mentality that accompanies it. I buy nearly all of my home and personal care items in big, bulk-size packages. The small containers, jars, balm tins, and spray bottles I use to package and store my finished products are all indefinitely reusable—either glass, metal, or heavy-duty plastic.

When you are just getting started with DIY home and personal care, I recommend reusing packaging from stuff you already have on hand. The small metal tins used to package breath mints can be great for creams and balms (wash them out well or you might find minty freshness someplace unexpected!). I often use the four-ounce mason jars and eight-ounce widemouthed mason jars for lotions, and use five-hundred-milliliter bail-closing glass jars for scrubs. Reuse spray bottles from your old cleaning products and glass jars for your lotions and you might never need to buy packaging for packaging's sake ever again.

In the long run, going the bulk-purchase route saves a ton of money, so if you do like this kind of thing, it can make sense to invest in some reusable containers you love.

Plastic spray bottles are the way to go for everyday cleaning solutions. While I totally understand the motivation to get away from plastic as much as possible, cleaning up typically involves water, slippery stuff like soap, and (hopefully) some quick movement to get the job done. I've dropped my cleaning sprays more than once and have been very grateful they simply bounced and sloshed.

For personal care containers, I generally prefer anything but plastic. If you like the convenience of twist-up deodorant or capped lip balm, you can also find new, unfilled plastic versions of those containers online and reuse them many times. I use a plastic twist-up deodorant tube, but otherwise prefer little metal tins with twist-on or lug closures (slip-fit closures loosen over time) because they are easier to get very clean for long-term reuse.

I am in the habit of mixing and cooling my lye solution in the sink, and I think you should adopt this habit too. If lye solution splashes, overflows, or tips over, there is far less potential for damage if that solution is in the sink rather than on a counter.

If lye, lye solution, or uncured soap splashes on you, wash the area thoroughly with a full running stream of cold water. If you are splashed over a large area of your body or the burning sensation does not abate with rinsing, call 911.

Never make soap when young children or pets are around—ever. If you have young children, wait until someone else can watch them or they are asleep to make your soap. Homemade soap is never worth taking your child to the emergency room, so don't get careless when you are dealing with lye, even for a minute.

essential equipment

To make cold-process bar soap, you will need:

+ Protective gear: goggles, gloves, long sleeves, etc.

+ Oils and fats, as called for in the recipe.

+ Pure, 100 percent sodium hydroxide lye. This is typically sold as a granular drain cleaner in hardware stores. Make sure it contains nothing but sodium hydroxide.

+ An accurate digital scale.

+ One quart-size, heat-resistant plastic or Pyrex pitcher for holding the lye solution. If you use plastic, mark this LYE, keep it out of reach of children, and don't use it for anything but holding your lye solution.

+ One small, pint-size stainless steel bowl or plastic container for measuring out the dry lye. If you use plastic, mark this LYE, keep it out of reach of children, and don't use it for anything but measuring your lye.

+ An old plastic or stainless steel spoon, or disposable wooden chopsticks, for stirring the lye solution.

+ A large, stainless steel (never aluminum!) pot, for melting fats and oils and blending soap. This pot should be large enough that the total volume of fats and lye solution together do not fill the pot more than halfway.

+ An instant-read thermometer for checking the temperature of fats and lye solution.

+ A cheap immersion blender you can dedicate to soap making (see page 96).

+ A soap mold. I like silicone molds, but a plastic-wrapped lined cardboard box works great too.

- A scrap of heavy cardboard slightly bigger than your soap mold.

- A small cooler (optional, but handy if you have it).

- Vinegar, for cleanup.

- Several old, large rags or towels.

basic steps

1. Empty your sink if necessary, and put on all your protective gear (eye goggles, gloves, long sleeves, etc.). Make sure kids, pets, and any other trip hazards are out of your work space. Prepare your soap molds (see page 96).

2. Measure water into your heat-resistant plastic or Pyrex pitcher. Set the pitcher in your sink. This will contain any overflow that might occur during the water-lye reaction. Precisely measure the lye into a small stainless steel bowl, then carefully add the lye to the water. *(Never add water to lye!)* Do not lean over the lye solution or inhale the fumes from the lye water! The water will become cloudy and will get quite hot. It may even "smoke" a bit—this is normal. Stir to fully dissolve the lye, then let the lye solution sit to cool as you melt the oils.

3. Carefully weigh your fats and oils and add them to a large, stainless steel pot. Never use aluminum in soap making. Melt fats and oils slowly together over medium-low heat, stirring occasionally. The oils just need to fully melt; you don't want them to get any hotter than necessary. Remove the melted oil from the heat and allow to cool.

4. When the lye and the oils are within 15 degrees of each other and are both around 110 degrees F or the temperature called for in the recipe, move the pot of warm oil into the sink and carefully pour the lye solution into the oil. *(Never add the oils to the lye!)*

5. Stir the mixture gently with your immersion blender to help bring the oils and lye together, then turn the immersion blender on its lowest speed. Blend the soap thoroughly, moving the immersion blender around the pot, until your soap thickens and achieves trace (see page 97).

6. When the soap achieves trace, add any essential oils as desired, blend to fully incorporate, and pour and scrape the soap into your prepared mold or molds.

7. Cover the soap with a layer of plastic wrap, then insulate or chill it as desired, to achieve a fully gelled or a no-gel soap (see page 97).

8. Leave your protective gear on and clean your soap-making equipment and work area very well. Finish cleanup by lightly wiping down anything that may have come in contact with lye with undiluted vinegar.

9. After twenty-four hours, check your soap. Put on a pair of disposable gloves, give your soap a gentle press, and check to see if the soap easily pulls away from the edges of the mold. If the soap is firm, turn the soap out of the mold. If not, give the soap another twenty-four hours to cure in the mold before turning out.

10. If necessary, slice the soap into bars. Set the soap in a cool, out of the way place on a wire rack. Cover it with a loose, lint-free cloth to keep dust off, and turn the soap periodically. Cure soap for at least four weeks before using.

a few notes on cold-process soap making

the immersion blender as soap maker's tool

Using an immersion blender to make cold process soap makes the process quite simple and quick. I recommend getting a dedicated secondhand immersion blender from your local thrift store or Freecycle-type community. It doesn't have to be pretty, it just has to work. If your immersion blender has a stainless steel wand, you can use it for both soap making and food preparation purposes so long as you wash it very, very thoroughly.

soap molds

Anything that will contain your soap as it cures and release it easily, can be pressed into service as a soap mold. If you have silicone muffin tins or loaf pans, or a clear plastic shoebox, those work great. Otherwise, a metal loaf pan or small cardboard box covered with a layer of plastic wrap, then a layer of parchment paper, makes a perfectly serviceable mold for your soap. Don't let your uncured soap touch anything aluminum—this can ruin both the soap and the aluminum container.

Fill your mold or molds, smooth the top of the mold, then lift the mold about a half-inch off the counter and rap the mold firmly but carefully back down to help release any air bubbles that might be trapped in the soap. Repeat this two or three times, then cover the soap with plastic wrap and smooth out any surface wrinkles or bubbles.

trace

You'll know the soap is ready to pour into molds when it reaches "trace." Trace is a full emulsification of the oils and the lye. It's the point at which the soap will no longer separate back out into oil and water components.

Traditionally, trace took a long time to achieve because the oils and lye solution were stirred together by hand. Old-time soap makers watched for the point when they could drizzle a bit of their soap down onto their batch and see a "trace" of that drizzle left on the surface. Using an immersion blender, trace can be achieved much more quickly, often in just a few minutes. Watch for your soap to thicken to a texture like thin pudding, and become quite creamy and opaque. If in doubt, the old test still works great—just drizzle some soap off your immersion blender or a spoon onto the surface of your batch and watch for that "trace" of soap to stay visible on the surface. Once the soap mixture achieves trace, thoroughly blend in any fragrance you're using, then quickly pour and scrape your soap solution into your prepared molds.

gel soap versus no-gel soap

When the saponification reaction starts, your soap really wants to heat up via an exothermic reaction typically called the "gel phase" by soap makers. During gel phase, the soap undergoes rapid saponification, hardens, and takes on a slightly darker and more translucent look. A fully gelled soap is ready to use sooner, and will tend to be longer lasting at the sink or in the shower.

To encourage a full gel, start with warmer oils and lye (around 120 degrees F) and insulate your soap during the gel phase to keep it very warm. I do this by lifting the filled, plastic-wrap-covered molds into a small cooler, then setting a piece of sturdy cardboard over the mold, and topping the cardboard with old kitchen rags. I lid the cooler and set it out of the way for twenty-four hours.

Soap that doesn't undergo a gel phase takes longer to fully cure and has a paler, more creamy and opaque look. This is encouraged by starting with cooler oils and lye solution (about 90 degrees F) and keeping the soap chilled through the gel phase. Soaps made with dairy products like goat milk, or with honey or sugar, are typically made with the no-gel method so the sugars in those ingredients don't caramelize and darken. No-gel soaps are also gentler on the scents of volatile essential oils, which can be driven out by the heat of the gel phase.

To encourage a no-gel soap, use smaller molds, such as individual soap molds instead of a loaf pan mold. Gently cover the filled molds with plastic wrap and transfer the soap carefully to the freezer for several hours, then transfer to the fridge for the remaining twenty-four to forty-eight hours of initial cure.

If you neither insulate nor chill your soap, nothing bad will happen but you may end up with partially gelled soap—soap that reaches gel at the warmer center of the bar, but not all the way to the edges. This can give a bulls-eye look to your soap. Although partially gelled soap is functionally fine, most soap makers consider the inconsistent look of this soap less desirable, and try to avoid a partial gel.

Both gel and no-gel soaps have their fans, and both methods make good soap. I fully gel my soaps because I like that look, and I don't want to find room in the freezer for soap! But gel versus no-gel is simply a matter of preference.

unmolding and curing

After an initial twenty-four to forty-eight hours in the mold, your soap will be, well, soap! Most of the lye will be saponified, and the bar should be firm enough to unmold but not so hard that it will shatter if you slice it.

But your soap isn't done yet—there's still too much residual lye and water in the soap. Slip on a pair of gloves, bring your soap to room temperature if necessary, and unmold your soap carefully onto a cutting board. At this point, if you molded your soap in something like a loaf pan or box, you'll need to cut your soap into bars. A sharp knife should slice through your soap just fine, though some people do cut soap with a metal dough scraper.

To cure your soap fully, set the bars on a wire cooling rack or piece of parchment paper someplace out of the way, and cover them with a piece of lint-free cloth to keep off the dust. Leave the bars for four weeks for a final cure, flipping them once a week or as you remember. After four weeks, your soap will be fully cured and ready to use, store, or gift. With additional aging, your soap will continue to get even harder and milder.

palm problems

Before it became (relatively) cheap and easy to process plants for vegetable oils, nearly all soap was made from a base of lard (pork fat) or tallow (beef fat). Castile soap, traditionally made with 100 percent olive oil, is the notable exception. If you have no personal or religious reasons to avoid them, soaps that incorporate hard animal fats as base oils typically make great bar soaps: cleansing, moisturizing, long-lasting, and with good lather.

Palm oil has replaced tallow and lard as the "hard fat" in many recipes for soap making. This highly saturated, semisolid fat is extracted from the fruit of the tropical oil palm tree and behaves much like tallow, producing a long-lasting, hard bar of soap with excellent lather and cleansing ability. (Palmolive soap is so named because it was originally formulated with palm and olive oils.)

The problem with palm oil is that the palm industry has a very spotty reputation. The majority of commercial palm oil is exported from Indonesia and Malaysia. Well-managed palm oil harvesting can provide jobs in areas that desperately need them, but when poorly managed, the palm oil industry is terribly destructive to native rainforests, indigenous people, and threatened wildlife. It's a complicated issue, and one soap makers need to research.

I choose not to use palm oil in my own soap making. If you do, I encourage you to seek out third-party-verified sustainable and ethically sourced palm oil.

Year-Round

Cooking

THOUGHTS ON VERSATILE BASICS

I'm going to share a secret with you. I probably shouldn't say this, since I'm about to start handing down recipes, but it's important that you know this. It's the key to mastering the fundamental life skill of being able to feed yourself. *Confident cooks rarely rely on recipes.*

Remember that time you asked a coworker of yours who always seems to bring great dishes to the company potluck if you could get his recipe for orzo salad? Or the time you asked a friend for the secret to her awesome flank steak marinade? The response was almost certainly, "Oh, you know, I just kind of made it up. I don't really use recipes." And perhaps you thought to yourself, stop hoarding the damned recipe and just share your sources!

Well, your coworker or friend, the "natural" in the kitchen, isn't lying. People who learn to be comfortable with food and cooking (and I count myself in this group) are culinary improvisers. Whether consciously or through repetition, we've learned that there just aren't that many ways to cook food. You bake, you roast, you grill, you sear, you fry, you braise, or you sauté. You steam or boil or simmer something starchy if you need a side. You finish with a vinaigrette or a pan sauce or an emulsion. This is all very predictable because there just aren't that many distinct techniques in cooking.

Oh, sure there are a million variations on everything from roast chicken to pumpkin bread if you go looking, but this just muddies and complicates matters. Good cooking isn't searching for that perfect recipe but mastering a few basic techniques, and then adapting those techniques to the seasons and circumstances of your day.

Good, confident, flexible cooking requires that we engage our senses while increasing our mastery of those few key techniques. Unless you are drawn to the cutting-edge, rarified world of molecular gastronomy, a recipe simply points the way to greater mastery of a technique. Once you have a few techniques under your belt, it's not intimidating to tweak a bit here or a bit there. And pretty soon you're one of those people who cook without recipes too.

flatbread

THE DOUGH FOR THIS FLATBREAD HAS been MacGyvered into everything from a soft, puffy gyro stuffed with leftover lamb and dill yogurt, to skillet fry bread topped with cheese and served alongside tomato soup, to grilled pizza topped with peanut sauce, shredded chicken, and a Thai cucumber salad. It's saved me from the siren call of takeout more times than I can count.

MAKES 4 TO 8 FLATBREADS

4 cups all-purpose or whole wheat flour

1¾ cups warm water, or 2 cups warm water if using whole wheat flour

¼ cup extra-virgin olive oil, plus more for brushing

1 teaspoon active dry yeast

1 teaspoon kosher salt, plus more for sprinkling

+ In a large bowl, combine all the ingredients. Stir the mixture with a strong wooden spoon until the dough comes together into a soft but cohesive ball.

+ To use the dough today, cover the bowl with a damp towel or a layer of plastic wrap and set it someplace warm until the dough is puffy and has doubled in size, 2 to 4 hours, depending on how warm your kitchen is.

+ To use the dough tomorrow, or any time in the next week, transfer the dough ball to a large ziplock freezer bag or 1-gallon or larger air-tight container. Refrigerate and let the dough rise in the refrigerator at least 12 hours, or up to 1 week. Bring the dough to room temperature before proceeding.

+ After the dough has risen, turn it out onto a smooth, lightly floured surface. With floured hands, gently fold and pat the dough into a disk shape.

+ Divide the disk into 4 to 8 equal pieces, depending on how large you want your finished flatbreads. Form each piece into a ball, covering the dough balls lightly with a lint-free towel or plastic wrap as you go, to prevent them from drying out.

+ Reflour the work surface to form the flatbreads. Working with one dough ball at a time, pat or gently roll the dough into a ¼-inch-thick disk. Repeat with the remaining dough balls.

+ Lightly brush the flatbreads with oil and, if desired, sprinkle with salt.

COOK IN ONE OF THE FOLLOWING WAYS:

+ To skillet-fry the flatbreads, preheat a cast-iron skillet over medium heat. Place a flatbread on the skillet and cook until golden brown, bubbly, and firm, about 3 minutes. Flip the flatbread and cook on the second side until the bottom is golden brown and the flatbread is fully cooked, about 3 minutes. Repeat with the remaining flatbreads.

+ To grill the flatbreads, preheat a grill to medium-high heat. Place a flatbread on the grill and cook until it is golden and a bit charred on the first side, 3 to 4 minutes. Flip the flatbread and grill the second side until the bottom is golden brown and the flatbread is fully cooked, 3 to 4 minutes. Repeat with the remaining flatbreads.

picnic bread

SOMEWHERE BETWEEN A BAGUETTE AND CIABATTA, this versatile bread is excellent alongside winter soups, topped with asparagus as a spring tartine, or slathered with butter and homemade jam in the early morning. We call it picnic bread because we build a giant sandwich from a loaf and slice it up to take along on picnics.

MAKES 2 MEDIUM LOAVES

2¼ cups room-temperature water

3 cups all-purpose flour

2 cups whole wheat flour

1 tablespoon active dry yeast

1 tablespoon kosher salt, plus more for sprinkling

Extra-virgin olive oil, for brushing

+ In a large bowl, add the water, flours, yeast, and salt and stir well with a strong wooden spoon until the dough is fully combined. There should be no dry flour spots in the dough, and it will be tacky and shaggy but should partially pull away from the sides of the bowl.

+ Cover the bowl with plastic wrap or a damp lint-free towel. Transfer the dough to the refrigerator and let it rise for 8 to 24 hours, until bubbly and at least doubled in size. The longer the rise time, the more complex the flavor development will be.

+ Line a sheet pan with lightly greased parchment paper. Set aside. Scrape the dough out onto a floured surface and divide the dough into 2 pieces. Fold and gently roll each piece into a long cylinder several inches shorter than your sheet pan. Place the dough cylinders on either side of the pan, lightly dust them with flour, and cover them with a damp lint-free towel. Let the dough rise for 2 hours in a warm place, or until the loaves are doubled in size.

+ While the loaves are rising, move an oven rack to the center position and preheat the oven to 425 degrees F.

+ Brush each loaf with a bit of oil and sprinkle lightly with salt. Cut three or four long, diagonal slashes along each loaf with a serrated bread knife and transfer the sheet pan to the oven.

+ Bake until the loaves are golden brown and crunchy on the outside and sound hollow when you tap them, about 30 minutes. Transfer the loaves to a wire rack to cool completely.

flour tortillas

"Taco Tuesday" is something of a loose tradition around my house. With a pantry full of Heat-and-Eat Pork Shoulder (page 297) and pressure-canned black beans (see page 352), tacos are true homemade fast food. When time allows, we like to make our tortillas fresh from pantry basics. The kids like flour, I like corn (see page 108). Try them both and see which one you prefer.

MAKES 16 TORTILLAS

+ In a small bowl, mix together the flour, salt, and baking powder. Add the water and oil and stir with a fork or sturdy wooden spoon until the mixture forms a thick dough. Turn the dough out onto a smooth, lightly floured surface and knead until the dough is smooth and silky, about 2 minutes.

+ Divide the dough into 16 equal pieces and form each piece into a ball about the size of a walnut. Cover the dough balls with a clean, barely damp lint-free towel and let the dough rest for 15 to 30 minutes.

+ Heat a large cast-iron skillet over medium-high heat.

+ Lightly flour a smooth surface and rolling pin, and roll each dough ball into a thin circle about 6 inches in diameter and ⅛ inch thick.

+ Cook the tortillas one at a time in the preheated skillet. Cook until the underside begins to bubble and brown, about 1 minute, then flip and continue to cook until the tortilla is speckled with browned patches on the second side, another 30 seconds to 1 minute. Set the cooked tortillas aside in a stack under a clean cloth as you cook the remaining tortillas.

3 cups all-purpose or whole wheat flour, or a combination

1 teaspoon kosher salt

1 teaspoon baking powder

1 cup room-temperature water

⅓ cup neutral-flavored vegetable oil or melted lard

corn tortillas

CORN TORTILLAS ARE MADE FROM A special kind of corn flour called masa harina. You'll find it at larger supermarkets and it's quite inexpensive. Don't try to substitute American-style cornmeal or Italian-style polenta in this application—it'll suck. A tortilla press makes corn tortillas far easier to turn out, and is a fun way to get kids involved in dinner. At ten to fifteen dollars, they're fairly inexpensive.

MAKES 12 TORTILLAS

2 cups masa harina

1¼ cups room-temperature water, plus more as needed

1 tablespoon neutral-flavored vegetable oil

½ teaspoon kosher salt

+ In a medium bowl, mix together all the ingredients and stir with a fork or sturdy wooden spoon until the mixture forms into a thick dough. If the dough is crumbly and doesn't pull from the sides of the bowl, add a few drops of water at a time until a thick, puttylike consistency is achieved. Turn the dough out onto a smooth, lightly floured surface and knead lightly until the dough is smooth, about 2 minutes. Return the dough to the bowl, cover with plastic wrap, and set aside at room temperature for 30 minutes to rest.

+ Heat a medium cast-iron skillet to medium-high heat.

+ Line each side of a tortilla press with parchment paper or a plastic freezer bag slit up the sides. Pinch off about 2 tablespoons of dough, roll it into a ball about the size of a walnut, and press it between the parchment or plastic in the tortilla press. You'll be left with a thin, 5- to 6-inch disk.

+ Put the tortilla in the hot skillet. If the dough is the right consistency, the tortilla will release from the parchment or plastic easily. If it's too crumbly, add a few more drops of water. If it sticks, work in a bit more masa.

+ Cook on the first side until the tortilla is set and just starting to brown on the bottom, 30 seconds to 1 minute. Flip the tortilla with a thin metal spatula and cook on the second side until the tortilla browns in patches and puffs lightly, about 30 seconds. Repeat with the remaining dough. Set the cooked tortillas aside in a stack under a clean cloth to allow them to steam as they finish cooking.

one-hour ricotta cheese

I LOVE HAVING A SIMPLE, VERSATILE homemade cheese on hand for adding to sandwiches or pasta, or to dollop on fruit. This farmer cheese fits the bill and can be made without any special cheesemaking equipment.

Officially, ricotta is made from "reboiling" the whey left over from other kinds of cheesemaking, but, unofficially, it's a super simple fresh cheese requiring nothing more than milk, heat, and acid. If you've ever added both lemon and milk to your tea (I have—oops) then you know that acidic ingredients will curdle milk. In this ricotta recipe we take advantage of this, and use common acidic ingredients to make cheese.

The three biggest determinants to the final flavor of your ricotta are the quality of the milk you start with, the acid you choose, and the amount of time you allow your cheese to drain. Start with very fresh dairy. Pasteurized milk and cream are fine, but skip ultra-high-temperature pasteurized options; these often fail to form a nice curd.

After thirty to sixty minutes of draining, this ricotta is thick enough to spread on toast or serve with fruit. If you drain it long enough, or press it under weight to get even more liquid out, it will become firm and crumbly, much like Mexican queso fresco or Indian paneer.

Save the whey that drains off your cheese—you can use it to replace some or all of the water used in bread making and other baking. It adds a nice tang and extra protein.

MAKES ABOUT 1 GENEROUS CUP

✦ In a heavyweight, nonreactive saucepot, combine all the ingredients. Stirring occasionally, gently bring the mixture to a simmer over medium heat and watch for the mixture to begin to curdle. You may see some curds very early in the cooking process, but between 185 and 200 degrees F, the curds will become quite distinct from the whey and will float to the surface. Watch for the whey to change from white and milky to yellowish-clear with only a bit of milky haze. When you note district curds and mostly clear whey, remove the pot from the heat and let sit, undisturbed, for 30 minutes.

BASIC RICOTTA

1 quart whole milk

1 cup heavy cream

3 tablespoons white distilled vinegar

1 teaspoon kosher salt

(continued)

+ Line a mesh strainer with a damp paper towel, several layers of cheesecloth, or a clean, damp lint-free towel. Set the strainer over the bowl and pour the curds and whey through the strainer. Let sit for at least 30 minutes to drain.

+ Check the texture. The longer you strain the cheese, the firmer it will get. If you plan to strain longer than 1 hour, transfer the cheese to the refrigerator and strain chilled.

+ For an even firmer texture, drain the mixture until the curd holds its shape, then form it into a disk shape and lightly salt the outside of the cheese. Wrap the cheese in a clean towel or several layers of cheesecloth and set the cheese on a plate. Place another plate on top of the cheese, and then set something heavy—like a big can of pumpkin or a jar of tomatoes—on top of the plate to weight the cheese. Transfer the whole contraption to the refrigerator. Periodically check for whey that has pooled on the bottom plate and discard it. Drain the cheese until it has reached the desired firmness, up to 12 hours.

+ When the ricotta is ready, transfer it to a clean container with a tight-fitting lid and keep it chilled. It's best eaten fresh but will keep for about 1 week in the refrigerator.

ricotta variations

Try these ricotta variations. Simply follow the instructions above, but substitute these ingredients.

LEMON RICOTTA	LIME RICOTTA
1 quart whole milk	1 quart whole milk
1 cup heavy cream	1 cup heavy cream
3 tablespoons freshly squeezed lemon juice	3 tablespoons freshly squeezed lime juice
1 teaspoon kosher salt	1 teaspoon kosher salt
Zest of 1 lemon	Zest of 1 lime

basic chicken broth

To make this much broth in one pot, you will need a really, really big stockpot (at least sixteen quarts). If this quantity is way beyond what you will use or just far larger than your biggest pot can accommodate, simply halve the recipe.

MAKES 6 QUARTS

8 pounds assorted chicken trimmings

2 gallons water

6 cups mild-flavored assorted vegetable trimmings such as carrot, parsnip, celery, onion, and leek

1 large bunch flat-leaf parsley

3 garlic cloves

1 to 2 teaspoons whole black peppercorns

Kosher salt

+ In a sixteen-quart stockpot, combine the chicken, water, vegetables, parsley, garlic, and peppercorns and bring to a bare simmer. Half cover the pot, adjust the heat to maintain a barely bubbling simmer, and cook for at least 3 hours. If you're hanging around the house anyway, you can let this simmer for even longer, up to 8 or 12 hours, though the final yield may be slightly less due to evaporation.

+ Taste the broth periodically, adding a bit of salt to the tasting spoon to help you assess the final flavor. When the flavor is clean and nicely chicken-y and the broth is a golden-yellow color, ladle the broth off the chicken and vegetables through a fine-mesh sieve into a 10- or 12-quart stockpot or a very large bowl. (I prefer not to pour the broth through a sieve—this tends to force a lot of cloudy sediment into the final broth, and it's fairly dangerous to go tipping over huge pots of very hot broth anyway. I use a small saucepan to ladle the broth quickly off the trimmings, and as the pot empties I tip it over to get the last of the clear broth off the bottom.)

+ To defat the broth, pop the entire pot of strained broth in the refrigerator for several hours or overnight. The fat will rise to the top and harden considerably, and you can spoon it off and save it for another use. If you can't make room in your refrigerator for a big pot of broth, just carefully ladle off as much of the floating liquid fat as possible while leaving behind the broth. If the chicken trimmings included a lot of skin, there will be more fat on the broth than if the trimmings were mostly lean meat and bone.

+ Now the broth is ready to pressure can (see page 192), freeze, or reduce further, if desired.

One of my best friends worked for a chef who was widely regarded as the best classical saucier in Seattle. Great broth is the foundation of great sauces, so I asked her what Mr. Famous Chef's trick was to get the best broth. Did he follow a recipe? Did they order in a special cut of chicken or beef just for the broth?

"Oh God no," she said. "We just throw everything in there and the stuff simmers for days." So don't overthink or overcomplicate your broth too much. It's not rocket science, it's just one of many delicious things that developed as a way to use up scraps and stretch food as far as possible.

I save up carcasses from chickens I've cut up or roasted and toss the leftover bones, necks, and scalded feet into the freezer until I have enough to make this process worthwhile. I do the same with mild-flavored vegetable trimmings—things like carrot peels, onion skins, leek greens, parsley stems, or the thick bottoms of celery. I have a container of these kinds of broth trimmings in my freezer, and I just add to it until it's full, and then I make broth.

I do believe you need a bit of meat to make a really good chicken broth, so if your bones are picked quite clean, add in a few purchased chicken legs, wings, or necks to give the broth a nice balance.

This recipe makes a lot of broth with the idea that this big batch will then be pressure canned (see page 192). However, you can just transfer your broth to freezer-safe containers and freeze instead.

If freezer space is limited, another good storage option is to reduce the broth by half or more, then freeze it in ice-cube trays or muffin tins (the silicone pans are great for this). When the broth is frozen, pop it out and transfer it to a freezer bag. When you want homemade broth, treat the frozen cubes or pucks like bouillon. Add a few to hot water, bring to a simmer, and proceed with your recipe.

magic mayonnaise

I ADORE MY IMMERSION BLENDER. In the professional kitchens where I spent a few years, we had these enormous heavy-duty immersion blenders that were big enough to puree the soup at the bottom of a fifty-five-gallon kettle. At home, I've always had excellent luck with inexpensive immersion blenders.

In addition to making pureed soups and sauces super simple, my immersion blender gets pulled into service every week as a DIY mayonnaise maker. In cooking classes, I've demonstrated how to make mayonnaise at home using this immersion blender trick, and people go crazy for it once they see how quick and easy it is. Commercial mayonnaise is filled with cheap and often rancid oils, added sugar, and preservatives. Homemade mayo tastes better than the store-bought variety, allows you to control the quality of the eggs and oil you use, and saves money. Once you see how easy it is, I bet you'll never go back!

MAKES ABOUT 1 CUP

1 large egg

1 tablespoon freshly squeezed lemon juice

1 tablespoon white wine vinegar

1 teaspoon Dijon mustard

½ teaspoon kosher salt

1 cup neutral-flavored vegetable oil

+ For the traditional method, in a small bowl, whisk the egg, lemon juice, vinegar, mustard, and salt together. While whisking continuously, slowly drizzle the oil into the egg mixture. The mayonnaise should transform into a thick, creamy white spread.

+ For the magically fast immersion blender method, in a wide-mouthed pint mason jar, combine all the ingredients. Give the mixture a few seconds for the egg to settle to the bottom of the jar, then insert an immersion blender and turn to medium speed. Keep the immersion blender at the bottom of the jar; it will slowly pull the oil down and into the egg, forming a strong emulsion. When almost all of the jar has magically turned into mayo, slowly pull the immersion blender up and out of the jar, pulsing a few times to emulsify any oil still floating at the top. The mayonnaise will keep in an airtight in the refrigerator for up to 1 week.

basic vinaigrette

THE MOST ELEMENTAL OF THE SALAD dressings is the vinaigrette. At its most basic, a vinaigrette contains just three ingredients: oil, vinegar or other acid, and an emulsifier. Emuls-what? Ah, I'm glad you asked. We all know that oil and water don't mix—they separate. Well, vinegar, being mostly water, doesn't mix with oil, either. No matter how vigorously you whisk oil and vinegar together, within a few minutes, the oil and vinegar will separate. An emulsifier is any ingredient that convinces the oil and vinegar to stay combined. The best emulsifier for vinaigrettes is mustard, which has a strong emulsifying property and works well from a flavor perspective.

Any vinaigrette will turn out pretty well if you keep the oil-to-acid ratio at about 3:1. If you like a tangier dressing, two parts oil for each part acid will give you more bite. Start with three tablespoons oil to each tablespoon vinegar and go from there—you'll never buy another bottled dressing again.

MAKES ABOUT ½ CUP

+ To prepare the vinaigrette by whisking, in a small bowl, add the vinegar and mustard and whisk to combine. While whisking, drizzle in the oil. Your vinaigrette should emulsify nicely. If it looks "broken," whisk it vigorously for another 30 seconds. If that doesn't work, add ½ teaspoon more Dijon mustard and whisk again. Season the vinaigrette to taste with salt and pepper and serve immediately, or transfer the dressing to a clean jar and refrigerate. Basic vinaigrette will last for several weeks in the refrigerator but may start to lose its punch after about 1 week.

+ To prepare the vinaigrette by shaking, add all the ingredients to a clean half-pint jar and cap with a very tight-fitting lid. Shake the jar vigorously until the dressing is smooth, about 1 minute. I like making my dressings in small jars like this because I avoid dirtying a bowl and it's easy to store in the fridge.

2 tablespoons red wine vinegar or champagne vinegar

1 teaspoon Dijon mustard or ¼ teaspoon dry mustard powder

6 tablespoons extra-virgin olive oil

Kosher salt and freshly ground black pepper

never buy salad dressing again

Growing up, there were exactly four salad dressings in the refrigerator, all made by Kraft: Catalina for my mom, blue cheese for my dad, ranch for us kids, and zesty Italian for when my mom made pasta salad with salami and provolone cheese.

The bottle in the refrigerator is convenient, sure, but there are a lot of good reasons to make DIY dressing.

1. Salad dressings aren't hard to make and you probably already have all the ingredients on hand to whip up everything from a basic vinaigrette to a creamy honey-Dijon dressing. Acid + Fat = Salad Dressing. It's pretty simple.

2. Making your own dressing allows you to control the quality of the ingredients. Seed oils, like those used in most commercial salad dressings, go rancid very quickly, but the strongly flavored ingredients in most dressings can make this hard to detect.

3. Do it your way, baby! You like your dressing a bit creamier, or a bit tangier, or a bit spicier? When you make your own, you make it exactly how you like it.

< Pictured: Basic Creamy Herb Dressing, page 120 (left) and Basic Vinaigrette, page 115 (right)

vinaigrette variations

By playing around with your fat, acid, and seasonings, an unlimited number of vinaigrette variations are fast and easy. Here are a few of my favorites to get you started—just follow the directions for Basic Vinaigrette (page 115).

DRESSING	OIL	ACID	EMULSIFIER	FLAVORINGS
A VERY FRENCH VINAIGRETTE	6 tablespoons extra-virgin olive oil	2 tablespoons sherry or red wine vinegar	1 teaspoon Dijon mustard	1 tablespoon finely minced shallot, 1 tablespoon minced chives, 1 tablespoon minced parsley, kosher salt and freshly ground black pepper to taste
MOM'S ITALIAN VINAIGRETTE	6 tablespoons mild vegetable oil	1 tablespoon white wine vinegar, 1 tablespoon red wine vinegar	1 teaspoon Dijon mustard	2 tablespoons grated Parmesan cheese, 1 teaspoon sugar, 1 teaspoon dried basil, 1 teaspoon dried oregano, ½ teaspoon minced garlic, pinch of red pepper flakes, kosher salt and freshly ground black pepper to taste
TANGY GREEK FETA VINAIGRETTE	6 tablespoons extra-virgin olive oil	1 tablespoon red wine vinegar, 1 tablespoon freshly squeezed lemon juice	1 teaspoon Dijon mustard	2 tablespoons crumbled feta, 1 tablespoon minced fresh oregano, 1 tablespoon minced fresh parsley, 1 teaspoon minced garlic, kosher salt and freshly ground black pepper to taste
BALSAMIC-HERB VINAIGRETTE	6 tablespoons extra-virgin olive oil	2 tablespoons balsamic vinegar	1 teaspoon whole grain mustard	1 tablespoon minced fresh basil, 1 teaspoon minced fresh oregano, 1 teaspoon minced fresh parsley, ½ teaspoon minced garlic, kosher salt and freshly ground black pepper to taste
LIGHT CITRUS-BASIL VINAIGRETTE	6 tablespoons mild vegetable oil	1 tablespoon freshly squeezed lemon juice, 1 tablespoon freshly squeezed lime juice	1 teaspoon Dijon mustard	2 tablespoons minced fresh basil, 1 teaspoon lemon zest, 1 teaspoon maple syrup, kosher salt and freshly ground black pepper to taste

DRESSING	OIL	ACID	EMULSIFIER	FLAVORINGS
CURRY VINAIGRETTE	6 tablespoons extra-virgin olive oil	1 tablespoon apple cider vinegar, 1 tablespoon freshly squeezed lime juice	1 teaspoon Dijon mustard	1 teaspoon curry powder, 1 teaspoon light brown sugar, ½ teaspoon minced garlic, ½ teaspoon minced fresh ginger, kosher salt and freshly ground black pepper to taste
ANY JAM VINAIGRETTE	6 tablespoons mild vegetable oil	2 tablespoons apple cider vinegar or rice wine vinegar	1 teaspoon Dijon mustard	2 tablespoons any fruit jam, kosher salt and freshly ground black pepper to taste
SMOKY BACON VINAIGRETTE	4 tablespoons mild vegetable oil, 2 tablespoons melted bacon fat	2 tablespoons apple cider vinegar	1 teaspoon whole grain mustard	3 tablespoons minced cooked bacon, 1 teaspoon smoked paprika, 1 teaspoon light brown sugar, ½ teaspoon minced garlic, kosher salt and freshly ground black pepper to taste
ORANGE-WALNUT VINAIGRETTE	6 tablespoons walnut oil or extra-virgin olive oil, or a blend	2 tablespoons freshly squeezed orange juice, 1 tablespoon rice wine vinegar	1 teaspoon Dijon mustard	2 tablespoons finely minced walnuts, 1 tablespoon orange zest, 1 teaspoon finely minced onion or shallot, 1 teaspoon honey, kosher salt and freshly ground black pepper to taste
SWEET-AND-SOUR THAI VINAIGRETTE	4 tablespoons mild vegetable oil	2 tablespoons rice wine vinegar, 1 tablespoon freshly squeezed lime juice		2 tablespoons Thai sweet chili sauce, 1 teaspoon fish sauce or soy sauce, ½ teaspoon minced garlic, kosher salt and freshly ground black pepper to taste
PEANUT-MISO DRESSING	3 tablespoons peanut or vegetable oil 1 tablespoon, toasted sesame oil	2 tablespoons rice wine vinegar		1 tablespoon honey, 1 tablespoon peanut butter, 1 tablespoon white miso paste, 1 teaspoon soy sauce, ½ teaspoon minced fresh ginger

basic creamy herb dressing

LIKE VINAIGRETTES, CREAMY DRESSINGS—blue cheese, Caesar, ranch, and the like—also contain oil, an acid like vinegar, and an emulsifier. Most creamy dressings use egg yolk as an emulsifier, because one of the components in egg yolk is lecithin, a particularly strong emulsifier. This allows for the thick, almost whipped texture that is desirable in creamy dressings.

Although we tend to think of it as a sandwich spread, the most basic creamy dressing is mayonnaise. Mayonnaise relies on eggs to emulsify oil with lemon juice or vinegar and a few flavorings. I make Magic Mayonnaise (page 114) and use that as a base for other creamy dressings, but store-bought mayonnaise will work just as well in these recipes.

Some creamy dressings (Caesar, most famously) skip the intermediary of mayonnaise and rely on raw egg yolk directly for its emulsifying properties. If you are uncomfortable using raw egg in your dressings, you can substitute two tablespoons commercial mayonnaise for each raw egg yolk in a recipe.

MAKES ABOUT ½ CUP

¼ cup mayonnaise

2 tablespoons plain yogurt, sour cream, or buttermilk

2 tablespoons minced soft green herbs, such as parsley, chives, basil, or dill

2 teaspoons apple cider vinegar, plus more as needed

1 teaspoon Dijon mustard

Kosher salt and freshly ground black pepper

✦ In a small bowl, whisk together the mayonnaise, yogurt, herbs, vinegar, and mustard. Season to taste with salt, pepper, and additional apple cider vinegar, if desired. Serve immediately, or transfer the dressing to a clean jar and refrigerate. Creamy dressings made with commercial mayonnaise will last for about 1 week in the refrigerator, and those made with raw egg mayonnaise should be used within a few days.

creamy dressing variations

Have fun experimenting with variations on creamy dressings. Add cheeses, swap sour cream for yogurt, or play around with seasonings. Here are a few of my favorite creamy dressings to get you started—just follow the directions for Basic Creamy Herb Dressing (see opposite page).

DRESSING	BASE	ACID	FLAVORINGS	TRY IT WITH . . .
CREAMY GARLIC DRESSING	¼ cup mayonnaise, 2 tablespoons sour cream or thick yogurt	1 tablespoon apple cider vinegar, 1 tablespoon freshly squeezed lemon juice	2 teaspoons minced garlic, ½ teaspoon Dijon mustard, ½ teaspoon paprika, kosher salt and freshly ground black pepper to taste	Roasted asparagus
CAESAR DRESSING	¼ cup extra-virgin olive oil plus 1 egg yolk, whisked together	2 tablespoons freshly squeezed lemon juice	¼ cup grated Parmesan cheese, 1 teaspoon anchovy paste, 1 teaspoon Dijon mustard, 1 teaspoon Worcestershire sauce, ½ teaspoon minced garlic, kosher salt and freshly ground black pepper to taste	Romaine, more Parmesan, and homemade croutons, of course!
SOUR CREAM RANCH	¼ cup mayonnaise and 2 tablespoons sour cream or thick yogurt	1 tablespoon white wine vinegar	1 tablespoon each minced fresh chives, dill, and parsley; 1 teaspoon sugar; ½ teaspoon minced garlic; kosher salt and freshly ground black pepper to taste	Go old-school with a chopped iceberg salad with black beans, corn, red peppers, and shredded cheddar cheese, or let the kids dip away!
BASIL GREEN GODDESS DRESSING	¼ cup mayonnaise; 2 tablespoons sour cream or thick yogurt	1 tablespoon white wine vinegar or tarragon vinegar	1 tablespoon each minced fresh basil, arugula, tarragon, parsley, and chives; ½ teaspoon minced garlic; ½ teaspoon anchovy paste; ½ teaspoon Dijon mustard; kosher salt and freshly ground black pepper to taste	Bibb lettuce, walnuts, and roasted beets

(continued)

year-Round

DRESSING	BASE	ACID	FLAVORINGS	TRY IT WITH . . .
BLUE CHEESE DRESSING	¼ cup mayonnaise, 2 tablespoons sour cream or thick yogurt	1 tablespoon distilled white vinegar	¼ cup crumbled Gorgonzola cheese, a few drops of Worcestershire sauce, kosher salt and freshly ground black pepper to taste	As a dip for chicken wings or to top a classic Cobb salad. Heck, what doesn't taste good with blue cheese dressing?
CURRIED HONEY DIJON DRESSING	¼ cup mayonnaise, 2 tablespoons sour cream or thick yogurt	1 tablespoon freshly squeezed lemon juice	1 tablespoon poppy seeds, 1 tablespoon Dijon mustard, 1 tablespoon honey, 1 teaspoon curry powder, kosher salt and freshly ground black pepper to taste	Grilled chicken, or a salad with pear and red onion
CREAMY LIME-MINT DRESSING	¼ cup mayonnaise, 2 tablespoons sour cream or thick yogurt	1 tablespoon freshly squeezed lime juice	2 tablespoons minced fresh mint, 1 teaspoon lime zest, ½ teaspoon minced garlic, ½ teaspoon sugar, kosher salt and freshly ground black pepper to taste	Snap peas or cucumbers
THAI LOUIE	¼ cup mayonnaise, 2 tablespoons sour cream or thick yogurt	2 tablespoons freshly squeezed lime juice	2 tablespoons minced fresh cilantro, 1 tablespoon Thai sweet chili sauce, 1 tablespoon minced fresh mint, 1 teaspoon fish sauce, kosher salt and freshly ground black pepper to taste	Prawns, crab, or salmon, or any salad that includes them
CHIPOTLE HONEY DRESSING	¼ cup mayonnaise, 2 tablespoons sour cream or thick yogurt	1 tablespoon freshly squeezed lime juice	1 minced chipotle pepper in adobo, 1 teaspoon adobo sauce, 1 teaspoon honey, ½ teaspoon finely minced garlic, ¼ teaspoon ground cumin, kosher salt and freshly ground black pepper to taste	Grilled steak or grilled kebabs with peppers, summer squash, and onions
ANY JAM CREAMY DRESSING	¼ cup mayonnaise, 2 tablespoons sour cream or thick yogurt	1 tablespoon distilled white vinegar	2 tablespoons any fruit jam, 1 teaspoon Dijon mustard, kosher salt and freshly ground black pepper to taste	Try a creamy orange marmalade dressing with pork, or drizzle over a summer fruit salad

choose-your-own-adventure granola

FORGET EXPENSIVE CEREALS FROM COMPANIES THAT spend more on their trademarked cartoon characters than they do on their ingredients. Homemade granola has been the happy-hippie solution to the quick-breakfast dilemma for hundreds of years.

I got tired of homemade granola that ended up more like toasted oats than a chunky, clumpy breakfast cereal. After playing around with a few techniques, I discovered the keys to a great clumpy granola. (1) Add oat flour, which acts as a binder to help the bigger oat-and-nut pieces stick together. (2) Pack your granola firmly in a pan. (3) Bake your granola at a very low temperature and skip all that tedious stirring.

The result was an awesome, homemade convenience item that kids love. This granola is great with yogurt (see page 132) in the morning, or as an on-the-go snack. We take it with us on so many adventures, and it's so easy to customize the flavor with different combinations of dried fruits, seeds, and nuts, that I started calling it Choose-Your-Own-Adventure Granola.

I make a batch of granola about every two weeks, and swap in whatever nuts, seeds, and dried fruit sound good at the time. Maple syrup is my sweetener of choice in this granola, but substitute honey if you prefer. As long as you stick to the basic proportions for each component—fruit, nuts and seed, oats, etc.—you can experiment to your heart's content. Sometimes, if the kids have been extra good, I'll sprinkle a few chocolate chips into the mix too.

MAKES ABOUT 2 QUARTS

+ Preheat the oven to 300 degrees F and line a sheet pan with parchment paper.

+ In a large bowl, combine the oats, coconut, pecans, almonds, sunflower seeds, and flour and stir.

+ In a small bowl, whisk together the oil, maple syrup, brown sugar, cinnamon, and salt until combined. Pour the oil mixture over the oat mixture and stir very well until every dry component is fully coated.

4 cups dry rolled oats

1 cup unsweetened coconut flakes

1 cup chopped pecans

1 cup chopped almonds

½ cup sunflower seeds

½ cup oat flour (see note)

(continued)

½ cup neutral-flavored
vegetable oil

½ cup maple syrup

¼ cup lightly packed light
brown sugar, or a bit
more if you prefer a
sweeter granola

1 teaspoon ground cinnamon

1 teaspoon kosher salt

1 cup dried cherries

1 cup dried cranberries

1 cup dark chocolate chips
(optional)

✦ Pour the granola mixture onto the prepared sheet pan, and with clean, lightly oiled hands, press down to make one firmly packed, even layer of granola.

✦ Bake on the center rack of the oven until the granola is uniformly golden brown, 30 to 40 minutes. If your oven has hot spots, rotate the sheet pan halfway through baking, but do not stir the granola.

✦ Remove the sheet pan from the oven and let the granola cool completely at room temperature. Transfer the granola to a large bowl, breaking it into random pieces and clumps as you go. Add the cherries, cranberries, and chocolate chips, if using, and toss everything together gently.

✦ Transfer the granola to an airtight container. It will keep at cool room temperature for at least 2 weeks.

NOTE: Oat flour can be purchased from specialty vendors like Bob's Red Mill, or you can make your own by food processing the heck out of rolled oats. Just let the blade run until the oats are mostly powdery. A rounded ½ cup rolled oats will yield about ½ cup oat flour.

fruit crisp for any season

IF YOU HAVE SEASONAL FRUIT and a few staples in your pantry, you can always make my favorite rustic dessert: a crisp. When I need a last-minute dessert, fruit crisp is always my go-to. It's so easy and so delicious.

You don't really need a recipe to make a great fruit crisp. You just need great fruit, a little sweetener, some spice, and plenty of crumbly oatmeal cookie–type topping. I like to use cornstarch or arrowroot powder to slightly thicken up juicy fruits, but if you don't have these starches on hand, all-purpose flour works fine too. Consider this a blueprint, with ideas for fruit crisps throughout the season, and combine fruits, play with spices, and experiment to find your own perfect crisp.

MAKES 6 TO 9 SERVINGS

For the topping:

¾ cup rolled oats

½ cup lightly packed light brown sugar

½ cup chopped walnuts, pecans, or almonds

½ cup all-purpose flour

½ cup (1 stick) unsalted butter, at soft room temperature

1 teaspoon ground cinnamon

Pinch of kosher salt

For the filling:

Filling ingredients (see opposite page)

Lightly sweetened whipped cream or vanilla ice cream, for serving (optional)

✦ Move an oven rack to the center position and preheat the oven to 350 degrees F. Lightly grease a 9-inch-square pan.

✦ In a small bowl, combine all the topping ingredients and mix together until it looks uniformly clumpy. Set aside.

✦ Choose a filling combination. In a medium bowl, toss the fruit, sweetener, thickener, and extras together, then pour the fruit mixture into the prepared pan.

✦ Sprinkle the crisp topping all over the filling, then bake until the fruit juices are thickened and bubbly and the topping is golden brown and crunchy, 40 minutes or up to 1 hour, depending on the fruit.

✦ Serve the crisp with a dollop of whipped cream or a scoop of ice cream, if desired.

NOTE: If you use frozen fruit, increase the amount of thickener you use a bit.

crisp fillings for any season

	FRUIT	SWEETENER	THICKENER	EXTRAS
APPLE	6 large baking apples, peeled, cored, and sliced into ¼-inch-thick rounds	¼ cup pure maple syrup or 2 tablespoons brown sugar	1 tablespoon cornstarch or arrowroot powder, or 2 tablespoons all-purpose flour	½ teaspoon ground cinnamon, ½ teaspoon ground ginger, and a pinch of freshly grated nutmeg
BLUEBERRY, BLACKBERRY, OR RASPBERRY	6 cups berries—use one kind or mix it up with a combo	2 tablespoons to ¼ cup sugar, depending on the natural sweetness of the berries	2 tablespoons cornstarch or arrowroot powder, or ¼ cup all-purpose flour	Juice and zest of 1 lemon
CHERRY	6 to 7 cups pitted dark sweet cherries	2 tablespoons sugar	2 tablespoons cornstarch or arrowroot powder, or ¼ cup all-purpose flour	½ teaspoon almond extract, and juice and zest of 1 lemon
PEACH OR NECTARINE	6 to 7 medium peaches or nectarines, pitted and sliced	2 tablespoons brown sugar	1 tablespoon cornstarch or arrowroot powder, or 2 tablespoons all-purpose flour	2 tablespoons dark rum or bourbon
PEAR	6 firm pears, such as Bosc or d'Anjou, peeled, cored, and sliced	¼ cup pure maple syrup or 2 tablespoons sugar	1 tablespoon cornstarch or arrowroot powder, or 2 tablespoons all-purpose flour	¼ cup chopped candied ginger and 1 teaspoon very finely minced fresh rosemary
PLUM	2 pounds Italian prune plums, or other firm, freestone plums, pitted and sliced	¼ to ½ cup sugar, depending on the natural sweetness of the plums	1 tablespoon cornstarch or arrowroot powder, or 2 tablespoons all-purpose flour	1 teaspoon vanilla or almond extract, and juice and zest of 1 lemon
RHUBARB	3 to 4 stalks tender rhubarb, sliced ½ inch thick (about 6 cups sliced rhubarb)	¾ cup sugar	2 tablespoons cornstarch or arrowroot powder, or ¼ cup all-purpose flour	Zest and juice of ½ orange and ¼ cup chopped candied ginger

Preserving

THOUGHTS ON LIVING CULTURES

I think the most interesting food preservation methods involve entering into a kind of contract with some collection of beneficial bacteria or yeasts. It's like our distant ancestors, living long before refrigeration or chemical preservatives like sodium benzoate, sat down with a collection of lactobacillus bacteria and said, "Hey, I'll make you a deal. You reliably turn this highly perishable milk into longer-lasting, smooth but tangy yogurt and I'll keep you and your family fed with fresh milk for the next, oh . . . ten thousand years or so. Whaddya say? Deal?"

And that's pretty much exactly what happened. It's not just yogurt—many traditional foods around the world involve this nurturing, almost protective relationship. There are stories of immigrant families from Eastern Europe bringing their sourdough starters with them into the United States. Many traditional fermented pickles rely on an inoculation with the last batch of brine to ensure the desired colony gets a strong shop. The strange, jellylike disk called a Mother of vinegar reliably converts fresh wine into delicious tangy vinegar as long as she's kept fed occasionally. (Most mothers will understand the desire for a periodic glass of wine—Mother of vinegar is no different.)

These are the living cultures. They exist on a strange spectrum between food preservation, culinary alchemy, and household pet. They are low care, but they do require some regular tending and use to keep them vital—kind of like a goldfish. Unlike a goldfish, you don't need to feel bad if your living cultures start to grow mold during a time of neglect, and you'll probably never have a hard talk with your kid about why her pet sourdough starter got flushed down the toilet while she was away at summer camp.

the cultured family

Yeasts, various beneficial lactic acid bacteria (LAB), and various acetic acid bacteria (AAB) are the most useful and frequently used living cultures for traditional methods of food preservation.

Yeasts are single-cell organisms in the fungi family, like mushrooms. They eat sugars—nearly all types of sugar have some strain of yeast that's evolved to consume it—and excrete ethanol (booze!) and carbon dioxide (bubbles!). We rely upon yeasts to create beer, wine, hard ciders, and leavened breads. Yeasts are everywhere. They are floating around in your home right now. Anywhere moisture and a sugary or starchy food source like fruit, juice, grains, potatoes, or corn come together, yeast is having a party.

Lactic acid bacteria are mostly friendly little guys that can handle low pH environments far better than most bacteria. LAB really prefer to work away from oxygen, and they are found in large quantities inside a healthy human gut. They chomp down on carbs and excrete tangy lactic acid as a byproduct of their metabolism. Lactic acid's preservative effect has been keeping yogurt, kimchi, and sour pickle lovers happy for thousands of years.

Acetic acid bacteria are always ready to party. They float around everywhere, just looking for booze, and when they find it they happily convert that ethanol into acetic acid (vinegar). The journey to vinegar, therefore, is a two-act play. Act one: Yeast convert sugars into booze. Act two: Acetic acid bacteria convert booze into vinegar. AAB love warm temperatures and lots of oxygen, and they frequently hitch a ride toward the nearest piece of overripe fruit or glass of wine on the feet of fruit flies. If your end goal is a ferment of vinegar, you'll love how easy it is to attract acetic acid bacteria. If you're trying to make booze, much of your sanitation efforts will be directed at keeping these ubiquitous beasties out of your brew.

notes on yogurt making

Yogurt is very easy to make—you simmer milk, then cool it, inoculate it with yogurt culture, and keep the inoculated yogurt at about 110 degrees F for four to eight hours. During the culturing period, the heat-loving beneficial bacteria in the yogurt eat milk sugars and give off tangy lactic acid. As this fermentation progresses, the milk gradually acidulates and forms a soft curd. After the yogurt has cultured, transfer it to the refrigerator, where it will last for 2 weeks or more, slowly getting more tangy and thick as it ages.

The most difficult part about making yogurt at home is figuring out how to keep a batch at 110 degrees F for several hours. I have a warming drawer under my oven that is great for making yogurt—other folks set their inoculated milk in a plastic cooler filled with warm water. Friends of mine have had good luck inoculating their milk in an oven with a pilot light. Still others wrap their yogurt well in a big blanket and set it on a heating pad set on low. Some folks swear by making yogurt in a Crock-Pot, though I'll admit this method has never worked well for me.

The point is, get creative. There are probably twenty ways you could use what you already have around your home to effectively hold your yogurt at around 110 degrees F for several hours. And if the proverbial spit-and-duct-tape solutions aren't your style, you can even buy commercial yogurt incubators that will manage the temperature for you.

The first time you make yogurt, you'll need a starter. I typically use plain, whole-milk, active-culture yogurt from the store. You can also buy dried yogurt cultures in some health food stores and online. The unique strains and blends of various beneficial lactic bacteria strains that turn milk into yogurt impart their own flavors to the yogurt, so if you start with commercial store-bought yogurt, choose a yogurt you enjoy.

Once you've make yogurt once, hold the last bit of your homemade yogurt aside as the starter for your next batch. Typically, I can get three to four batches of yogurt from an initial purchase of starter culture before that culture begins to degrade a bit and the results of the yogurt making become less predictable. If you invest in a more aggressive heirloom yogurt starter online, you may be able to maintain that culture indefinitely.

thick and creamy yogurt

YOGURT IS MORE VERSATILE THAN YOU might think. You can eat it plain, of course, or topped with a drizzle of maple syrup, a spoonful of strawberry jam, or a sprinkle of granola (see page 123). Strain it well and it makes a great substitute for sour cream. I marinate chicken in yogurt, and add it to meatloaf and lamb burgers to ensure juicy, tender meat. In summer, try slicing up cucumbers and adding a big dollop of yogurt and a scattering of dill for a fast and refreshing salad.

MAKES ABOUT 8 CUPS

½ gallon whole milk, not ultra-high-temp pasteurized

1 cup heavy cream

½ cup plain active-culture yogurt or dried yogurt culture

+ In a heavy Dutch oven or heavy, non-aluminum saucepot set over medium heat, bring the milk and cream to just under a simmer—about 190 degrees F. Maintain this temperature for 20 minutes, stirring frequently to prevent the milk from scorching on the bottom of the pan. Heating results in a thicker yogurt.

+ Cover the pot and remove it from the heat. Let the milk cool to 115 degrees F. Stir the starter yogurt together with about 1 cup of the warm milk until the mixture is smooth, without lumps, and about the texture of heavy cream. If using dried yogurt culture, follow the rehydration instructions on the package.

+ Add the yogurt mixture to the pot of warm milk and stir to combine. Ladle the inoculated milk through a strainer into clean, warm mason jars or other containers. Straining removes any bits of curdled milk protein. Lid the jars and culture the yogurt at 110 degrees F for 4 to 8 hours, until a curd forms (see Notes on Yogurt Making, page 131). Longer fermentation results in a firmer but tangier yogurt.

+ Transfer the jars to the refrigerator until completely chilled. The yogurt should last several weeks in the refrigerator.

notes on vinegar making

Vinegar is a very easy two-step ferment. The first step in fermentation is to convert a sugary liquid like grape or apple juice into something containing alcohol, like wine or cider. Because we actually want the wine or cider to "spoil" into vinegar, we can be pretty relaxed about that first fermentation. I typically rely on the wild yeasts living on the fruit to ferment it. If you start with premade wine, hard apple cider, beer, or any other non-distilled alcoholic ferment, this step is already done!

The second step in vinegar making is inoculating the fermented juice with beneficial acetobacter bacteria. Acetobacter converts alcohol to acetic acid, which gives vinegar its lovely tang. Acetobacter and cellulose will eventually form a jellylike disk in vinegar that's called the Mother. It's a little weird looking, but it's harmless (and many believe it confers health benefits). Think of the Mother as the vinegar equivalent of a sourdough bread starter: once it forms, you can keep it alive nearly indefinitely if you keep it fed with fresh wine or other fermented juice. The Mother will grow and multiply, so once you have a healthy, happy Mother, you can supply all your friends with vinegar starter too!

You can buy a Mother of vinegar from most brewing or winemaking supply stores, or you can inoculate your fermented juice with unpasteurized vinegar that contains the Mother, such as Bragg's apple cider vinegar. The raw vinegar route is a bit slower than inoculating with the Mother, but is a good option if a Mother of vinegar is hard to find in your area. It's best to keep the vinegar Mother consistent with the fermented juice you'll be feeding it, so if you want to inoculate red wine, seek out raw, unpasteurized red wine vinegar, typically a fancy one from France.

The acetic acid conversion is an aerobic fermentation, which means that the vinegar Mother needs oxygen while it ferments. Use a widemouthed jar for lots of surface area and cover the jar with a breathable, lint-free cloth rather than a tight-fitting lid. I save my husband's old dress shirts for this and cut squares from them as needed to cover ferments.

The flavor and acid content of your homemade vinegar can vary from mild to biting depending on the acidity in the fruit you are using and the starting alcohol content of your ferment. This means you cannot use your homemade vinegar for canning projects, but it's great in salad dressings, as a seasoning, or sweetened with sugar or honey for a delicious fruit vinegar shrub.

simple never-ending red wine vinegar

IF YOU ENTERTAIN, OR JUST ENJOY a single glass of wine every once in a while, chances are you find yourself with half-full bottles of wine on occasion. Rather than letting that extra wine go to waste, start a never-ending vinegar jar to keep yourself supplied with handcrafted vinegar.

Feel free to combine various end pours from several bottles of wine. Just make sure the wine hasn't turned sour before you start your vinegar. For best results, use wine without preservatives and distilled water.

MAKES A VARIED AMOUNT

+ In a spotlessly clean widemouth jar that leaves several inches of headroom above the ingredients, combine all the ingredients. Cover the jar with a clean lint-free cloth or several layers of cheesecloth and secure tightly with a rubber band or length of kitchen twine.

+ Set the vinegar aside in a warm, dark place for several weeks. Acetobacter works best at temperatures between 75 and 85 degrees F. The vinegar is ready when it has a rich, pungent, vinegar smell and taste.

+ Once the Mother gets going, feed it by adding leftover wine to the jar periodically as you have it.

+ When the jar gets too full to add more wine, pour off about three-quarters of the finished vinegar and strain it through a fine-mesh sieve to catch any bits of the Mother. Return any Mother to the vinegar jar.

+ Taste and adjust the strength of the vinegar by adding a bit of water if the vinegar is too pungent. If desired, pasteurize the vinegar by bringing it just to a simmer in a nonreactive pot. I don't bother pasteurizing my vinegar, but it will keep a bit longer if you do. Decant the vinegar into sanitized dry bottles and lid tightly. Store in a cool, dark place for up to 1 year.

2 cups red wine

1 cup water, ideally distilled

1 (8-ounce) jar red wine Mother of vinegar, or 1 cup unpasteurized red wine vinegar with the Mother

cores and scraps fruit vinegar

THIS IS A VERY ECONOMICAL VINEGAR because you can use trimmings, peels, cores, and scraps of fruit from other recipes and projects. When I make applesauce, I always have a lot of peels and trimmings left over. This vinegar is a great way to turn those trimmings into something useful. Use fruit scraps without mold or severe bruising. Some bruising or browning from oxidation is fine, but discard anything showing signs of actual decay. Once you've made this fruit vinegar, you can use vinegar from an unpasteurized older batch to inoculate a new batch instead of relying on store-bought apple cider.

MAKES 1 QUART

About 8 ounces of cores, peels, or trimmings from fresh fruit, chopped roughly into bite-size chunks (apple, pear, peach, plum, and pineapple will all work well)

1 quart warm water

¼ cup sugar

1 cup raw, unpasteurized apple cider vinegar with the Mother

+ In a clean 1-quart widemouthed glass jar, add the fruit trimmings. The fruit should half fill the jar. In a pitcher, mix the water and sugar together until the sugar dissolves, then pour enough of the sugar water into the jar to cover the fruit trimmings and mostly fill the jar. Leave 1 inch of headroom at the top of the jar to allow for fermentation.

+ Place a clean lint-free cloth or several layers of cheesecloth over the top of the jar and secure it tightly with a rubber band or length of kitchen twine. Set the jar aside at warm room temperature. Within 48 hours, you'll be able to hear the bubble and fizz of fermentation.

+ Let the fruit mixture ferment for about 1 week, until signs of bubbly fermentation have slowed. The mixture should smell fruity and boozy. Strain the liquid off the fruit trimmings into a clean 1-quart jar or crock. You should have about 3 cups liquid.

+ Add the apple cider vinegar to the liquid and cover the jar with a clean lint-free cloth, paper towel, or several layers of cheesecloth. Secure it tightly with a rubber band or length of kitchen twine.

✦ Set the vinegar aside in a warm, dark place for several weeks. Acetobacter works best at temperatures between 75 and 85 degrees F. The vinegar is ready when it has a rich, pungent fruit vinegar smell.

✦ Taste the vinegar and adjust the strength by adding a bit of water if it's too pungent. If desired, pasteurize the vinegar by bringing it just to a simmer in a nonreactive pot. I don't bother pasteurizing my vinegar, but it will keep a bit longer if you do. Decant the vinegar into a sanitized dry bottle and lid tightly. Store in a cool, dark place for up to 1 year.

infused vinegar

INFUSE ADDITIONAL FLAVORS INTO YOUR VINEGAR (homemade or purchased) and you'll have fast, cheap ways to splash on flavor. Classic infused vinegars like tarragon and raspberry make simple oil-and-vinegar salad dressings a snap. But there's a lot of room for creativity in your infusing too.

Play around with fruit, herbs, and spices and find the flavors that work best with your style of cooking. I also like taking flavor inspiration from classic sauces like chimichurri, an herbal Argentinian steak sauce, and mignonette, a traditional accompaniment to oysters served on the half shell.

For an easy and refreshing summer drink, mix a fruit-infused vinegar (I like blackberry) with a little simple syrup and a pour of still or sparkling water. You'll have what's called drinking vinegar or a shrub—a traditional heirloom drink that's been enjoying a huge revival as folks have discovered this great soda or juice alternative.

MAKES A VARIED AMOUNT

✦ Choose an infused vinegar flavor from the chart on page 141. Prepare the flavoring ingredients as necessary. All fruit and herbs should be as fresh as possible, and in top condition. Discard any ingredients with signs of mold or decay. Wash and thoroughly dry your fresh ingredients.

✦ Clean and sanitize a glass jar that will be large enough to hold the vinegar and flavor ingredients comfortably. I typically use pint or quart mason jars.

✦ Combine the vinegar and flavor ingredients in the jar. Make sure there is enough vinegar to fully cover all the flavoring ingredients. If not, add a bit more vinegar to the jar.

✦ Lid the jar and let the vinegar sit in a cool, dark place for 3 to 4 weeks. Taste the vinegar; when the flavor has developed to your satisfaction, it's done!

Vinegar, homemade
(see pages 135 or 136)
or store-bought

Flavor ingredients
(see page 141)

Sugar (optional)

(continued)

✦ Strain the vinegar through a fine-mesh sieve to remove any big chunks, then filter the vinegar through a strainer lined with a paper coffee filter, clean lint-free cloth, or layered paper towels.

✦ If desired, sweeten the vinegar slightly. Many fruit vinegars taste more rounded with about 1 tablespoon sugar added per 1 cup finished vinegar. This is totally optional.

✦ Transfer the vinegar to sanitized dry bottles. Lid tightly and store the vinegar in a cool, dark place. It will keep for about 1 year.

infused vinegar flavors

	VINEGAR	FLAVOR INGREDIENTS
CRANBERRY VINEGAR (quart jar)	2 cups white wine vinegar or red wine vinegar	1 pound fresh or frozen cranberries, lightly crushed
STONE FRUIT VINEGAR (quart jar)	2 cups rice wine vinegar	1 pound fresh or frozen peaches, nectarines, plums, or a combination, pitted and chopped
ANY BERRY VINEGAR (quart jar)	2 cups white wine vinegar, rice wine vinegar, or apple cider vinegar	1 pound fresh or frozen blueberries, blackberries, raspberries, or a combination, lightly crushed
APPLE OR PEAR VINEGAR (quart jar)	2 cups white wine or apple cider vinegar	1 pound fresh apples or pears; peels, cores, and trimmings are fine
CITRUS VINEGAR (pint jar)	1½ cups white wine vinegar or rice wine vinegar	½ cup peeled zest (no pith!), lightly packed, from 6 to 7 lemons, 6 to 7 limes, or 3 to 4 oranges
ZESTY GARLIC AND HERB VINEGAR (pint jar)	1½ cups red wine vinegar	4 to 6 cloves garlic, peeled and lightly crushed; ½ bay leaf; 1 (4-inch) sprig fresh rosemary; several sprigs fresh oregano and thyme
TARRAGON VINEGAR (pint jar)	1¾ cups white wine vinegar or champagne vinegar	8 to 10 sprigs fresh tarragon
CHIMICHURRI VINEGAR (pint jar)	1½ cups red wine vinegar	½ cup each minced fresh cilantro and parsley; 2 cloves garlic, lightly crushed; ½ teaspoon ground cumin; ½ teaspoon freshly ground black pepper; ½ teaspoon red pepper flakes
GREEN HERB VINEGAR (pint jar)	1½ cups white wine vinegar, champagne vinegar, or apple cider vinegar	1 cup lightly packed fresh chives, basil, dill, fennel, lemon balm, mint, or other soft green herb
MIGNONETTE VINEGAR (pint jar)	1¾ cups champagne vinegar or rice wine vinegar, and 1 cup red wine vinegar	1 to 2 fresh shallots, sliced; 1 tablespoon freshly ground black pepper; zest of 1 lemon

Home Care

glass cleaner

VODKA: IT'S NOT JUST FOR HAPPY HOUR any more. The solvent qualities of alcohol are excellent for streak-free glass cleaning. If you can't get cheap vodka or prefer not to keep it in the house, you can use one cup rubbing alcohol in this recipe and increase the distilled water to three cups. Rubbing alcohol is pretty stinky and definitely not good to inhale, but it's cheaper. Your call.

I add a drop of blue food coloring to this spray so it's the universal "glass cleaner" color and my kids won't mistake it for plain water. I also use this for cleaning stainless steel and chrome—basically "shiny metal"—because it does such a great job at polishing up sinks and fixtures without leaving any residue.

MAKES 1 QUART

✦ Add all the ingredients to a 32-ounce heavy-duty spray bottle. Tightly lid the bottle and give it a few turns to mix everything together. Label the bottle and store the cleaner tightly lidded and out of reach of kids. The cleaner will last for at least a year, though the essential oil scent may fade over time.

To use:

✦ Shake the glass cleaner well, then spray onto a clean lint-free towel or the surface you wish to clean. Wipe the glass, mirror, or polished metal clean, then polish the surface dry with a soft, lint-free rag (old cut-up cotton t-shirts are great for this).

NOTE: Less is more when it comes to cleaning glass. You will not get a better result if you spray the heck out of it.

2 cups cheap vodka

2 cups distilled water

½ teaspoon baking soda

30 drops peppermint essential oil

1 drop blue food coloring (optional)

all-purpose cleaner

For all-purpose cleaning of counters; hardwood, laminate, or tile floors; painted or stained woodwork and painted walls; and even spot touch-up cleaning of mirrors and stainless steel, I use this alkaline, residue-free cleaner. I have a bottle in both my upstairs and downstairs cleaning totes and keep another under the kitchen sink for fast access. This is as simple and thrifty as it gets for routine cleaning. I add a drop of green food coloring to this spray, so it matches the fresh peppermint scent and my kids never mistake it for water.

MAKES 1 QUART

2 tablespoons borax

½ teaspoon liquid castile soap

Hot water

30 drops peppermint essential oil or other essential oil of choice

1 drop green food coloring (optional)

+ Add the borax and castile soap to a 32-ounce heavy-duty spray bottle. Add enough hot water to fill the bottle, lid tightly, and give the bottle a good shake to dissolve the borax. Let the mixture cool, then add the peppermint essential oil and food coloring, if using. Label the bottle and store out of reach of kids. The cleaner will last for at least a year, though the essential oil scent may fade over time.

To use:

+ Lightly spray the cleaner onto a clean lint-free towel or directly onto the surface you wish to clean, then wipe away the grime. To clean sealed hardwood floors, spray floors very lightly and immediately wipe them with a microfiber mop.

acidic bathroom cleaner

BATHROOMS OFTEN SUFFER FROM MINERAL BUILDUP or hard-water spots, and this acid-based cleaner works great against inorganic grime. When mixing this up, distilled white vinegar works fine, but for even more cleaning power, try this with the Citrus Vinegar Concentrate (page 362). Don't use vinegars with the Mother for cleaning—save those for cooking!

I like the fresh citrus combo of essential oils here, and they complement the citrus vinegar I use. When made with citrus-infused vinegar, this cleaner will naturally be a warm yellow color. If you are using distilled vinegar, consider adding a drop of yellow food coloring to the cleaner so kids never mistake it for water.

MAKES 1 QUART

2½ cups water

1½ cups distilled white vinegar or Citrus Vinegar Concentrate (page 362)

20 drops lemon or lemongrass essential oil

10 drops grapefruit essential oil

1 drop yellow food coloring (optional)

✦ Add all the ingredients to a 32-ounce spray bottle. Lid the bottle tightly, then give it a few turns to mix everything together. Label the bottle and store out of reach of kids. The cleaner lasts indefinitely, though the essential oil scent may fade over time.

To use:

✦ Spray the cleaner onto bathroom tile, tub surroundings, bathroom countertops, etc. Gently scrub stubborn areas of dirt or hard-water buildup. Wipe the surface clean with a lint-free cloth.

customize your acidic cleaner with science!

At this dilution, your vinegar cleaner is about 2 percent acetic acid. While this doesn't sound like much, I've found this concentration is perfectly effective for regular maintenance cleaning. If you are dealing with long-standing mineral or hard-water buildup, a more concentrated solution might be needed. Undiluted distilled white vinegar is typically 5 percent acetic acid and will clean all but the very worst mineral, rust, and lime-scale buildup. If you need an even more powerful acidic cleanser, dilute ½ cup citric acid in 4 cups straight 5 percent distilled white vinegar, and you'll boost the overall acid concentration to about 20 percent. Do take special care with a cleaner that strong—wear gloves and be careful which surfaces you clean. Even though it's homemade, it's powerful!

greasy grime spray

year-round

WHEN I NEED TO TACKLE REALLY greasy grime in the kitchen or around the house, I use this spray. Adding washing soda and grease-cutting orange essential oil to a generous squeeze of castile soap makes this a powerful formula. It takes care of even tough grease like the buildup on kitchen vent hoods and stovetop grime. I label this spray and add a drop of orange food coloring to match the punchy citrus scent and so my kids never mistake it for water.

MAKES 1 QUART

1 tablespoon liquid castile
   soap

2 teaspoons washing soda

About 4 cups warm water

30 drops sweet orange
   essential oil

1 drop orange food coloring
   (optional)

✦ Add the soap and washing soda to a 32-ounce heavy duty spray bottle. Add enough warm water to fill the bottle, leaving an inch of room at the top. Add the essential oil and food coloring, if using. Lid the bottle tightly, then give it a few turns to mix everything together. Label the bottle and store out of reach of kids. The spray will last for at least a year, though the essential oil scent may fade over time.

To use:

✦ Spray onto a clean lint-free towel to wipe delicate surfaces of grease, or spray directly onto hard surfaces and then scrub. Wipe the surface again as necessary, then dry.

basic scrubbing powder

SOMETIMES THE ONLY THING TO DO is scrub the dirt off. Think bathtub rings, ground-in mystery grime on the tile floor, or dried egg goo in the sink. That's where this scrubbing powder comes in. Just add a bit of water and a bit of elbow grease and this scrub will clean through just about anything. It does a nice job on stainless steel, too, restoring a light polish to sinks. While this formulation isn't likely to scratch hard surfaces, test this scrub in an inconspicuous space if you aren't sure about the durability of your surface.

MAKES 3 CUPS

+ Add all the ingredients to a widemouthed quart mason jar and stir together. Store in the jar with a Mason Jar Shaker Lid (see note). The powder will last indefinitely, though the essential oil scent may fade over time.

1 cup baking soda

1 cup borax

1 cup kosher salt

20 drops lemon essential oil

20 drops sweet orange essential oil

To use:

+ Sprinkle a bit of the powder on a damp cellulose sponge or lint-free cloth. Scrub away at the dirty surface. Rinse the surface well, then wipe dry.

mason jar shaker lid

For everything from Potty Powder (page 150) to Carpet Freshener (page 198), shaker lids make powdered cleaning products easy to dispense. Make your own shaker lids inexpensively from readily available plastic mason jar lids. Just drill 15 to 20 small holes in the cap with a 1/32-inch drill bit. If you want to go even cheaper, cut a thin cardboard round to exactly fit on the mason jar. Poke 15 to 20 small holes in the cardboard with a heavy-gauge needle or push-pin. Use the ring from a two-piece mason jar lid to hold the cardboard in place.

potty powder

THERE ARE REALLY TWO WAYS TO go when it comes to toilet cleaners. Acidic toilet cleaners do a great job at removing rust stains and hard-water buildup, and highly alkali cleaners do away with even the grossest "biological" stains (how's that for a euphemism?). You'll find extreme, corrosive ingredients like hydrochloric acid (strong acid) and sodium hypochlorite (bleach—strong alkali) in various commercial toilet cleaners, but there's really no need to employ that stuff for routine home cleaning.

Most of the bio stains you're likely to find in a toilet bowl will come clean with plain ol' water—they don't call H_2O the "universal solvent" for nothing—so I opt for this mild acidic cleaner when I'm cleaning a toilet. A simple mix of granulated citric acid and some of the most effective antimicrobial essential oils deal with inorganic soil while freshening up this potentially stinky space. You can substitute other essential oils of your choice, if desired

MAKES 2 CUPS

2 cups granulated citric acid

20 drops tea tree essential oil

20 drops cinnamon essential oil

20 drops clove essential oil

✦ Add all the ingredients to a widemouthed pint mason jar and stir together. Store the powder in the jar with a Mason Jar Shaker Lid (page 149). The powder will last indefinitely, though the essential oil scent may fade over time.

To use:

✦ Shake about 1 tablespoon of the powder into the toilet bowl, give it a swirl with a toilet brush to help the powder dissolve in the water, and let it sit for several minutes. After soaking, a quick scrub with the toilet brush should be all it takes to get the toilet bowl clean.

Personal Care

peppermint tooth powder

WHEN YOU ARE USED TO TOOTHPASTE that tastes like an after dinner-mint, transitioning to a baking soda–based tooth cleanser can take a little getting used to. But, oh, how clean it leaves your teeth!

Tooth decay happens when bacteria in your mouth eat sugar on your tooth surfaces and convert it to an acid (this is not unlike how yogurt and sauerkraut are made). This acid can slowly eat away at your alkaline tooth enamel. When the pH of the mouth returns to its healthy, alkaline state, mineral ions dissolved in the saliva help rebuild the damaged tooth enamel. This recipe is distinctly alkaline, has a healthy dose of calcium to assist in the re-mineralization of your tooth enamel, and adds the dental-friendly sweetener called xylitol.

If you don't want in invest in calcium carbonate or xylitol, you can get squeaky-clean teeth by brushing with pure baking soda. I brushed with plain baking soda for years and came to really like how fresh it left my mouth feeling, but the taste can be pretty off-putting at first.

MAKES ½ CUP

✦ In a small bowl, mix all the ingredients together until thoroughly blended. Store the tooth powder at room temperature in a small tin or a widemouthed 4-ounce jar with a tight-fitting lid. If kept dry, the powder will last indefinitely, though the essential oil scent may fade over time.

To use:

✦ Run your toothbrush under water, then tap off any excess. Sprinkle the tooth powder onto the brush and gently scrub your pearly whites clean.

4 tablespoons baking soda

3 tablespoons food-grade calcium carbonate powder

2 tablespoons granulated xylitol

4 to 6 drops food-grade peppermint oil or food-grade peppermint essential oil

basic lard bar soap

THIS ALL-PURPOSE, FIRM, GENTLE WHITE SOAP recipe is a great one for beginners because the results are consistent and the fats are easy to find. Use clean rendered lard: either lard you've rendered yourself or lard from the supermarket will work. Lavender essential oil in this recipe is nice.

MAKES ABOUT 1½ POUNDS SOAP AFTER CURING

9 ounces cold water

3.4 ounces pure granular lye

10 ounces lard

7 ounces coconut oil

7 ounces olive oil

1 to 2 tablespoons essential oils (optional)

+ Before you begin, read the basic steps of soap making and all safety information and notes on page 92. Empty your sink if necessary, get on your protective gear (eye goggles, gloves, long sleeves, etc.), and make sure kids, pets, and other trip hazards are out of your work space. Prepare a 2-pound soap mold.

+ In a heat-resistant pitcher, add the water. Set the pitcher in the sink. In a small stainless steel bowl, precisely measure the lye. Carefully add the lye to the water. *(Never add water to lye!)* The water will become cloudy and will get quite hot. It may even "smoke" a bit— this is normal. Do not breathe the fumes from this reaction. Stir with an old plastic or stainless steel spoon, or disposable wooden chopsticks, to fully dissolve the lye, then let the lye solution sit to cool while you melt the oils.

+ In a large stainless steel pot over medium heat, carefully add the lard and coconut and olive oils. Warm them slowly together, stirring occasionally until just melted. Remove the oil mixture from the heat and set aside to cool.

+ When the lye and the oils are both around 110 degrees F—anything from about 90 to 120 degrees F is fine, but the lye and the oil should be within about 15 degrees of each other—set the pot in the sink and carefully pour the lye solution into the oil. *(Never add the oil to the lye!)*

+ Stir the mixture gently with an immersion blender (not turned on) to help bring the oils and lye together, then turn the immersion blender on the lowest speed. Blend the soap thoroughly, moving the blender around the pot, until the mixture thickens and achieves trace, 8 to 15 minutes.

+ Add any essential oils as desired, blend to fully incorporate, then pour and scrape the soap into the prepared mold. Cover the soap with a layer of plastic wrap, then insulate or chill soap as desired, to achieve a fully gelled or a no-gel soap.

+ Leave your protective gear on and clean your soap-making equipment and work area very well. Finish cleanup by lightly wiping down anything that may have come in contact with lye with undiluted vinegar.

+ After 24 hours, check the soap. Put on a pair of disposable gloves and give the soap a gentle press to see if it easily pulls away from the edges of the mold. If the soap is firm, turn the soap out of the mold. If not, give the soap another 12 to 24 hours to cure in the mold before turning out.

+ If necessary, slice the soap into bars. Set the soap in a cool, out-of-the-way place on a wire rack. Cover it loosely with a lint-free cloth and turn the soap periodically. Cure for 4 weeks before using.

To use:

+ Use at the sink or in the shower for general purpose cleaning of hands or body.

honey-rosemary hair wash

YOU CAN GET A GOOD DIY shampoo with just honey, liquid castile soap, and a few essential oils. But I like playing personal care chemist, so I add a few other ingredients too. In this formula, the vegetable glycerin improves the "slip" of the shampoo to reduce hair breakage during washing, the castor oil and vitamin E condition the hair and scalp, the kaolin clay helps remove impurities and buildup from hair, and the citric acid lowers the pH.

MAKES ABOUT 8 FLUID OUNCES

½ cup (4 ounces) pure honey

6 tablespoons (3 ounces) liquid castile soap

1 tablespoon vegetable glycerin

1 tablespoon castor oil

1 tablespoon kaolin clay

⅛ teaspoon granulated citric acid

10 drops vitamin E oil

15 drops rosemary essential oil (for light-blond hair, substitute chamomile essential oil)

10 drops lavender essential oil

8 drops peppermint essential oil

+ Slightly warm the honey, if necessary, to make it easier to mix. In a 10- to 12-ounce squeeze or pump bottle, add all the ingredients, lid tightly, and shake to combine. The hair wash will last for about 3 months as long as water isn't added to the mixture.

To use:

+ Shake the shampoo. Rub a teaspoon or so of the hair wash in the palms of your hands, then lather it evenly through your hair and scalp. Rub gently, then rinse hair thoroughly with warm water. Squeeze any excess water from your hair, then spray with pH-Balancing Rosemary Hair Spritz (page 159).

notes on hair care science

The high-powered, oil-stripping detergents, chemical preservatives, and artificial fragrances found in nearly all commercial shampoos aren't doing you any long-term favors. If you want to avoid that gunk and DIY your hair care, it helps to understand a bit about what hair is and how it responds to a good washing.

Hair is composed primarily of a tightly packed bundle of fine, strong strands made of keratin. These strands are called the cortex. The cortex is protected by the outer layer of hair, called the cuticle. The cuticle forms smooth scales that overlap tightly, like clay roof tiles. The cuticle is your hair's defense against pollution, breakage, damage, and excessive moisture. A healthy, smooth, flat cuticle reflects light, making hair look shiny. A rough, damaged hair cuticle makes hair looks dull, coarse, and frizzy.

Our hair's natural conditioner is called sebum. This is a type of oil manufactured in the sebaceous oil glands of the skin. Sebum coats the hair (and skin) with a microscopically thin layer of a protecting, waterproofing wax. Sebum has an acidic pH between 4.5 and 5.5 and—unsurprisingly—this is the pH range best suited to hair care products.

Alkaline, high-pH products open up the hair cuticle and leave hair rough and more prone to tangling and breakage, while moderately acidic products help close the hair cuticle and leave hair smooth, just like natural sebum. For DIY-shampoo enthusiasts, this can be a problem, because natural soaps, including my beloved liquid castile, are always alkaline, with a pH of around 9.0.

In my search for a good DIY shampoo, I wanted a gentle liquid cleanser with a nice lather that I didn't have to make fresh before every shampooing. I also wanted a pH level that was healthy for my hair and left it feeling good.

I found the solution in honey. This sticky substance has been used to clean, condition, and beautify skin since at least Cleopatra's time. Honey has a pH of between 4 and 6, which makes it acidic enough to temper the alkalinity of natural soaps, but perhaps because of the viscosity of the mixture, it doesn't undermine saponification.

This honey-based hair wash cleans well without drying hair, is mild, and has plenty of "slip" so your hair won't feel like angry straw as you wash it. It's not sticky at all, and it rinses cleanly away in warm water. After shampooing, I finish up with the pH-Balancing Rosemary Hair Spritz (see opposite page). This decidedly acidic spray firmly closes the hair cuticle, leaving hair smooth and shiny. The combination of the two is the best, most natural way I've found to clean my hair.

pH-balancing rosemary hair spritz

THIS HAIR SPRITZ IS IDEAL FOR dark-haired folks. The rosemary is particularly good at adding sheen and deepening brunette tones in hair. If you have light or blond hair, the herb for you is chamomile, which can very subtly lighten hair pigments and enhance that sun-kissed look.

MAKES ABOUT 16 FLUID OUNCES

+ In a medium pot, bring the water to a simmer. Remove from the heat, add the rosemary and citric acid, stir, and cover the pot tightly. Set aside for 30 minutes to steep, then strain and discard the rosemary sprigs.

+ Once the infusion has cooled completely, add the vegetable glycerin, vitamin E oil, jojoba oil, and essential oils. Transfer the spritz to a 16-ounce spray bottle. Add water to fill if necessary. The hair spritz will last for at least 3 months, though the essential oil scent may fade over time.

To use:

+ After washing your hair with Honey-Rosemary Hair Wash (page 156) or your shampoo of choice, shake the spritz bottle and spray generously onto damp hair. Work the spritz through your hair. Don't rinse it out. Dry and style hair as usual.

2 cups distilled water

3 (5-inch) sprigs fresh rosemary (for light or blond hair, substitute ¼ cup chamomile blossoms or 4 teabags chamomile herbal tea)

1¼ teaspoons granulated citric acid

½ teaspoon vegetable glycerin

¼ teaspoon vitamin E oil

½ to 1 teaspoon jojoba, apricot kernel, or sweet almond oil (optional, for dry hair)

15 drops rosemary essential oil (for light-blond hair, substitute chamomile essential oil)

10 drops lavender essential oil

8 drops peppermint essential oil

creamy bar deodorant

DEODORANT DOESN'T STOP SWEAT, BUT IT does help absorb it and control the bacteria that makes it stinky. With baking soda, mineral and clay powders, skin-soothing oils, and antibacterial essential oils, this is a gentle but powerfully effective nontoxic deodorant.

MAKES TWO 2.5-OUNCE BARS OF DEODORANT

3 tablespoons baking soda

2 tablespoons magnesium carbonate (see notes)

1 tablespoon cream of tartar

2 tablespoons kaolin clay

4 to 5 tablespoons coconut oil (see notes)

4 tablespoons shea butter

4 tablespoons beeswax (pastilles or finely grated)

8 drops vitamin E oil

40 drops tea tree oil

12 drops peppermint essential oil

10 drops lavender essential oil

8 drops rosemary essential oil

✦ In a small bowl, combine the baking soda, magnesium carbonate, cream of tartar, and kaolin clay, making sure the powders are finely ground and free of lumps. Set aside.

✦ In a medium microwave-safe bowl, combine the coconut oil, shea butter, and beeswax. In the microwave, heat the oil mixture on medium power until just melted, 2 to 3 minutes, depending on the power of your microwave. Alternatively, melt in a double boiler set over a pot of simmering water.

✦ Add the powder mixture to the oil mixture and whisk to combine. Working quickly before the deodorant sets up, add the vitamin E oil and essential oils. Whisk well. Divide the mixture evenly into 2 clean twist-up deodorant containers. Let the deodorants cool completely. At cool room temperature, the deodorant will last for a year, though the essential oil scent may fade over time. Avoid storing the deodorant someplace very hot, like inside your car in summer, as the oils can melt and cause the deodorant to separate.

To use:

✦ Apply the deodorant lightly to clean underarms. If you have sensitive skin, avoid applying within 8 hours of shaving.

notes on diy stink stopping

✦ Perhaps our national war on sweat has been a little too aggressive. After all, sweat itself is basically odorless. It's only when hungry little bacteria get ahold of it that it ferments into the stink we know as BO. Commercial stink stoppers are generally antiperspirants that rely on various aluminum salts to keep your pits fresh. The aluminum salts form little plugs that stop up your skin pores and prevent sweat from making it to the surface. The poor underarm—it has to be the only area of the body where we deliberately attempt to clog our pores.

✦ The magnesium carbonate in this formula is a natural mineral used as a nutritional supplement. It's also called "gym chalk," because it's used by weight lifters and gymnasts to absorb sweat and oils from their hands and ensure a slip-free grip on rings and bars. The sweat-absorbing property and supersmooth texture of magnesium carbonate make it perfect for DIY deodorant. You'll find gym chalk most inexpensively in superstores and athletic supply stores—just look for 100 percent magnesium carbonate. It's also available as a finely ground powder online.

✦ Additional coconut oil leads to a slightly softer bar. Use less if your ambient room temperature is fairly warm, in the mid-70s or above, and more if your ambient room temperature is fairly cool, in the mid-60s or below. This quantity can be adjusted seasonally as needed too.

✦ Empty twist-up deodorant containers can be ordered online, or just clean and reuse the container from an empty store-bought deodorant.

Cooking

THOUGHTS ON GREEN AND WILD THINGS

After months of winter and meals made from sturdy greens, cabbages, and dense root vegetables, spring shoulders her way in with perennial shoots, tender greens, and vibrant herbs. Seasonal eating in spring is green eating.

The first greens to appear are always the wildlings that we've not quite succeeded in domesticating for our own use. Freed of the breeder's expectation of year-round succulence, nettle, dandelion, and wild garlic are the first to poke up, deep green and fearless. Watercress, chickweed, miner's lettuce, and goosefoot follow quickly, soft for wild plants, but always with an undercurrent of raw minerality, like eating butter lettuce while licking a penny.

When I eat these foods, there is a sense of rejuvenation in the meal, as if the nutrition of these plants has been building slowly underground all winter and serves to restore the energy I too will need to grow strong and bold in the upcoming year.

I don't live far from a small stream, and though the area is fully developed, the perennial greens manage to keep going in the most humble of spaces. In the dark muck alongside that stream, nettles and wild watercress flourish, and I pick them greedily. Tender young dandelion grows a bit farther out, a good addition to early salads or quick sautés, and I gather wild blackberry leaves to dry for tea.

These greens do not stay gentle for long—prioritizing survival as all the wildlings will, they will grow rapidly, stretch tall, and begin to toughen up or head toward seed in just a few weeks. But by then, the more refined garden crops fill the need. Spinach, arugula, mustards, pea vines, asparagus, radishes, and herbs of all kind are available fresh from the garden or farmers' market, and these will sate our need for fresh greens until the longing of our palate changes again and we realize, four weeks before it could reasonably happen, that what we really want is a sweet, ripe summer tomato.

But for now, everything is verdant and emerald. If ever there was a time to put on heavy socks and waterproof boots and tramp around outside in search of a tonic for body and soul, this is it. The ground is springy, and if you step too close to the puddles, the mud will suck at your feet. Once summer rolls into dominance everyone will be out, staining their lips purple and scratching their hands as they casually pick wild blackberries. But for now, the only foragers are those of us who love the herbs and tender shoots and plain green leaves of spring.

watercress salad with stir-fried beef and peanuts

I LIVE ACROSS THE STREET FROM a small stream that boasts several thriving patches of wild watercress. In the spring, before my own garden has much in the way of lettuce or salad greens to offer, the wild watercress is tender, crunchy, and perfectly peppery. I love it, and I ignore the sideways glances from passing neighbors as I squat down in the stream-side mud with my harvesting scissors. They have no idea that this delicious and healthy salad green is right there, free for the taking, which I suppose is all the better for me.

MAKES 4 SERVINGS

+ In a medium bowl, combine the beef, onion, vinegar, fish sauce, sugar, garlic, ginger, and red pepper flakes and stir well to coat. Cover the bowl with plastic wrap and set aside at room temperature to marinate for 20 minutes.

+ While the beef is marinating, put the watercress and cilantro in a large heat-resistant bowl. Heat a wok or large skillet over medium-high heat. Add 1 tablespoon of the oil and the peanuts to the skillet and cook, stirring constantly, until the peanuts are lightly toasted.

+ Scrape the peanuts into the bowl with the watercress and return the wok to high heat. Add the remaining 2 tablespoons of oil to the skillet. When the oil shimmers, add the marinated beef along with the onion and all the liquid. Cook without stirring for 2 minutes to allow the beef to sear, then stir and continue cooking until the beef is cooked through.

+ Scrape everything from the skillet into the bowl with the watercress. The watercress will wilt slightly—that's normal. Season to taste with salt and pepper, then divide the salad evenly between four plates. Serve a wedge of lime on the side of each plate.

1 pound lean beef, very thinly sliced across the grain

1 small red onion, peeled, cored, and thinly sliced

2 tablespoons rice wine vinegar

2 tablespoons fish sauce

1 tablespoon sugar

1 clove garlic, minced

1 tablespoon minced fresh ginger

Pinch of red pepper flakes

2 bunches watercress, trimmed

1 bunch fresh cilantro, trimmed

3 tablespoons neutral-flavored vegetable oil, divided

½ cup shelled raw peanuts

Kosher salt and freshly ground black pepper

1 lime, quartered

snap peas with mint, feta, and walnuts

REALLY FRESH SNAP PEAS ARE ONE of the best reasons I know to have a garden. In late spring, when my own pea patch starts producing, I frequently make variations of easy sautéed snap peas. This version, with mint, feta, and walnuts is a favorite. It's an excellent side dish, or add a bit of cooked pasta or couscous to turn it into a light vegetarian meal.

MAKES 4 TO 6 SERVINGS AS A SIDE

2 tablespoons butter

2 pounds sugar snap peas, stemmed, with tough strings removed

¼ cup chopped walnuts

Kosher salt and freshly ground black pepper

½ cup chopped fresh mint

4 ounces feta, crumbled

+ In a large sauté pan over medium heat, melt the butter. When the butter foams, add the snap peas and walnuts and cook, stirring frequently, until the snap peas are bright green and crisp-tender and the walnuts are toasted, about 5 minutes. Season to taste with salt and pepper, then toss in the mint and cook for just a few seconds to wilt it.

+ Spoon the snap pea sauté into a large bowl, toss it with the crumbled feta, and serve immediately.

forager spring greens soup

AT SOME POINT DURING THAT TRANSITION from late winter to early spring, I will inevitably feel a thickness behind my eyes and in my sinus cavities—the warning that I'm about to get sick. That's when I know to make this soup. I make it every year, and it is like a tonic—I swear it helps me fight off seasonal colds.

If you wildcraft, the punchy early spring greens like nettles, wild arugula, lambs quarters, or baby dandelion leaves are good in this soup. Use a mix of mild and spicy greens for the best flavor. If you're picking up your greens at the store, spinach and a bit of arugula are nice, but as long as the greens are tender, fresh, and still seem to have some life in them, you can use what you like. Don't make this ahead of time—the beauty of this soup is how bright and vivid green it is.

MAKES 6 TO 8 SERVINGS

2 tablespoons extra-virgin olive oil

1 medium onion, chopped

2 medium leeks, trimmed and sliced

2 cloves garlic, minced

1 medium potato, peeled and diced

6 cups vegetable broth

Zest of ½ lemon

1 pound tender spring greens

1 bunch fresh cilantro, trimmed and roughly chopped

Kosher salt and freshly ground black pepper

+ In a large heavy stockpot set over medium heat, warm the oil. Add the onion, leeks, and garlic and cook, stirring occasionally, until the onion is translucent, 5 to 6 minutes.

+ Add the potato and broth to the pot and bring the soup to a simmer. Adjust the heat to maintain a bare simmer and cook, covered, until the potato is falling-apart tender, about 30 minutes.

+ Add the lemon zest, greens, and cilantro and cook until the greens turn bright and vivid, 1 to 2 minutes. Using an immersion blender, puree the soup to a smooth consistency, or transfer the soup to a blender and very carefully puree the soup in batches before returning it to a clean pot. (If using a blender, vent the lid by removing the center pour cap, place a clean kitchen towel over the lid of the blender, and hold the towel-covered lid down firmly while pureeing.)

+ Season the soup to taste with salt and pepper. Ladle into wide, shallow bowls and serve immediately.

roasted asparagus and ricotta tartine

GROWING UP, MY MOTHER TURNED NEARLY every food into a melt. We had tuna melts, apple-cheddar melts, and asparagus melts. I'm not sure if this is a term used only in our family, so I'll explain. A "melt" is any open-faced sandwich topped with cheese and popped under the broiler.

When I took my first trip to France, I fell in love with tartines—wide slices of perfectly French bread topped with ingredients *en saison* and served open-faced. It was like a grown-up version of the melts Mom used to make. This tartine is delicious with freshly made Lemon Ricotta (page 111), but you can substitute store-bought ricotta, brie, or goat cheese if you like.

MAKES 4 SERVINGS

✦ Move an oven rack to the center position and preheat the oven to 475 degrees F. Line a sheet pan with parchment paper.

✦ To prepare the asparagus, wash and trim the asparagus by holding a few at a time in one hand about midstalk and snapping the tough ends off with the other hand. The asparagus will break at its natural tender point. After trimming, you should have about 1 pound of asparagus.

✦ Place the asparagus in a medium bowl. Add the oil, salt, and pepper to taste and toss to coat. Transfer the asparagus to the sheet pan. Spend a minute arranging the asparagus so the spears sit in a single layer.

✦ Roast until the asparagus is bright green and tender with a bit of caramelization, 8 to 12 minutes, depending on the thickness of the stalks. Set aside.

✦ Spread the bread with a thin layer of butter. Season the bread with salt to taste and toast it in the oven until golden brown and lightly crunchy, about 10 minutes, flipping the bread over halfway through.

✦ To assemble the tartines, top each piece of toast with about ¼ cup of the lemon ricotta and a generous serving of asparagus and serve immediately.

For the asparagus:

1½ pounds fresh asparagus

2 tablespoons extra-virgin olive oil

Kosher salt and freshly ground black pepper

4 large slices rustic bread

Butter or extra-virgin olive oil

Kosher salt

1 cup Lemon Ricotta (page 111)

green herb and peanut pork meatballs in lettuce cups

OVER TEN YEARS AGO, I PLANTED a little four-inch pot of adorable lemon balm in a moist, partially sunny location in my garden. It grew rapidly into a patch of lemon balm that threatened to overtake my garden. Beyond drying the leaf for tea, I was at a bit of a loss for how to use it all up and how to contain the herbal monster I had created. It took a few years, but eventually I realized that lemon balm is great as a temperate-climate substitute for the lemongrass used throughout Southeast Asian cooking. Now I keep my patch of lemon balm in check using recipes like these Thai-inspired meatballs.

My lemon balm is at its most fresh and lovely in the spring, when the lettuce, mint, and first cilantro of the season are just getting large enough to harvest. Later in the year, I use lemon verbena. Either of these lemony herbs work well here.

MAKES 4 SERVINGS

+ Move an oven rack to the center position and preheat the oven to 400 degrees F. Line a sheet pan with parchment paper.

+ In the bowl of a food processor fitted with the metal blade, combine the onion, garlic, peanuts, lemon balm, mint, cilantro, fish sauce, brown sugar, and chili sauce. Pulse until the mixture resembles a course paste, about the texture of pesto, 30 seconds to 1 minute.

+ Scrape the herb mixture into a medium bowl, then add the pork and mix together until well combined.

+ Use a 1-ounce portion scoop or your clean hands to form the pork mixture into meatballs about the size of golf balls. Evenly space the meatballs on the sheet pan and bake until the meatballs are cooked through and lightly browned, 15 to 20 minutes, turning once halfway through.

(continued)

For the meatballs:

¼ medium white onion, roughly chopped

2 cloves garlic, peeled

½ cup unsalted peanuts

½ cup lightly packed fresh lemon balm or lemon verbena

½ cup lightly packed fresh mint

½ cup lightly packed fresh cilantro

1 tablespoon fish sauce

1 tablespoon lightly packed light brown sugar

1 tablespoon Thai sweet chili sauce

1 pound ground pork

Spring

For the sauce:

3 tablespoons freshly squeezed lime juice

2 tablespoons water

2 tablespoons fish sauce

2 tablespoons sugar

Asian-style chili paste or pepper sauce

2 medium heads butterhead lettuce, separated into leaves

½ cup shredded carrot

½ cup sliced or shredded radishes

1 thinly sliced serrano or jalapeño pepper

Additional fresh mint and cilantro

✦ While the meatballs are cooking, prepare the sauce. In a small bowl, add the lime juice, water, fish sauce, and sugar and stir until the sugar is dissolved. Add a bit of chili paste or Asian-style hot chili sauce if you like a bit of spice. Set aside.

✦ Set out the lettuce, carrot, radishes, serrano, and herbs on a tray or large plate.

✦ When the meatballs are fully cooked, transfer them to a serving plate. Let everyone assemble their own wraps with several leaves of butterhead lettuce, a scattering of fresh vegetables and herbs, a meatball or two, and a drizzle of sauce.

NOTE: Lettuce wraps like these can be messy. We serve them outside on a warm spring day when eating with your hands and drippy sauce will just add to the fun. If this is too messy for your house (or your kids!) just turn the components into a lovely, light salad. Tear the lettuce up a bit, top with the herbs and shredded vegetables, finish with the meatballs, and use the sauce as a dressing.

green herb lamb chops with preserved lemon aioli

LAMB CHOPS ARE A PRICEY CUT to serve as a main meal, but a single rack can make a nice hors d'oeuvres for four people on a special occasion. Back in my catering days, this was a very popular choice for my clients who wanted a passed starter. The chops come with a kind of built-in handle, and the marinade keeps them tender and flavorful.

When I serve these plated, I like to cross two chops over a dollop of the preserved lemon aioli and add a little color to the plate with a salad of fresh flat-leaf parsley leaves lightly dressed with olive oil, a drop of lemon juice, and a bit of salt. It looks fancy, but all the components are really simple, so the last-minute work is quite minimal.

MAKES 4 SERVINGS AS AN APPETIZER OR 2 AS AN ENTRÉE

For the aioli:

2 wedges (½ lemon) Salt-Preserved Meyer Lemons (page 347), rind only, very finely minced

1 clove garlic, very finely minced

½ cup mayonnaise

2 tablespoons chopped parsley

½ teaspoon freshly ground black pepper

2 wedges Salt-Preserved Meyer Lemons (page 347), seeds removed but flesh intact

3 cloves garlic

1 cup coarsely chopped fresh parsley

✦ To make the aioli, in a small bowl, add the preserved lemon, garlic, mayonnaise, parsley, and pepper and whisk to combine. Cover and refrigerate several hours to allow the flavors to marry. The aioli can be made up to 3 days ahead.

✦ Next, make the herb paste to season the lamb. In the bowl of a food processor fitted with the metal blade, chop the lemons, garlic, parsley, oregano, rosemary, oil, and mustard until the mixture is coarsely pureed and resembles thick pesto.

✦ Slice the rack of lamb between each rib. You should have 8 or 9 individual chops. Place the chops in a shallow baking dish or gallon-size ziplock bag, and completely coat the lamb chops with the herb paste. Cover the dish with plastic wrap or seal the bag, and transfer to the refrigerator to marinate for at least 1 hour and up to 12 hours. The flavor of the lamb gets better as it marinates, but after 12 hours the texture of the meat is compromised by the acid in the lemons. I think it's ideal to marinate these in the morning and broil them that evening.

+ Move an oven rack to the top position and preheat the broiler. Set a rack on a sheet pan. Remove the lamb from the marinade and shake off any excess. Some marinade still clinging to the lamb forms a nice crust on the chops, though, so don't wipe them clean. Place the lamb chops on the sheet pan and broil until chops are nicely browned, 3 to 5 minutes. Flip them over and broil on the second side until the chops are medium rare, 2 or 3 more minutes, or until cooked to desired doneness.

+ Serve the lamb hot with a dollop of the aioli.

¼ cup coarsely chopped fresh oregano

2 tablespoons minced fresh rosemary

¼ cup extra-virgin olive oil

1 tablespoon Dijon mustard

1 (8-rib) rack of lamb, bones cleaned of any excess meat or fat

---

NOTE: If you are feeding a crowd, consider doubling the marinade and using it to flavor a whole butterflied leg of lamb. Marinate the leg of lamb for at least 24 hours, then cook by slow-roasting or indirect grilling for a similar flavor profile at a lower cost per pound.

roasted salmon with yogurt-herb crust

SALMON IS SOMETHING OF A RELIGION to Pacific Northwesterners, and late spring marks the beginning of the wild Alaskan king salmon season. There is simply no fish in the world as excellent as a perfectly fresh, line-caught king salmon. Alder-planked, stovetop smoked, simply grilled with salt and lemon: I love all respectful preparations of salmon. This is one I return to, time and again, because it's easy, fast, and foolproof: simply smear a boneless fillet of salmon with a herby, tangy yogurt paste and bake it in a hot oven. The yogurt keeps the salmon very moist, and the bright-pink salmon against the green crust of herbs looks gorgeous.

MAKES 4 SERVINGS

1 (2-pound) boneless center-cut salmon filet

Kosher salt and freshly ground black pepper

For the crust:

1 teaspoon kosher salt

2 cloves garlic

1 bunch dill, leaves and tender stems chopped

1 bunch scallions, trimmed and chopped

1 bunch parsley, leaves and tender stems chopped

¼ cup extra-virgin olive oil, plus more if needed

1 medium lemon, zested then quartered

½ cup thick plain yogurt

+ Move an oven rack to the center position and preheat the oven to 450 degrees F. Line a sheet pan with parchment paper and set the salmon, skin-side down, on it. Season the salmon generously with salt and pepper and set aside.

+ In the bowl of a food processor fitted with the metal blade, add the salt, garlic, dill, scallions, parsley, oil, and lemon zest. Pulse until the mixture is very well blended and resembles a thick pesto. The sauce should be thick, but drizzle in a bit more oil to loosen it as needed. Add the yogurt and pulse a few times just to combine. Add in a good squeeze of lemon juice from one of the quarters—enough to make the sauce taste bright without being overly tart—and adjust seasonings with salt, pepper, or a bit more lemon juice as desired.

+ Spread the yogurt-herb paste over the salmon, like you are frosting a cake, so the fillet is covered with a layer about ¼ inch thick.

+ Place in the oven and roast until salmon is just cooked through and slightly translucent in the center, 10 to 15 minutes, depending on the thickness of the filet.

+ Remove from the oven and let the salmon rest for 5 minutes. Cut the fillet into 4 portions and serve hot.

vanilla cream tart with fresh strawberries

Spring

THIS IS A SPECIAL-OCCASION DESSERT. It's really quite simple, but you have to plan ahead. I consider the first big homegrown strawberry harvest a pretty special occasion, so that's when we celebrate with a generous slice of this tart.

The vanilla pastry cream and shortbread crust both need to be made several hours ahead of time. If you'd like, you can make the pastry cream up to three days in advance. Once the components are done, the assembly is very simple. This tart base is equally good when topped with fresh raspberries, blueberries, blackberries, or thinly sliced apricots, nectarines, or peaches.

MAKES 8 TO 10 SERVINGS

For the vanilla cream:

3 cups whole milk

3 egg yolks

1 whole vanilla bean

½ cup sugar

⅓ cup cornstarch

¼ teaspoon kosher salt

1 tablespoon softened unsalted butter

1 teaspoon vanilla extract

For the crust:

1¾ cups all-purpose flour

1 cup (2 sticks) unsalted butter, at room temperature, plus more for greasing

½ cup powdered sugar

2 tablespoons cornstarch

½ teaspoon fine sea salt

Zest of 1 lemon

✦ To make the vanilla cream, in a medium bowl, whisk together the milk and egg yolks until completely blended and smooth. Split the vanilla bean in half lengthwise and scrape all the seeds from the bean. Add the vanilla seeds and bean to the milk mixture and stir to distribute the seeds.

✦ In a large, heavy stainless steel pot, add the sugar, cornstarch, and salt. Add about ½ cup of the milk mixture to the pot and whisk until perfectly smooth. Add the rest of the milk mixture while whisking to ensure no lumps form.

✦ Stirring frequently, bring the milk mixture to a simmer over medium-low heat. This will take about 20 minutes, and the cream will thicken as it cooks. When the cream is very thick like pudding, remove from the heat and whisk in the butter and vanilla extract. Immediately strain the pastry cream through a fine-mesh sieve into a clean bowl or container. Press plastic wrap down onto the surface of the pastry cream and refrigerate for several hours, or until completely chilled. The pastry cream can be made up to 3 days in advance.

✦ To make the crust, lightly butter a 10-inch round tart pan with removable bottom. Set the pan on a sheet pan.

+ In the bowl of a food processor fitted with a metal blade, combine the flour, butter, sugar, cornstarch, salt, and lemon zest. Pulse in 5- to 10-second bursts until the dough comes together in a ball and the butter is evenly mixed throughout the dough.

+ Using your fingers, press the dough evenly into the tart pan and up the sides. The dough should feel a lot like Play-Doh. If at any point the dough starts to get sticky and hard to press out, just pop it in the refrigerator for 10 minutes. The crust should be about ⅜ inches thick when you are done. Take you time and pat it smooth and even—this dough isn't like a pie crust that can easily be overworked into oblivion. When you are happy with your crust, place it in the refrigerator for 30 minutes to chill.

+ Move an oven rack to the center position and preheat the oven to 325 degrees F. Line the chilled tart crust with parchment, then top with pie weights or dry beans.

+ Bake the crust until it's pale golden, about 25 minutes, then remove the pie weights and parchment, and continue baking until the crust is uniformly golden brown and baked all the way through, another 15 to 20 minutes.

+ Let the crust cool completely at room temperature. The crust may be made up to 1 day ahead. Cover the cooled crust lightly with foil and store in a cool and dry place.

+ To assemble the tart, rinse and thoroughly dry the strawberries. Hull and then thinly slice, quarter, or halve the berries, depending on their size.

+ Spoon the chilled pastry cream into the tart crust and level it gently with an offset spatula. Arrange the fresh berries over the pastry cream. At this point, the tart can be chilled for up to 3 hours or served immediately. Just before serving, dust with powdered sugar.

1 pound fresh strawberries

Powdered sugar, for dusting

Preserving

apricot barbecue sauce

TANGY, A LITTLE SWEET, AND A LITTLE SMOKY, this barbecue sauce is excellent mopped on grilled meats or spooned over chicken, turkey, or pork. It also makes a fantastic braising sauce and punchy ketchup alternative.

MAKES 6 HALF-PINT JARS

+ If this is your first time water-bath canning, please review the basics on page 25. Prepare a water-bath canner, 6 half-pint jars, and their lids.

+ In a large, wide saucepan set over medium-high heat, combine all the ingredients. Stirring frequently, bring the sauce to a simmer. Cook until the sauce thickens, about 25 minutes, reducing the heat if needed to maintain a gentle simmer.

+ Ladle the sauce into the prepared hot jars, leaving ½-inch headspace. Remove any air bubbles, wipe the jar rims, and set the jar lids and bands according to the manufacturer's directions.

+ Carefully lower the filled jars into the simmering water-bath canner. When the water has returned to a boil, cover the kettle and set a timer for 20 minutes. When the jars have processed for 20 minutes, remove the canner from the heat and allow the jars to cool in the water for 5 minutes, then use a jar lifter to transfer the jars onto a clean kitchen towel to cool and set their seals.

+ Leave the jars alone until they have fully cooled—at least 8 but no more than 24 hours—then check the seals. Any jar that hasn't sealed should be refrigerated and used within 2 weeks. Jars with solid seals may be washed, labeled, and stored in a cool, dark place where they will keep for about 1 year.

PROCESSING AT A GLANCE
Method: Water-bath canning
Headspace: ½ inch
Processing time: 20 minutes in a boiling water-bath canner; adjust for altitude

6 cups finely chopped apricots

1 cup finely chopped yellow onion

1 cup finely chopped red bell pepper

1 medium red jalapeño or Fresno pepper, seeded and finely minced

1 tablespoon minced garlic

1 cup apple cider vinegar

¾ cup lightly packed light brown sugar

1 tablespoon chipotle pepper powder

2 teaspoons kosher salt

1 teaspoon ground cumin

½ teaspoon ground ginger

strawberry preserves in balsamic–black pepper syrup

SEVERAL YEARS AGO, EVERYONE IN THE food world went absolutely crazy for the traditional Italian pairing of strawberries and balsamic vinegar. I was no exception, so I began playing around with easy ways to capture those flavors in a jar.

This isn't your childhood strawberry jam. Whole berries are cooked in a sweet-tart syrup with balsamic vinegar and a kick of black pepper, for a distinctly grown-up take on spring's most canonical preserve. Warm a few of these strawberries in their syrup to spoon over vanilla ice cream, use the preserve as an accompaniment to a dark chocolate tart, or serve them with goat cheese on a water cracker for an easy appetizer.

MAKES 4 HALF-PINT JARS

PROCESSING AT A GLANCE
Method: Water-bath canning
Headspace: ¼ inch
Processing time: 10 minutes in a boiling water-bath canner; adjust for altitude

6 cups washed and stemmed small strawberries

3 cups sugar

¼ cup balsamic vinegar

½ teaspoon finely ground black pepper

1 tablespoon lemon zest

+ If this is your first time water-bath canning, please review the basics on page 25. Prepare a water-bath canner, 4 half-pint jars, and their lids.

+ In a large stainless steel bowl, gently fold together the strawberries and sugar. Cover with plastic wrap and set in the refrigerator to macerate for 8 to 12 hours, or overnight.

+ In a large, wide saucepan set over medium-high heat, scrape the berries and any juice from the bowl. Add the vinegar, pepper, and lemon zest. Stirring frequently, bring the mixture to a simmer and cook until it thickens, about 35 minutes, reducing the heat if needed to maintain a gentle simmer.

+ Ladle the preserves into the prepared hot jars, leaving ¼-inch headspace. Remove any air bubbles, wipe the jar rims, and set the jar lids and bands according to the manufacturer's directions.

✦ Carefully lower the filled jars into the simmering water-bath canner. When the water has returned to a boil, cover the kettle and set a timer for 15 minutes. When the jars have processed for 15 minutes, remove the canner from the heat and allow the jars to cool in the water for 5 minutes, then use a jar lifter to transfer the jars onto a clean kitchen towel to cool and set their seals.

✦ Leave the jars alone until they have fully cooled—at least 8 but no more than 24 hours—then check the seals. Any jar that hasn't sealed should be refrigerated and used within 2 weeks. Jars with solid seals may be washed, labeled, and stored in a cool, dark place where they will keep for about 1 year.

rhubarb syrup

IT'S NICE TO SEE RHUBARB HAVING a bit of a culinary revival. This syrup is floral and delicious and such a lovely soft-pink color. It's great in a cocktail (see page 188) or mixed into lemonade or sparkling water for a delicious, sweet-tart alternative to commercial soda.

MAKES 6 HALF-PINT JARS

✦ If this is your first time water-bath canning, please review the basics on page 25. Prepare a water-bath canner, 6 half-pint jars, and their lids.

✦ Chop the rhubarb stalks into 1-inch sections. In a small saucepan over medium heat, combine the rhubarb, water, and sugar. Cover and bring the rhubarb mixture to a simmer.

✦ Simmer until the rhubarb is very soft, about 15 minutes. Strain the rhubarb syrup through a fine sieve. Allow the syrup to drip through the sieve without pressing on the solids for the clearest syrup, and leave behind the soft rhubarb puree (which is delicious when used like apple-sauce or added to quick breads).

✦ Transfer the syrup to a clean saucepan, add the lemon juice, and bring to a simmer. Ladle the syrup into the prepared hot jars, leaving ¼-inch headspace. Remove any air bubbles, wipe the jar rims, and set the jar lids and bands according to the manufacturer's directions.

✦ Carefully lower the filled jars into the simmering water-bath canner. When the water has returned to a boil, cover the kettle and set a timer for 10 minutes. When the jars have processed for 10 minutes, remove the canner from the heat and allow the jars to cool in the water for 5 minutes, then use a jar lifter to transfer the jars onto a clean kitchen towel to cool and set their seals.

PROCESSING AT A GLANCE

Method: Water-bath canning

Headspace: ¼ inch

Processing time: 10 minutes in a boiling water-bath canner; adjust for altitude

---

2 pounds fresh or frozen rhubarb stalks (about 6 large stalks)

4 cups water

3 cups sugar

¼ cup freshly squeezed lemon juice

(continued)

+ Leave the jars alone until they have fully cooled—at least 8 but no more than 24 hours—then check the seals. Any jar that hasn't sealed should be refrigerated and used within 2 weeks. Jars with solid seals may be washed, labeled, and stored in a cool, dark place where they will keep for about 1 year.

the rhubarb 75

2 ounces gin

1 ounce Rhubarb Syrup

½ ounce freshly squeezed lemon juice

About 1 ounce champagne or dry sparkling wine

+ Shake the gin, syrup, and lemon juice together with cracked ice and strain it into a chilled cocktail glass. Add the champagne and garnish with a peel of fresh rhubarb stalk, if desired. So delicious!

pickled asparagus

FRESH LOCAL ASPARAGUS IS A FLEETING joy, so it's nice to pickle up a few jars for later in the year. I munch on pickled asparagus straight out of the jar, but it's also a shockingly good addition to a gooey, melty grilled cheese sandwich. I recommend the tall twelve-ounce jars for pickling asparagus. They look like standard half-pint jars that have had a crazy growth spurt, and the extra height makes them lovely for the elegant stalks of asparagus. Pack your asparagus tip-down for the best appearance; often asparagus will float a bit in the jar, and if you pack them right-side up, the delicate tips can break off.

MAKES FIVE 12-OUNCE JARS

✦ If this is your first time water-bath canning, please review the basics on page 25. Prepare a water-bath canner, 5 twelve-ounce jars, and their lids.

✦ Wash the asparagus and trim the bottoms so that the spears will fit in the jars with a generous ½-inch headspace. Remove the sanitized jars from the canning kettle to your workspace. To the bottom of each jar, add 1 garlic clove, 1 teaspoon dill seed, ½ teaspoon mustard seed, ½ teaspoon peppercorns, and ¼ teaspoon red pepper flakes.

✦ Tightly but gently pack the trimmed asparagus spears, tip-down, into the jars. The easiest way to do this is to bundle a jar's worth of asparagus spears in your hand and slide the whole bundle into the jar as one unit. Then, if you have extra room, carefully snuggle a few extra spears down into the jar to fill any gaps.

✦ While you are preparing the jars, in a medium saucepan, bring the vinegar, water, sugar, and salt to a boil.

✦ Ladle the brine over the asparagus, leaving ½-inch headspace. Remove any air bubbles, wipe the jar rims, and set the jar lids and bands according to the manufacturer's directions.

(continued)

PROCESSING AT A GLANCE

Method: Water-bath canning

Headspace: ½ inch

Processing time:
10 minutes in a boiling water-bath canner; adjust for altitude

---

5 pounds asparagus

5 large cloves garlic, peeled and halved

5 teaspoons dill seed, divided

2½ teaspoons mustard seeds, divided

2½ teaspoons whole black peppercorns, divided

1¼ teaspoons red pepper flakes, divided

2¼ cups apple cider vinegar

2¼ cups water

3 tablespoons sugar

2 tablespoons fine sea salt

+ Carefully lower the filled jars into the simmering water-bath canner. When the water has returned to a boil, cover the kettle and set a timer for 10 minutes. When the jars have processed for 10 minutes, remove the canner from the heat and allow the jars to cool in the water for 5 minutes, then use a jar lifter to transfer the jars onto a clean kitchen towel to cool and set their seals.

+ Leave the jars alone until they have fully cooled—at least 8 but no more than 24 hours—then check the seals. Any jar that hasn't sealed should be refrigerated and used within 2 weeks. Jars with solid seals may be washed, labeled, and stored in a cool, dark place where they will keep for about 1 year.

pressure-canned chicken broth

ONE TIME I WENT OUT TO the garage freezer and six gallon-size bags of frozen chicken broth tumbled out from the top shelf of the freezer onto my bare feet. I was not quite fast enough to jump back and ended up with a nasty bruise.

Many choice words were yelled, and very soon after this incident, I bought a pressure canner. The first thing I pressure canned was chicken broth, and it was love at first not-having-to-thaw. Pressure canning broth is fast (by pressure-canning standards) and creates a versatile, ready-to-grab, and shelf-stable product.

MAKES 6 QUART JARS

PROCESSING AT A GLANCE

Method: Pressure canning

Headspace: 1 inch

Processing time:
25 minutes at 11 PSI;
adjust for altitude

---

6 quarts Basic Chicken Broth (page 112) (see note)

Kosher salt (optional)

Distilled white vinegar

+ If this is your first time pressure canning, please review the basics on page 32.

+ Prepare a pressure canner, 6 quart-size jars, and their lids.

+ In a stainless steel pot large enough to generously hold the broth, bring it to a simmer over medium heat. If desired, lightly salt the broth to taste. Often basic broths like this are left unseasoned or only lightly seasoned with the expectation that they will be seasoned further as part of a soup or sauce. I add a bit of salt to my chicken broth, but not as much as I would use for a broth-based soup. Your call.

+ Ladle the broth into the prepared hot jars, leaving 1-inch headspace. Dampen a clean lint-free towel with hot water and a bit of vinegar (this helps cut through any grease on the jar), wipe the jar rims thoroughly, and set the lids and bands according to the manufacturer's directions.

+ Double-check the water level in the pressure canner and adjust as necessary. Carefully lower the filled jars into the pressure canner. Fasten the canner lid securely, increase the heat to high, wait for a full stream of steam to vent from the vent pipe or petcock, and fully exhaust the canner for 10 minutes. After exhausting the canner, set a counterweight or weighted gauge on the vent pipe or close the petcock to bring the canner up to pressure. Follow the manufacturer's directions for regulating heat to maintain the correct pressure throughout the processing time.

+ Process the jars for 25 minutes, then turn off the heat and allow the canner to naturally cool and completely depressurize.

+ After the canner has fully depressurized, open the pressure canner according to the manufacturer's directions, being careful of escaping steam. (I like to allow the jars to cool for 30 minutes in the canner after removing the weight from the vent pipe but before opening and unloading—I've found this cuts down on siphoning and leads to more reliable seals.)

+ Lift the jars straight up from the canner with a jar lifter and set them down on a clean kitchen towel to cool and set their seals. Let the jars cool undisturbed for at least 12 hours and up to 24. Any jar that hasn't sealed should be refrigerated and used within 3 days. Jars with solid seals may be washed, labeled, and stored in a cool, dark place where they will keep for about 1 year.

NOTE: Make sure you've defatted the chicken broth prior to canning, for safety reasons.

lacto-fermented curried cauliflower

I ADORE THE COMBINATION OF CURRY and cauliflower. Roasted, braised, pureed in a soup, or, as here, made into a probiotic-rich fermented pickle, it's a winning flavor combo. When you make this, cut or pull the cauliflower into small florets. These ferment more quickly and evenly than large pieces.

MAKES 1 QUART JAR

+ If this is your first time fermenting vegetables, please review the basics on page 41.

+ Prepare a widemouthed quart-size jar, its lid, and a fermenting weight.

+ If the cauliflower has any thick green wrapper leaves, pull those off carefully and set them aside. Remove the tough core of the cauliflower, then cut the head into very small florets. You should have about 3 cups.

+ Add the jalapeño and garlic to the prepared jar. Add the cauliflower florets and press down to compact the vegetables. The cauliflower should come to about 2 inches from the top of the jar.

+ In a medium bowl, combine the water, salt, curry powder, and ginger, and stir until the salt is fully dissolved. Pour this brine over the cauliflower to within 1 inch of the top of the jar. Make sure all the vegetables are tucked down under the liquid, then add the reserved cauliflower wrapper leaves to the top of the ferment to help hold all the little bits under the brine.

+ Weight the ferment well, cover, and ferment for at least 3 days at cool room temperature, out of direct sunlight, and up to 1 week. Vent the lid as necessary to prevent pressure from building up in the jar.

+ Taste the cauliflower frequently throughout the fermentation and, when it loses the squeak and opacity of rawness and tastes tangy, it's done. Remove the weight, lid the jar, and move it to the refrigerator, where the fermented cauliflower will keep for at least 4 months.

1 small head cauliflower
(about 2 pounds)

2 medium jalapeños, halved,
seeded, and thinly sliced

2 cloves garlic, smashed

3 cups water

2 tablespoons fine sea salt

1 tablespoon mild
curry powder

1 teaspoon ground ginger

korean-spiced turnips

Spring turnips are milder than their winter cousins, with smooth white skin. They are typically sold bunched with leaves intact and are about golf-ball size. This juicy root vegetable ferments into one of my very favorite spicy pickles. If you like kimchi, try this Korean-influenced turnip pickle. Once fermented, the turnips lose their punch and become pleasantly spicy and tangy. If you can't find spring turnips, large breakfast radishes or daikon make a fine substitute.

MAKES 1 QUART JAR

1½ pounds mild spring turnips, greens removed

1 bunch green onions, thinly sliced

8 cloves garlic, minced

2 teaspoons red pepper flakes (see note)

3 cups water

2 tablespoons fine sea salt

2 to 3 fresh grape or oak leaves (optional)

+ If this is your first time fermenting vegetables, please review the basics on page 41.

+ Prepare a widemouthed quart-size jar, its lid, and a fermenting weight.

+ Scrub, trim, and peel the turnips, then halve or quarter them. You want small, bite-size pieces. In the prepared jar, mix the turnips with the green onions, garlic, and red pepper flakes and pack together. Press the turnips down. They should come about 2 inches from the top of the jar.

+ In a medium bowl, mix the water with the salt to make a brine and stir until the salt is completely dissolved. Pour the brine over the turnips. Make sure all the vegetables are submerged in the liquid, then add a few grape leaves to the top of the ferment to help hold all the little bits under the brine.

+ Weight the ferment well, cover, and ferment for at least 3 days at cool room temperature, out of direct sunlight, and up to 1 week. Vent the lid as necessary to prevent pressure from building up in the jar. Taste the turnips frequently throughout the fermentation, and when they lose their opacity and become juicy-tender throughout, they are done. Remove the weight, lid the jar, and move it to the refrigerator, where the fermented turnips will keep for at least 4 months.

NOTE: If you can find Korean-style chili powder, use it instead of the red pepper flakes—and be generous with it.

Home Care

carpet freshener

ONE DAY WHEN MY SON WAS about three, I turned from doing the dishes to see that he had taken a large bulk container of cinnamon out of a kitchen drawer, opened it, and proceeded to methodically—almost lovingly—grind every teaspoon of the spice into my favorite area rug in the living room. There was a splotch of dusky reddish brown stretching from one end of the carpet to the other, and my son looked as if he'd spent the afternoon rolling in the red dirt of Georgia. I'm happy to say that six thorough vacuumings and a bath later, there wasn't too much trace of the cinnamon on either my rug or my son.

The funny thing is, my carpet smelled great after that. Twenty dollars' worth of bulk cinnamon worked a treat in freshening up the fibers of the carpet. I got to thinking that maybe an odor-absorbing powder would be a good way to keep my wall-to-wall carpets and rugs fresh in between deeper cleanings. This carpet-refreshing formula kills dust mites (which love your carpet almost as much as your bed), works even better than cinnamon, and it's much, much cheaper.

While essential oils are optional, they're a nice addition. Dust mites particularly hate eucalyptus, cinnamon, tea tree, and clove.

MAKES 1 QUART

3 cups baking soda

1 cup borax

2 to 3 teaspoons essential oil (optional)

+ In a medium bowl, combine the baking soda, borax, and essential oil of your choice, if using. Mix well, then transfer to a widemouthed quart mason jar fitted with a Mason Jar Shaker Lid (page 149). The freshener will last indefinitely, though the essential oil scent may fade over time.

To use:

+ Generously sprinkle the carpet freshener all over a manageable-size section of carpet. (Don't do your entire house at once!) Run your vacuum cleaner over the freshener without turning the vacuum on; the rotating bristles of the vacuum will help work the powder down into the carpet fibers. When the powder has been worked into the entire section, let it sit for an hour or so. Vacuum the carpet (power on this time) to suck up the carpet powder, dead dust mites, and funky odors. Repeat with other sections of carpet.

NOTE: Don't allow kids or pets into an area you are treating with this carpet freshener. You don't want four-legged friends or enthusiastic crawlers transferring it from their paws or hands to their mouths. If you have any concerns about pets or kids getting into this, just use plain baking soda instead. While I use this carpet freshener without issue on all the carpeted areas in my home, do test this in an inconspicuous spot to make sure it's compatible with your carpet materials and dyes before you pour it all over your priceless, handwoven heirloom Persian rug.

leather cream

OVER TIME, LEATHER FURNITURE CAN LOSE its luster and get dried out. An occasional rubdown with this conditioner will help restore oils to the leather and add a soft shine. Clean the leather with a damp cloth or a very dilute castile soap solution and let dry before conditioning. Applied sparingly, this also adds a nice shine to wood tables.

MAKES ABOUT ½ CUP

3 tablespoons coconut oil

1 tablespoon beeswax pastilles

2 tablespoons jojoba oil

15 drops eucalyptus essential oil

15 drops lemon essential oil

+ In a small heatproof bowl, melt the coconut oil and beeswax pastilles. Add the jojoba oil and essential oils and stir until the mixture comes together and thickens slightly. Scrape the leather cream into a clean, widemouthed half-pint mason jar or other small container and let cool. The cream will last about 6 months.

To use:

+ Rub a pea-size amount onto a clean lint-free rag, then rub the cream into leather furniture. Be careful not to use too much, especially over areas of stitching, because a thick layer of cream will look waxy on your furniture. Buff the leather until no residue remains.

grout cleaner

MOST TILE IS PRETTY EASY TO keep clean, but porous grout seems to suck dirt to it like a sponge. Because grout is made mostly from soft, powdered, alkaline rock minerals, acidic cleaners can damage grout over time by literally etching it away. They're effective in the short-term, but mean frequent re-grouting or possible water damage if used long-term. For a safer grout cleaner, baking soda and borax work very well, and powdered oxygen bleach increases the stain-removal capability of this cleaner. You can scale this recipe as needed for larger areas.

MAKES ABOUT ½ CUP

+ In a small bowl, mix the borax, baking soda, and oxygen bleach. Add just enough hot water to make a thick paste and stir to combine. Once the hot water is added, use the cleaner immediately.

To use:

+ Spread the paste over dirty, moldy, or mildewy grout. Let it sit for 30 minutes, then scrub gently with a toothbrush and rinse.

¼ cup borax

¼ cup baking soda

2 tablespoons powdered oxygen bleach

Hot water

Personal Care

two-in-one facial exfoliant and moisturizer

THIS SIMPLE, TWO-INGREDIENT MOISTURIZING EXFOLIANT does an amazing but gentle job of removing dirt and rough skin from the face and lips (I stay away from my eyes and recommend you do too) and leaves skin super soft. It's gentle enough to use daily or as desired.

MAKES ABOUT ½ CUP

+ In a small bowl, combine the coconut oil and baking soda and mix well, until the exfoliant is thoroughly blended and frosting-like in appearance. If desired, add the essential oil and stir to combine. Store the moisturizer in a tin or widemouthed half-pint jar with a tight-fitting lid. The exfoliant will last for at least 6 months, though the essential oil scent may fade over time.

To use:

+ Rinse your face with warm water. Rub a tablespoon or so of the exfoliant between your hands to warm it, then gently rub your face and lips with the exfoliant. Rinse your face well with warm water, then pat dry.

½ cup coconut oil, melted or very soft

½ cup baking soda

10 drops lavender essential oil or other oil of choice (optional)

everyday, everybody scrub

SPRING CLEAN YOUR SKIN WITH A POLISHING SCRUB customized for your skin's needs. Body scrubs are easy to make as needed and last for several months. Make this basic all-purpose scrub, which is great for all skin types and doesn't require any exotic oils or fine clay powders, or play around with polishing agents, oils, and essential oils that are just right for your skin type. If you want to experiment, I've found using about two cups of dry scrubby ingredients to half a cup of oils or moisturizing ingredients gives me the firm, scoopable consistency I prefer in a body scrub. If you like a thinner, more pourable scrub, just add a bit more oil to the mixture. For skin-specific scrubs, see the variations that follow.

MAKES ABOUT 2 CUPS

+ In a medium bowl, stir together all the ingredients. Transfer the scrub to a pint-size mason jar or other moisture-proof container. If water isn't added to the mixture, the scrub will last for about 6 months, though the essential oil scent may fade over time.

1 cup sugar

1 cup baking soda

½ cup sweet almond or extra-virgin olive oil

20 drops lavender essential oil

To use:

+ In the shower, scoop about ¼ to ½ cup of the scrub into your hand and rub all over your body, avoiding your face and delicate areas. Be careful if your shower floor gets slippery from the scrub. Rinse your body with warm water and pat dry.

(continued)

body scrub variations

Try these variations for skin-specific body scrubs. Follow the same directions for the Everyday, Everybody Scrub, but substitute these ingredients.

FOR OILY OR ACNE-PRONE SKIN:

1½ cups fine sea salt

¼ cup baking soda

¼ cup kaolin clay

6 tablespoons grapeseed oil

2 tablespoons castor oil

20 drops tea tree essential oil

10 drops peppermint essential oil

10 drops rosemary essential oil

10 drops lemon essential oil

FOR SENSITIVE SKIN:

1 cup granulated sugar

1 cup light brown sugar

6 tablespoons sweet almond oil

2 tablespoons apricot kernel oil

1 tablespoon vitamin E oil

20 drops lavender essential oil

10 drops Roman chamomile essential oil

10 drops jasmine essential oil

FOR VERY DRY SKIN:

1¾ cups sugar

¼ cup extra-virgin olive oil

2 tablespoons avocado oil

2 tablespoons shea butter, melted

1 tablespoon honey

1 tablespoon vegetable glycerin

20 drops chamomile essential oil

12 drops cedarwood essential oil

6 drops lemon essential oil

FOR MATURE SKIN:

1 cup light brown sugar

½ cup baking soda

½ cup kaolin clay

½ cup jojoba oil

1 tablespoon honey or vegetable glycerin

1 tablespoon castor oil

1 tablespoon borage seed oil

16 drops lavender essential oil

16 drops clary sage essential oil

8 drops bergamot essential oil

silicone-free shine spray for hair

COMMERCIAL HAIR-SMOOTHING SERUMS ARE ALMOST ENTIRELY made of silicone and preservatives. Silicone looks good at first—it shrink-wraps hair in something like plastic, making it look smooth. Unfortunately, silicone builds up with use unless really harsh detergents are used to strip it off the hair. Buildup makes hair heavy, flat, and dull, which makes dedicated product junkies think the answer lies in more silicone! Get off the shrink-wrapped hair bandwagon with this completely natural and hair-nourishing shine spray.

MAKES ABOUT ¼ CUP

✦ In a 2-ounce spray bottle, combine all the ingredients. Lid tightly and shake well to combine. The shine spray will last about 3 months, though the essential oil scent may fade over time.

To use:

✦ Shake the shine spray well, then spray the tips of your hair to tame split ends and frizziness. For all-over smoothing, or to protect your hair before styling, spray throughout your hair. For best results, avoid spraying your roots.

1 tablespoon water

1 tablespoon jojoba oil

1 tablespoon vegetable glycerin

2 teaspoons distilled white vinegar

10 drops vitamin E oil

10 drops lemon essential oil

6 drops orange essential oil

6 drops bergamot essential oil

Cooking

THOUGHTS ON BOUNTIFUL FRUITS AND FAST FOOD

As I write this, it is August. The fruits, both the ones we think of as fruits—blackberries, blueberries, figs, currants, peaches, Asian pears, raspberries, melons, and more—and the ones that are fruits only botanically—tomatoes, peppers, tomatillos, green beans, summer squash, and cucumbers—are all in a tumbling race to ripen and overwhelm me with their goodness.

Fast food at this time of year is fresh food. If you think about it, fruit is the only thing that really, truly wants us to eat it. Fruit is a natural packet of sugar wrapped around the genetic material of the next generation. It's basically a sweet bribe from nature to get us to eat (and distribute) plant seeds. Everything else, from leaves to roots to grains to animals, would really prefer not to become our dinner, but fruit wants to be snacked upon and makes doing so easy. Nothing is faster to nourish and takes less effort to prepare than the bountiful fruits.

My domestic duty at this time of year is fruit wrangler. At mealtime, it's easy to snack my way through the day on raspberries and peaches and cucumbers right in the garden. I thank the heavens that my children like tomatoes and peppers, and even "proper" meals are heavy on the botanical fruits, maybe garnished with a bit of cheese and a slice of bread.

No time of year offers more culinary variety and goodness, but who wants to run the oven for hours or stand over a stove any longer than absolutely necessary? Outside beckons, and how could we refuse? And so we keep it easy, pulling apart juicy nectarines or sprinkling cool cucumbers with salt and herbs. Finally we fire up the grill, set a table outside, and make dinner a picnic.

This seems the only sensible way to eat when the sun warms our shoulders so late into the day. Smoky corn and steak, eggplant and peppers, summer squash of every color, or a skewer of prawns come off the grill. Unfussy salads are served family style, plopped down in big bowls at the center of the table. The kids are sent into the garden to pick yet more fruit for dessert, while the adults raise a glass of wine or beer in the warm evening air.

There is a thin line between bounty and bludgeoning, and in a good year the fruits dance across it. We do our summer best to eat on and on, and let the juice drip sticky on our chin. And when finally, exhaustedly, we've had our fill, we turn our hands to preserving so that we may capture the sweetness and light of the seasonal fruits like a firefly in our humble canning jars.

summer garden gazpacho soup

Summer

IF, LIKE ME, YOU LOVE SALSA—so much so that you'll happily skip the chips and just spoon it into your mouth—I urge you to try this cold soup with a Spanish pedigree. There are two tricks to this soup. The first is to not skimp on the olive oil or the vinegar—both are needed to really bring out the flavors. The second trick is to make the soup a few hours before you intend to serve it and let the flavors meld as the soup chills.

MAKES 6 TO 8 SERVINGS

4 ounces chewy rustic bread without crusts, fresh or a bit stale, plus more for serving

5 medium juicy beefsteak tomatoes (about 2 pounds)

2 medium cucumbers (about 1½ pounds)

1 large white onion (about 1 pound)

1 medium green bell pepper, seeds and pith removed

1 medium red bell pepper, seeds and pith removed

2 medium red jalapeño peppers

3 cloves garlic, smashed

½ cup extra-virgin olive oil, plus more as needed

1 tablespoon kosher salt, plus more as needed

3 to 4 tablespoons red wine or sherry vinegar

Freshly ground black pepper

+ Cut the bread into cubes and add it to a very large bowl. Roughly chop the tomatoes, cucumbers, onions, bell peppers, jalapeño, and garlic. Add the chopped vegetables plus the oil and salt to the bowl. Stir to combine, cover, and set aside to allow the vegetables to release some of their juice, about 30 minutes.

+ Working in batches, transfer the mixture with its liquid to a blender. Puree the soup, adding a bit more oil or a bit of water to the blender as needed to ensure a smooth consistency. Transfer the pureed soup to a large serving bowl.

+ When all the soup is pureed, season to taste with the vinegar, additional salt, and pepper. For best results, cover the bowl and chill the soup for at least 30 minutes before serving.

+ To serve, ladle the chilled soup into wide, shallow bowls and drizzle with a few drops of oil. Serve with additional rustic bread for dipping.

cucumber and garbanzo bean salad with feta

IN SUMMER, I CAN LIVE ON this salad. I make it in big batches when the cucumbers are growing so fast I can practically see them mature. It keeps well in the refrigerator for several days, and I spoon myself a bowl whenever I get hungry. Add what you have, leave out what you don't—but do allow the onions several minutes to marinate in the vinaigrette.

MAKES 4 GENEROUS SERVINGS

✦ In a large bowl, add the oil, vinegar, mustard, and garlic. Add the onion and let it soak in the vinaigrette for about 10 minutes. Whisk the mixture into a dressing.

✦ Add the cucumber, garbanzo beans, tomato, feta, basil, and oregano and stir gently to combine. Season with salt and pepper to taste, then divide the salad among 4 bowls and garnish with a bit more feta and herbs.

¼ cup extra-virgin olive oil

3 tablespoons balsamic vinegar

1 teaspoon Dijon mustard

1 teaspoon minced garlic

½ red onion, finely sliced

2 large cucumbers, diced (about 4 cups)

2 cups cooked garbanzo beans, drained

1 large tomato, diced

½ cup crumbled feta, plus more for garnish

½ cup chopped fresh basil

¼ cup chopped fresh oregano

Kosher salt and freshly ground black pepper

grilled nectarines with red onion, basil, mint, and blue cheese

GRILLING FRUIT CARAMELIZES THE SUGARS, adds a sweet, toasty component to a meal, and brings out the aroma of the fruit. Plus, prime fruit season coincides so perfectly with prime grilling season! It's really a match made in heaven. If you're firing up the barbecue for a main course of grilled steak or vegetable, try grilled fruit in a salad like this beforehand.

MAKES 4 SERVINGS

1 cup loosely packed fresh basil

½ cup loosely packed fresh mint

¼ cup freshly squeezed lime juice

¼ cup extra-virgin olive oil, plus more for brushing

1 tablespoon honey

4 firm-ripe nectarines, halved

1 small red onion, very thinly sliced

2 ounces creamy blue cheese, such as Gorgonzola, crumbled

Kosher salt and freshly ground black pepper

+ To make the dressing, in a blender or food processor, combine the basil, mint, lime juice, oil, and honey and pulse until the herbs are well chopped and the dressing has combined. Set aside.

+ Preheat a very clean grill to high, or set a grill pan over high heat. Lightly brush the cut side of the nectarines with oil and grill them cut-side down. Don't fiddle with the nectarines—they need to sear until dark, caramelized grill marks form on the flesh or they will stick. This will take 3 to 5 minutes.

+ Carefully lift the nectarine halves from the grill with a thin metal spatula. Arrange 2 nectarine halves on each of 4 plates, then drizzle the nectarines with about 2 tablespoons of the dressing, a small handful of red onion, and ½ ounce of cheese. Season with salt and pepper to taste.

grill-roasted corn with adobo-honey butter

GRILLED CORN IS PERFECT DURING THOSE few weeks in the summer when I can harvest ripe corn directly from my garden or buy it picked same-day from local farmers. The faster corn travels from the field to your taste buds, the better and sweeter and juicier it is.

The adobo-honey butter isn't nearly so seasonal. In the winter, spread it on the skillet cornbread you serve with chili. Mix it with a bit of fresh lime juice and toss it with hot rice for an easy side dish, or use it instead of mayonnaise on a simple ham sandwich.

MAKES 4 SERVINGS AS A SIDE

+ To make the honey butter, in a small bowl, whisk the butter, chipotle, honey, salt, and vinegar together until fully combined. Use right away, or transfer the butter to an airtight container and refrigerate it for up to several weeks. Bring the butter to room temperature before serving.

+ Prepare and preheat a grill to high heat. Shuck the corn, pulling back the husk and silk. Try to pick most of the little bits of silk off the corn.

+ Grill the corn with the grill lid on until it is tender with patches of yummy caramelized kernels, about 10 minutes, rotating the corn occasionally.

+ Immediately roll the corn in the honey butter and sprinkle it with a bit of salt and a squeeze of lime. Garnish the corn with a few herbs, if desired. Serve the corn very hot, with additional adobo-honey butter on the side.

½ cup (1 stick) unsalted butter, at room temperature

1 tablespoon minced chipotle in adobo sauce

1 tablespoon honey

½ teaspoon kosher salt

A few drops apple cider vinegar

4 ears very fresh sweet corn

1 lime

A few sprigs fresh chives, parsley, or cilantro, for garnish (optional)

grilled prawns and cherry tomatoes with avocado-basil salad

EVERYTHING ABOUT THIS MEAL SAYS AUGUST to me. There's not much better on a warm evening than a few skewers of prawns eaten right off the grill, and the accompanying salad is like summer in a bowl. I developed this salad because I have a thing about avocados. I'm glad they are so conveniently packaged, because one avocado equals one serving, as far as I'm concerned. The salad is excellent with the shrimp-and-tomato skewers but I've been known to eat it alone as well.

For this recipe, you'll need eight large bamboo or metal skewers. I like the thick, eight-inch-long bamboo skewers often sold as corn dog sticks. They don't scorch as easily as the thin skewers, and food doesn't roll around on them as much. If you use the thin bamboo skewers, consider soaking them in water for thirty minutes before threading the prawns so they scorch less. When I'm in a skewer pinch, I'll cut several long pieces of rosemary, strip them of most of their leaves, and use the twigs as my skewers.

MAKES 4 TO 6 SERVINGS

+ In a large bowl, combine the prawns, oil, garlic, orange zest, orange juice, salt, and pepper to taste. Stir well to combine—make sure the garlic and zest is evenly distributed all around the prawns. Cover and refrigerate for at least 30 minutes and up to 1 hour. This gives the prawns great flavor.

+ To make the salad, in another large bowl, add the corn, onion, garlic, lime juice, and oil and stir to combine. Gently fold in the avocado, beans, and basil. Season with salt and pepper to taste. Serve immediately, or cover and refrigerate for up to 2 hours.

+ Prepare and preheat a grill to medium heat.

24 jumbo prawns, peeled and deveined

¼ cup extra-virgin olive oil

1 tablespoon finely minced garlic

Zest of 1 large orange

1 tablespoon freshly squeezed orange juice

1 teaspoon kosher salt

Freshly ground black pepper

24 large cherry tomatoes

(continued)

For the avocado salad:

¾ cup fresh raw sweet
corn kernels

½ cup diced sweet onion

1 large clove garlic, smashed
and minced

¼ cup freshly squeezed
lime juice

¼ cup extra-virgin olive oil

2 avocados, cut into
½-inch dice

1 cup cooked black beans

1 cup fresh sweet basil,
chopped

Kosher salt and freshly
ground black pepper

✦ Meanwhile, assemble the skewers. Skewer the prawns and cherry tomatoes, alternating, on large bamboo skewers. I use thick, 8-inch skewers and get 3 prawn-tomato sets on each skewer. Don't bother leaving a handle on your skewer—just fill the thing up.

✦ Transfer the skewers to the grill and sear. After 2 to 3 minutes, the prawns will be pink on one side with some light grill marks and the cherry tomatoes will show a bit of char in places. Flip the skewers and grill for 2 to 3 more minutes, or until the prawns are cooked through and the tomatoes are hot.

✦ Remove the prawn skewers from the grill and serve hot. I like to serve the skewers right on top of the avocado salad on a big platter and let people help themselves.

japanese eggplant with hoisin glaze

THE TRICK TO THIS DISH IS to use young, firm Japanese-style eggplant. They are long and slender, and they aren't bitter or seedy when picked small. The skin is tender, too, so there's no need to peel. The fat Italian-style eggplant doesn't work so well in this application, so save it for baba ghanoush.

MAKES 4 SERVINGS AS A SIDE

+ To make the glaze, in a small bowl, combine the hoisin sauce, vinegar, soy sauce, sesame oil, and red pepper flakes. In a small saucepan or skillet over medium heat, heat the vegetable oil until it shimmers. Add the garlic to the pan and stir continuously to toast it. Remove the pan from the heat as soon as the garlic starts to take on a golden color—you don't want it to scorch. Scrape the garlic and all the oil into the hoisin mixture and stir to combine. Use the glaze immediately, or transfer to an airtight container and store for up to 1 week.

+ Prepare and preheat a grill to medium heat. Trim the eggplants and slice on an angle into ½-inch-thick slices. Most slices should be about 3 to 4 inches long, so cut at a fairly steep bias.

+ Toss the eggplant slices together with the vegetable oil, and season very generously with salt. Transfer the eggplant slices to the grill. After about 5 minutes, the eggplant should have nice char marks and be softening. Flip the eggplant slices carefully, and grill on the second side until the eggplant is just tender all the way through, 5 to 7 minutes.

+ Leave the eggplant slices on the grill and brush with the hoisin glaze, giving it a minute or so to dry slightly. Flip the eggplant and brush the other side with glaze. Let the glaze dry a bit. Flip and brush both sides of the eggplant with glaze one more time, to build up a nice coating. During this glazing stage, watch your eggplant carefully so that it doesn't scorch.

+ Transfer the eggplant slices to a serving platter and scatter the green onions over the top. Serve warm or at room temperature.

For the glaze:

¼ cup hoisin sauce

1 tablespoon rice wine vinegar

1 tablespoon soy sauce

1 tablespoon toasted sesame oil

1 teaspoon red pepper flakes

2 tablespoons vegetable or extra-virgin olive oil

2 cloves garlic, minced

3 to 4 medium Japanese eggplants

¼ cup vegetable or extra-virgin olive oil

Kosher salt

½ cup thinly sliced green onions

grilled strip steak with fresh herb chimichurri

IN LATE FALL OR WINTER, WHEN I pick up a side of beef, I typically ask for the strip loin to be left whole, and I cut it into thick steaks myself. These juicy, tender, flavorful steaks are precious, and on special occasions when I pull them from my deep freeze, I don't want to get too clever with them. My preference is to quickly sear the strip steaks and serve them with the Argentinean green herb steak sauce called chimichurri.

In summer, when my herb garden is producing, I make this sauce regularly—it comes together in minutes in a food processor. This amount of sauce may be more than you need for the steaks, but it lasts for a few days and is great dabbed (or poured) on nearly any kind of meat, fish, grain, or bean. If strips steaks aren't in the budget, any flavorful cut of beef suitable for grilling will work just as well. Try flap, tri-tip, flank, or teres major.

MAKES 4 TO 6 SERVINGS

For the chimichurri:

¼ large yellow onion, chopped

4 cloves garlic

2 cups lightly packed fresh parsley

½ cup lightly packed fresh cilantro

¼ cup lightly packed fresh oregano

½ cup extra-virgin olive oil

3 tablespoons red wine vinegar

2 tablespoons freshly squeezed lemon juice

1 teaspoon kosher salt

+ To make the chimichurri, in the bowl of a food processor fitted with the metal blade, pulse the onion, garlic, parsley, cilantro, and oregano until well chopped. Add the oil gradually and continue to pulse until everything is well incorporated, but do not allow the mixture to become a puree. Add the vinegar, lemon juice, salt, cumin, and red pepper flakes and pulse just to combine. Serve immediately, or transfer the sauce to an airtight container and refrigerate for up to 4 days. Bring the sauce to room temperature before serving.

+ To cook the steaks, prepare and preheat a grill to high heat.

+ Let the steaks sit, lightly covered, at room temperature for 30 minutes before grilling. Pat the steaks dry of any surface moisture, then lightly brush with oil and season generously with salt and pepper.

+ Transfer the steaks to the grill and sear. After about 5 minutes, the steaks should have nice char marks and a crispy, golden color. Flip the steaks and grill on the second side for 4 to 7 minutes for medium-rare to medium doneness. Remove the steaks from the grill when they are cooked to just under the desired doneness. Place the steaks on a clean plate and cover loosely with foil. Let the steaks rest for 5 to 10 minutes before serving.

+ Serve the steaks sliced across the grain, topped with the chimichurri sauce.

¼ teaspoon ground cumin

¼ teaspoon red pepper flakes

4 thick-cut New York Strip steaks, fat trimmed to about ¼ inch

Neutral-flavored vegetable oil, for brushing

Kosher salt and freshly ground black pepper

berries, cake, and cream

Summer

SOMETIMES SIMPLER REALLY IS BETTER, and it doesn't get much simpler—or much better—than berries, cake, and cream. Use whatever berries are perfectly sweet and ripe, or chop up some juicy peaches or plums instead.

MAKES 4 TO 6 SERVINGS

For the cake:

2 cups all-purpose flour

¼ teaspoon baking soda

1 cup (2 sticks) butter, very soft

1½ cups sugar

3 eggs

¼ cup plain yogurt

1 tablespoon whole milk

1 teaspoon almond extract

½ pound ripe berries

A few tablespoons sugar (optional), plus 2 to 3 tablespoons for whipping the cream

½ cup cold heavy whipping cream

A few drops vanilla or almond extract

+ Preheat the oven to 300 degrees F and move an oven rack to the center position. Grease and flour an 8-by-4-inch loaf pan.

+ Sift together the flour and baking soda and set aside.

+ In a stand mixer fitted with the paddle attachment, or with a hand-held mixer, beat the butter on medium-high until light, fluffy, and pale yellow in color. Add the sugar and continue to beat until the mixture is very airy. Add the eggs one at a time, and continue to beat until the batter is the texture of buttercream frosting. Reduce the mixer speed to low, then add the yogurt, milk, and almond extract. Carefully stir in the flour, mixing just to combine.

+ Scrape the batter into the prepared loaf pan, gently smooth the top with a spatula, and transfer to the oven. Bake until pound cake is golden brown and a skewer inserted in the center of the cake comes out clean, 90 to 110 minutes.

+ Remove the pan from the oven and set it on a wire rack. Cool the cake for 20 to 30 minutes in the pan, then carefully remove it from the pan and set on the wire rack to cool completely before cutting.

+ Toss the berries with a few spoonfuls of sugar, if desired. Set the berries aside while you whip the cream; the sugar will draw a bit of juice from the berries.

+ Whip the cream until soft peaks form. Add the vanilla and 2 to 3 tablespoons of sugar to taste. Continue whipping the cream until stiff peaks form.

+ To serve, cut generous slices of pound cake and top with the berries and whipped cream.

Preserving

THINKING OUTSIDE THE (PECTIN) BOX

Do you need a box of pectin to make jam? I used to think so.

I followed the recipe on the inside of the pectin box slavishly for seven years before I broke free of the pectin bonds. Every year, my strawberry jam tasted exactly like the strawberry jam of everyone else who followed the box recipe. The jam was never bad, but it was never really mine, either.

Making jam like that just wasn't fun for me. It was about following rigorous and strict recipes, adding in a ton of sugar to "ensure a good set," skimming diligently to remove foam, and crossing my fingers while timing that one minute of "hard rolling boil" down to the second.

That's what was required by the pectin box master, and I was terrified to change a thing lest I ruin an entire batch of jam.

Now, I'm a liberated jam maker who skips the pectin box, and I'd never go back. When I make preserves now, I work with my fruit, tasting and adjusting things like sugar and spice based on fruit ripeness and variety and juiciness and what sounds good. I reduce the water out of my preserves to get the consistency and depth of flavor I'm looking for. I reduce sugar levels and still produce a preserve that is full of sweetness and sunshine. My jams, each and every batch, are creative and unique.

The only things I slavishly adhere to now are the sanitation and processing standards and acidity levels, which ensure that while I'm having fun and getting to be creative jam-girl, I'm also producing a product that is faultlessly and impeccably safe for my family and friends to enjoy.

Over the years, I've developed a basic, highly adaptable formula for my easygoing preserves. This method will work with any fruit that is firmly high acid. Borderline acid fruits, including tomatoes, figs, melons, and most tropical fruit like guava require additional acid to be safely water-bath canned. Do not add borderline or low-acid ingredients—doing so may raise the pH of your jam to levels not safe for water-bath canning.

I'm a simple girl when it comes to my preserves. I like chunky and rustic, and I'm not bothered in the slightest by a soft-set jam. So you'll find no recipes for sparkling clear, blue-ribbon-winning jellies in here. While there's nothing wrong with those labor-of-love preserves, I like straightforward, spreadable fruit, personalized with zings of flavor that are fuss free and fun to make.

simple jam with flavor zings

Summer

THIS BASIC FORMULA CAN BE ADAPTED for all high-acid fruits. For jam making, you want fruit that is fully ripe and flavorful, but still a touch firm—fruit that, if you bit into it for fresh eating, you'd say, "Oh, this would have been just perfect tomorrow!"

If you are making jam with a low-pectin fruit, it can help to use some fruit that is a bit green and underripe, but the jam will require more sugar to taste balanced. You can also combine a low-pectin fruit with a high-pectin fruit to bump the overall natural pectin levels up. Green apples and citrus are good for this. Or, just don't worry about it, and enjoy that, in jam, some fruits express themselves more softly than others.

MAKES ABOUT 4 HALF-PINT JARS (VARIES BY FRUIT)

PROCESSING AT A GLANCE

Method: Water-bath canning

Headspace: ¼ inch

Processing time: 10 minutes in a boiling water-bath canner; adjust for altitude

---

3 pounds trimmed, peeled, seeded, and cored fruit

2 to 3 cups sugar

2 tablespoons freshly squeezed lemon or lime juice

¼ to ½ teaspoon dry zing (see page 232) (optional)

1 to 2 tablespoons wet zing (see page 232) (optional)

+ If this is your first time water-bath canning, please review the basics on page 25.

+ In a large bowl, toss together the fruit and 2 cups of the sugar. Cover and transfer to the refrigerator to macerate. Let the mixture sit overnight, or up to 24 hours. When the sugar and fruit rest, two things happen. One, the sugar pulls juice from the fruit and forms a syrup. Two, the cell structure of the fruit is firmed up, which means the fruit will stand up better to cooking without breaking down. After 12 to 24 hours, the sugar should be mostly dissolved and the fruit should have released quite a bit of juice.

+ When you're ready to make the jam, prepare a water-bath canner, 6 half-pint jars, and their lids.

+ Add the macerated fruit and all juices from the bowl to a large, wide, nonreactive pan. Stirring frequently, bring the jam to a simmer over medium-high heat. When the fruit has softened but not fallen apart, add the lemon juice and the dry zing component, if using.

+ At this point, decide what kind of texture you want the preserve to have. If the texture in the pan is too chunky or the pieces are too large, crush your fruit with a potato masher or puree as desired with an immersion blender.

+ Take a small spoon of jam, including some fruit and a bit of syrup together if the preserve is chunky, and taste it. Is it sweet enough? Does it need more sugar?

+ If the preserve is tart at this point, add a bit more sugar, up to an additional cup. You may need even more sugar if you are cooking something quite tart, like quince, currants, or gooseberries. Trust your judgment. If it is sweet enough to your taste, leave it alone. As the preserve cooks longer, the flavors, including the sugar, will taste more concentrated. Stir everything gently but consistently.

+ Continue cooking, stirring frequently, until the preserve is glossy, a bit darkened, and looks slightly thickened. When it reaches the gelling point at 220 degrees F (at sea level) and sheets off a spoon, it's done (see page 29 for more information about the gelling point).

+ At this point, reduce the heat to low and add the wet zing flavoring, if using. Stir well, taste the jam one last time with a clean spoon, and make any final adjustments to the sweetness. You may also add additional citrus juice at this point, if desired. (If a preserve tastes like it needs just a little something, usually that something is a few drops of lemon juice.)

+ Ladle the jam into the prepared hot jars, leaving ¼-inch headspace. Remove any air bubbles, adjust the headspace, wipe the jar rims, and set the jar lids and bands according to the manufacturer's directions.

+ Carefully lower the filled jars into the simmering water-bath canner. When the water has returned to a boil, cover the kettle, and set a timer for 10 minutes. When the jars have processed for 10 minutes, remove the canner from the heat and allow the jars to cool in the water for 5 minutes, then use a jar lifter to transfer the jars onto a clean kitchen towel to cool and set their seals.

+ Leave the jars alone until they have fully cooled—at least 8 but no more than 24 hours—then check the seals. Any jar that hasn't sealed should be refrigerated and used within 1 month. Jars with solid seals may be washed, labeled, and stored in a cool, dark place where they will keep for about 1 year.

wet and dry flavor zings

There is nothing wrong with a jam that has nothing but fruit, sugar, and a bit of lemon juice in it. The sublime simplicity of pure strawberry has a lot going for it, for example. But when you are ready to get creative with jam making, it is possible to turn a simple fruit preserve into something a bit more personalized. All you need to do is add a bit of flavor to enhance the fruit.

Some of my favorites include:

+ Pear with Rosemary and Maple Syrup

+ Sweet Cherry with Cinnamon and Vanilla

+ Nectarine with Lime and Cointreau

+ Plum with Cardamom and Port Wine

+ Apricot with Vanilla and Earl Grey Tea

+ Peach with Ginger and Bourbon

You can think of your jam flavoring options as either "dry zings" or "wet zings." Dry zings include ground spices, citrus zests, or dried herbs and are typically added in small quantities toward the beginning of the jam-cooking process. Wet zings are liquids like alcohols and liqueurs, vinegars, maple syrup, or citrus juices. They are added in slightly larger volume toward the end of jam making to keep their flavors bright.

Adding one dry zing and one wet zing to a basic preserve gives you lots of opportunities for creative jam making while avoiding a potential flavor muddle. Play around and you'll find your own favorite signature jams too.

Over the years, I've developed some opinions on what flavor zings tend to work best with what fruit. The chart that follows presents some flavors that will, when used in an appropriate quantity and paired correctly, taste good with the fruit they are supporting.

The chart of flavor zings is by no means exhaustive, but it's a good place to get started. Start with a few solid crowd pleasers, like blueberry and cinnamon, apricot with nutmeg, or blackberry with lemon zest and Grand Marnier before venturing into more unusual pairings, like strawberry with cocoa and Framboise, pear with curry and maple syrup, or apple with rosemary.

flavor zing suggestions

FRUIT	DRY ZING: SPICE OR HERB	WET ZING: BOOZE AND SUCH
APPLE	Allspice*, Cinnamon+, Ginger, Nutmeg, Cardamom, Clove*, Rosemary^, Black Pepper, Curry^, Lemon Zest, Five-Spice Powder	Rum+, Whiskey, Calvados, Sherry, Madeira, Maple Syrup
APRICOT, PEACH, AND NECTARINE	Cinnamon+, Ginger+, Cardamom, Nutmeg*, Lemon Zest, Vanilla Bean+, Black Pepper^, Orange Zest, Lime Zest (particularly for Nectarine), Lavender*, Mint	Ice Wine, Whiskey, Brandy, Amaretto and Almond+, Vanilla+, Kirsch, Earl Grey Tea Syrup (particularly for Apricot), Orange Juice, Grand Marnier and Cointreau, Tequila, Champagne, Rum
BLACKBERRY AND SIMILAR BERRIES	Cinnamon+, Ginger, Nutmeg, Cardamom, Clove*, Black Pepper, Mint, Vanilla Bean, Lemon Zest, Lime Zest, Sage^	Grand Marnier and Cointreau, Tequila, Lemon Juice, Lime Juice, Rose (Rose Hip Tea, Rosewater), Crème de Cassis, Brandy, Vanilla, Gin^
BLUEBERRY	Allspice, Cinnamon+, Thai Basil^, Cinnamon, Basil^, Ginger, Nutmeg, Lemon Zest+, Lavender*	Rum, Whiskey, Brandy, Amaretto and Almond+, Vanilla, Kirsch, Grand Marnier and Cointreau, Tequila, Cognac+, Balsamic Vinegar
CHERRY	Allspice*, Cinnamon, Ginger, Nutmeg, Cardamom, Clove*, Lemon Zest, Orange Zest, Lime Zest, Vanilla Bean, Mint	Kirsch+, Red Wine, Armagnac, Amaretto and Almond+, Brandy, Cognac, Grand Marnier and Cointreau, Whiskey, Balsamic Vinegar
PEAR	Cinnamon+, Ginger+, Nutmeg, Cardamom, Clove*, Mustard^, Allspice*, Lemon Zest, Orange Zest, Black Pepper^, Rosemary^, Star Anise^, Five-Spice Powder^, Vanilla Bean+, Fennel^, Curry^	Brandy, Whiskey, Red Wine, Maple Syrup, Gin^, Amaretto and Almond, Grand Marnier and Cointreau, Rum+, Champagne, Vanilla, Crème de Cassis, Maple Syrup+

FRUIT	DRY ZING: SPICE OR HERB	WET ZING: BOOZE AND SUCH
PLUM	Allspice, Anise, Cinnamon+, Ginger, Nutmeg, Cardamom, Clove*, Black Pepper^, Lavender*, Coriander^, Lavender*, Lemon Zest+, Nutmeg, Mint, Orange Zest, Sage^, Thyme^, Vanilla Bean+	Brandy, Whiskey, Amaretto, Gin^, Amaretto and Almond+, Frangelico, Kirsch, Grand Marnier and Cointreau+, Maple, Orange Juice, Dark Rum, Vanilla, Red Wine, Port
RASPBERRY AND SIMILAR BERRIES	Cinnamon, Ginger, Lemon Zest+, Lime Zest, Mint, Star Anise, Lemon Verbena	Kirsch, Lemon, Rose (Rose Hip Tea, Rosewater), Brandy, Champagne, Cognac, Grand Marnier and Cointreau, Crème de Cassis, Framboise, Rum, Tequila
STRAWBERRY	Black Pepper^, Basil, Thyme, Cardamom, Cocoa Powder, Clove*, Cinnamon, Ginger, Lemon Verbena, Nutmeg, Lemon Zest+	Balsamic Vinegar, Lemon, Lime, Amaretto and Almond, Kirsch+, Brandy, Champagne, Cognac, Crème de Cassis, St. Germain Elderflower Syrup, Grappa*, Frangelico, Grand Marnier and Cointreau, Framboise, Champagne+, Sherry, Port

+ This flavor is a classic. You can't go wrong with this.

* This flavor can be particularly strong. You may want to go easy on the amount you add.

^ This flavor is daring. Best left in the hands of advanced flavor-makers.

Note: All herbs and spices are dried.

tomato-ginger sauce

I MAKE A BATCH OF THIS tomato-ginger sauce every year because it makes dinner easy and yummy. Open the jar, pour the contents of the jar over fish, bake. Voilà, cod with tomato-ginger sauce. Or, sear some beef strips and broccoli in a skillet or wok, then pour the contents of the jar and a splash of soy sauce in with the meat. Tomato-beef stir-fry: done. This sauce is a tasty example of effort shifting that works: spend an hour or two putting up six jars of sauce that will payoff in nearly effortless dinnertimes half-a-dozen times over the course of the year.

MAKES ABOUT 6 HALF-PINT JARS

PROCESSING AT A GLANCE

Method: Water-bath canning

Headspace: ½ inch

Processing time: 15 minutes in a boiling water-bath canner; adjust for altitude

---

8 cups chopped tomatoes

1½ cups diced onion

1½ cups apple cider vinegar

¾ cup lightly packed light brown sugar

¼ cup finely chopped candied ginger

¼ cup freshly squeezed lemon juice

2 tablespoons kosher salt

1 tablespoon mustard seed

2 teaspoons ground ginger

½ teaspoon ground cumin

¼ teaspoon red pepper flakes

⅛ teaspoon ground cloves

✦ If this is your first time water-bath canning, please review the basics on page 25.

✦ Prepare a water-bath canner, 6 half-pint jars, and their lids.

✦ In a large nonreactive stockpot, add all the ingredients. Stirring frequently, bring the sauce to a simmer over medium heat and cook until the sauce thickens, about 30 minutes.

✦ Ladle the sauce into the prepared hot jars, leaving ½-inch headspace. Remove any air bubbles, adjust the headspace, wipe the jar rims, and set the jar lids according to the manufacturer's directions.

✦ Carefully lower the filled jars into the simmering water-bath canner. When the water has returned to a boil, cover the kettle, and set a timer for 15 minutes. When the jars have processed for 15 minutes, remove the canner from the heat and allow the jars to cool in the water for 5 minutes, then use a jar lifter to transfer the jars onto a clean kitchen towel to cool and set their seals.

✦ Leave the jars alone until they have fully cooled—at least 8 but no more than 24 hours—then check the seals. Any jar that hasn't sealed should be refrigerated and used within 2 weeks. Jars with solid seals may be washed, labeled, and stored in a cool, dark place where they will keep for about 1 year.

blueberry chipotle sauce

ONE YEAR, I WANTED A SAUCE to accompany some turkey burgers I was making for the grill, and my eyes fell to the laden blueberry bushes in my garden. That led to this straightforward, fruity, smoky sauce that's been a favorite ever since. It's awesome with pork and poultry (try it with duck) and makes a great glaze for ribs or meatloaf.

MAKES ABOUT 6 HALF-PINT JARS

✦ If this is your first time water-bath canning, please review the basics on page 25.

✦ Prepare a water-bath canner, 6 half-pint jars, and their lids.

✦ In a large nonreactive saucepot, add all the ingredients. Stirring frequently, bring the sauce to a simmer over medium heat and cook until the blueberries burst and the sauce thickens, about 30 minutes. Remove the pot from the heat and use an immersion blender to puree the sauce until smooth, then return to the heat and continue to simmer the sauce until it is fairly thick, like barbecue sauce.

✦ Ladle the sauce into the prepared hot jars, leaving ½-inch headspace. Remove any air bubbles, adjust the headspace, wipe the jar rims, and set the jar lids according to the manufacturer's directions.

✦ Carefully lower the filled jars into the simmering water-bath canner. When the water has returned to a boil, cover the kettle, and set a timer for 20 minutes. When the jars have processed for 20 minutes, remove the canner from the heat and allow the jars to cool in the water for 5 minutes, then use a jar lifter to transfer the jars onto a clean kitchen towel to cool and set their seals.

✦ Leave the jars alone until they have fully cooled—at least 8 but no more than 24 hours—then check the seals. Any jar that hasn't sealed should be refrigerated and used within 2 weeks. Jars with solid seals may be washed, labeled, and stored in a cool, dark place where they will keep for about 1 year.

PROCESSING AT A GLANCE
Method: Water-bath canning
Headspace: ½ inch
Processing time: 20 minutes in a boiling water-bath canner; adjust for altitude

8 cups blueberries

½ cup lightly packed light brown sugar

½ cup granulated sugar

¼ cup balsamic vinegar

¼ cup bourbon

2 tablespoons freshly squeezed lemon juice

1 tablespoon kosher salt

1 teaspoon mustard seeds

1 teaspoon Worchestershire sauce

½ teaspoon ground cumin

½ teaspoon ground allspice

1 cup finely diced onion

1 cup finely diced red bell pepper

2 tablespoons minced chipotles in adobo

2 cloves garlic, minced

1 cup distilled white vinegar

summer vegetable salsa

CORN, PEPPERS, AND ONIONS ARE ALL low-acid vegetables, which means you have to essentially pickle them to make them safe to water-bath can. Because of the added vinegar, it might not really be fair to call this a salsa, but that's how I use it. I add a pint-size jar of this salsa to a pint-size jar of drained, pressure-canned black beans (see page 352) and serve the combo as a corn-and-black-bean salsa. I just love it as a topping for grilled steak, alongside a bowl of corn chips, mixed into a bowl of brown rice, or spooned into tortillas with a bit of pulled pork or grilled chicken and lots of avocado.

MAKES 6 PINT JARS

PROCESSING AT A GLANCE
Method: Water-bath canning
Headspace: ½ inch
Processing time: 15 minutes in a boiling water-bath canner; adjust for altitude

5 cups diced tomatoes

4 cups cooked whole-kernel corn (cut from the cob)

3 cups diced onions

3 cups diced bell peppers

2 cups seeded and diced mild long green chilies, such as Anaheim

2 medium jalapeños, seeded and finely chopped

¼ cup chopped cilantro

+ If this is your first time water-bath canning, please review the basics on page 25.

+ Prepare a water-bath canner, 6 pint-size jars, and their lids.

+ In a large nonreactive saucepot, add all the ingredients. Stirring frequently, bring the salsa to a boil, then gently simmer until slightly thickened, about 20 minutes.

+ Ladle the salsa into the prepared hot jars, leaving ½-inch headspace. Remove any air bubbles, adjust the headspace, wipe the jar rims, and set the jar lids according to the manufacturer's directions.

+ Carefully lower the filled jars into the simmering water-bath canner. When the water has returned to a boil, cover the kettle, and set a timer for 15 minutes. When the jars have processed for 15 minutes, remove the canner from the heat and allow the jars to cool in the water for 5 minutes, then use a jar lifter to transfer the jars onto a clean kitchen towel to cool and set their seals.

+ Leave the jars alone until they have fully cooled—at least 8 but no more than 24 hours—then check the seals. Any jar that hasn't sealed should be refrigerated and used within 2 weeks. Jars with solid seals may be washed, labeled, and stored in a cool, dark place where they will keep for about 1 year.

2 cloves garlic, finely chopped

2¾ cups distilled white vinegar

1 cup lightly packed light brown sugar

¼ cup freshly squeezed lime juice

1 tablespoon fine sea salt

1 teaspoon ground cumin

1 teaspoon mild chili powder, such as ancho

lacto-fermented pico de gallo

I LIKE CANNED SALSA JUST FINE, but when it comes to a fresh pico de gallo, nothing that is cooked can possibly compare. That's why I make batches of this lacto-fermented pico de gallo through the summer. A jar will last several months or longer in the refrigerator—I've even had big gallon-size batches last over a year. As this salsa ages, it gets tangier, but it never loses that fresh quality I like so much.

Chopping all the ingredients is a snap if you use a food processor and pulse to get the right texture—just make sure to process each ingredient separately, then combine them in a big bowl, otherwise some ingredients will be overprocessed by the time others are just right.

MAKES 2 QUART JARS

+ If this is your first time fermenting vegetables, please review the basics on page 41.

+ In a large bowl, stir together all the ingredients until fully combined.

+ Divide the pico de gallo evenly between 2 scrupulously clean quart mason jars. With a clean spoon, press the ingredients down to release some of the juices. Do your best to press the solid ingredients under the juices, and weight the ferment.

+ Loosely seal the jars with standard 2-piece lids, leaving the ring just fingertip tight, as you would for canning, to allow the gases of the fermentation process to escape. Leave the pico de gallo at cool room temperature out of direct sunlight for 2 to 4 days. Check the ferment daily. Look for bubbles and other signs of fermentation, burp the lid to release any pent-up carbon dioxide in the jar, and taste the development of the salsa with a clean spoon.

+ When you like the taste, or after 4 days, lid tightly and transfer the pico de gallo to the refrigerator, where it will keep for at least 4 months.

2 pounds tomatoes, cored and chopped (about 4 cups)

1 pound onion, peeled and chopped (about 2 cups)

¾ pound green or red bell peppers, seeded and chopped (about 1½ cups)

2 medium jalapeños, seeded and chopped

2 cloves garlic, chopped

1 bunch fresh cilantro, trimmed and chopped

½ cup freshly squeezed lime juice

4 teaspoons fine sea salt

1 teaspoon ground cumin

lacto-fermented garlic dilly beans

GREEN BEANS ARE THE IDEAL PICKLING VEGETABLE. They are easy to work with and fit into jars, hold their shape well, and resist becoming mushy in the jar. These fermented dilly beans are a simple, healthy, and delicious way to handle the bounty of summer green beans without having to break out the canning kettle.

MAKES 1 QUART JAR

1 quart water

3 tablespoons fine sea salt

1 pound tender green beans

3 cloves garlic, halved

2 teaspoons dill seed

½ teaspoon red pepper flakes

½ teaspoon mustard seeds

2 fresh grape leaves (optional)

+ If this is your first time fermenting vegetables, please review the basics on page 41.

+ To make the brine, in a large bowl, stir together the water and salt until the salt fully dissolves. Set aside.

+ Trim the green beans to remove the stems and so that the beans will fit, snuggly packed, into the jar with about 2 inches of headroom.

+ Add the garlic, dill seed, red pepper flakes, and mustard seeds to the bottom of a scrupulously clean widemouthed quart-size jar. Pack the green beans tightly into the jar stem-side down. Get as many green beans in there as you can without damaging them.

+ Pour the brine into the jar so that it comes at least 1 inch above the beans and to within 1 inch of the top of the jar. Cover the beans with the grape leaves, if using, tucking down the sides a bit so that they act to hold the beans down. Weight the ferment so that all the green beans are fully submerged under the brine.

✦ Loosely seal the jars with standard 2-piece lids, leaving the ring just fingertip tight, as you would for canning, to allow the gases of the fermentation process to escape. Leave the green beans at cool room temperature out of direct sunlight for 3 to 5 days. Check the ferment daily. Look for bubbles, a milky color to the brine, and other signs of fermentation. Burp the lid to release any pent-up carbon dioxide and, after 2 to 3 days, taste the development of the green beans using clean tongs.

✦ When the beans are a dull-green color throughout and have a tang you like, transfer the jar to the refrigerator, where the beans will keep for at least 4 months.

walnut-lemon pesto

BREAK OUT THE FOOD PROCESSOR AND make a big batch of this pesto—it keeps beautifully in the freezer and it's a great match for seafood, chicken, pork, vegetables, and any number of starches. I've used it as a sauce for salmon and as the base for basil salad dressing and so many things in between, and it's never gone wrong. Use high-quality, flavorful olive oil for this recipe.

MAKES 7 HALF-PINT JARS

+ Process the garlic and walnuts separately in a food processor fitted with the metal blade. Process the basil and oil together, working in two batches if necessary so that the basil chops easily. As each ingredient reaches the consistency of coarse bread crumbs, or the texture you prefer, transfer it to a large bowl.

+ Add the lemon juice and zest to the mixture, and season with the salt and additional lemon juice to taste. Stir very well.

+ When the pesto tastes just right, transfer it to spotlessly clean half-pint jars, leaving ¼-inch headspace, and drizzle a bit of oil over the top. Tightly lid the jars. Label the jars and store in the freezer for up to 6 months.

20 cloves garlic, peeled

4 cups walnut halves

1 pound fresh basil

2 cups extra-virgin olive oil

½ cup freshly squeezed lemon juice

Zest of 2 lemons

2 to 3 tablespoons kosher salt

pesto variations

+ Use spinach, arugula, parsley, or "exotic" basils in place of some or all of the basil (think if you grew a pound of lemon basil for this recipe . . . lemony yum!).

+ Substitute almonds for the walnuts.

+ Add Parmesan cheese to the pesto (which would bring it closer to traditional). If you add cheese, you will likely need less salt.

oven-roasted herb confit tomatoes

I CAN ABOUT 100 QUARTS of basic crushed tomatoes every summer in a giant preserving push I call can-o-rama. One year, I was just over canning tomatoes. I was sick of the steamy kettle, sick of standing in front of my stove, sick of peeling tomatoes. It would have been a great time to take a break from preserving until the apples came ready.

Only one problem: I still had forty pounds of local Roma tomatoes on my counter, and they didn't care that it was high summer and my tired feet were so sweaty they were starting to smell like wet dog. I decided to come up with a way to process all those tomatoes while sitting down. This recipe is the result. The quantities given here are for one sheet pan's worth of tomatoes, but it's simple to scale the quantities to accommodate multiple batches if you have extra tomatoes on hand.

MAKES ABOUT 2 PINTS

+ Preheat the oven to 250 degrees F. Get a big sheet pan (or several, if you have a lot of tomatoes and a big oven) and line it with parchment paper. Drizzle 2 tablespoons of olive oil over the parchment.

+ Wash and core the tomatoes. Slice them in half lengthwise, and set the halves on the prepared sheet pans, seed cavities facing up. The tomatoes can be very snug on the pan because they will shrink as they cook, but they should be arranged in a single layer.

+ Scatter the garlic over the tomatoes, then drizzle the remaining 2 tablespoons oil over the tomato halves. Sprinkle the tomatoes generously with salt and pepper, then scatter whatever herbs you might have over the top—several sprigs of fresh thyme seem nearly essential, some oregano and basil are nice. If you have a bay leaf, drop that onto the pan, too. If you have no fresh herbs, a pinch each of dried thyme and dried basil will do just fine.

5 pounds thick-fleshed Roma or other canning-type tomatoes

10 large cloves garlic, peeled

¼ cup extra-virgin olive oil, divided

Kosher salt and freshly ground black pepper

Fresh or dried herbs, such as thyme, oregano, basil, or bay leaf

(continued)

✦ Put the tomatoes in the oven and roast for several hours—at least 3 but up to 7—depending on how big the tomatoes are and how soft and caramelized you like them. Roast until the tomatoes are collapsed and tender throughout and beginning to brown and caramelize nicely on the bottom.

✦ Pick out anything that looks unpleasant to eat like an herb twig or bay leaf, then fill wide-mouthed mason jars or plastic freezer bags with the tomatoes, garlic, and any herbs clinging to them. Divide all the lovely infused roasting oil from the sheet pan evenly into the jars with the tomatoes.

✦ Lidded tightly, the tomatoes will keep in the refrigerator for several days, and in my home a jar never lasts that long. I freeze most of the confit in widemouthed pint-size jars. If you make sure the tomatoes are submerged in juices and oil (add an extra glug of olive oil to the jar if needed) and press a layer of plastic wrap onto the tomatoes before lidding and freezing them, they will keep for at least 6 months. If you use freezer bags, simply squeeze out as much air as possible before sealing.

✦ To use, thaw the confit in the refrigerator overnight, and serve it as a sauce for pasta, alongside fish or chicken, or to top a little slice of bread smeared with goat cheese. In the winter, use it in place of anemic supermarket tomatoes on burgers, sandwiches, salads, and more. Mash it up for a lovely tomato spread that's excellent on flatbread or pizza, or for stirring into a bowl of white beans or lentils.

Home Care

ZEN AND THE ART OF LINE DRYING

There's something about line drying laundry that's almost meditative. You get outside for a few minutes of sunshine and gently stretch and move to reach and pin and hang your clothes. Your attention is directed to the arc of the sun or threatening rainclouds or helpful, gentle breezes. Simple things—the sharp crack of a briskly snapped pair of jeans or the springy tension in a well-made clothespin—transform a practical chore into a moment of respite.

ADVANTAGES OF LINE DRYING:

✦ Save loads of money and gain eco-cred with the massive energy conservation that comes with turning off the dryer.

✦ Enjoy a real fresh breeze scent without the disturbing chemical undertones or the endocrine disrupters that come with fake "fresh breeze" clothing and room sprays.

✦ Line-dried sheets are so smooth they look like they've been ironed (without the tedious ironing).

✦ Consistently line drying your clothes will make these items last far, far longer than machine drying. And ladies, good-quality delicates (bras, panties, nylons, etc.) aren't cheap—line drying really helps maintain the shape of your foundation garments and keeps the elastic snappy.

✦ Sunlight is the best free disinfectant we have—UV rays are quite effective at killing pathogens. Sunlight does an excellent job of killing bacteria that cause odors in clothing, and many organic stains can be faded or removed though sun bleaching.

There can be a bit of a learning curve with line drying. Like most other traditional skills, there's nothing particularly hard about hanging your clothes, but for best results it's good to know a few tricks:

1. Set up your clothesline someplace convenient to you. Not having to traipse through your house and across your yard with a heavy basket of wet laundry will make you more likely to take advantage of line drying. The ideal place for a clothesline is only a few steps from where you do laundry. Someplace with a nice breeze and sunshine will make your clothes dry much faster. Get creative—I turned a seldom-used covered patio into our clothes-hanging area and it's worked great.

2. If you don't have an outside area, there are many ways to line dry inside. The simplest is to set up a retractable clothesline in your shower. This is a common technique to dry clothes in crowded cities across Europe and Asia. Shirts can often be hung damp, directly from the washer, onto hangers, and hung to dry from a rod in the laundry area or bathroom. As long as they are hung with plenty of air circulation around them, they'll dry nicely. All manner of interior clothes racks can be DIY'd or purchased. The better designs all fold flat, collapse, or can be raised up out of the way when the drying rack isn't in use.

3. Be sensitive to indoor humidity levels when deciding how and when to dry inside. In arid climates, the additional moisture from drying clothes is a benefit; in very humid climates like mine, extra moisture can lead to mold, mildew, and rot (sadly, I know this from experience).

4. Your actual clothesline should be rot-and-mildew resistant and attached as high as you can comfortably reach. Make sure it's taut and well anchored to resist the pull of the heavy, wet clothes you'll be pinning to it.

5. Inexpensive wooden clothespins work fine. If you become a line-drying connoisseur, you can invest in heavy-duty artisan-made pins that hold more securely (and look super cool), but these aren't necessary.

6. Using a high-speed spin cycle in the washing machine will result in clothes with less moisture that take less time to line dry. This isn't appropriate for delicates, but jeans, T-shirts, towels, and sheets are usually fine with a high-speed spin.

7. Give clothes a good "snap" to release any wrinkles from the wash before hanging them to dry. Smooth and reshape delicate clothes like sweaters or camisoles.

8. Always hang clothes in the way least likely to cause pulling, stretching, or conspicuous clothespin marks. Hang most casual shirts like T-shirts upside down by the bottom hem. Dress shirts are typically best dried on a hanger. Most casual pants, jeans, and shorts are best hung upside down from the pant cuff so that the heavy, belt-loop area gets maximum airflow for faster drying. Hang towels from one end so the full length of the towel gets good air circulation instead of folding the towels in half over the clothesline. Sheets are often too big to hang freely. You don't want them hanging on the ground, after all. Hang sheets from their open edges along the clothesline, with each edge pinned separately from the other. The sheet will look a bit like a closed up hammock, and will catch airflow and breezes well.

9. Hang heavy items at the ends of your line and lighter weight items in the middle to cut down on line sag.

10. Remember to watch the weather and take your clothes in if rain threatens.

11. Line-dried towels have a very different texture than machine-dried towels. A vigorous towel-off after your morning shower with a line-dried towel is like a good body brushing session: it'll get your lymphatic system moving and (in time) you'll learn to love it. Or, you will hate it so much that absolutely no amount of eco-cred will convince you to use towels that feel like sandpaper. I like my towels with exfoliation fingers, but this is a personal call.

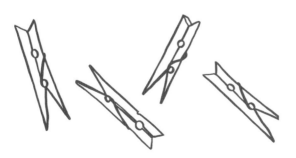

an old-fashioned mattress airing for a sunny day

ON THE BRIGHTEST, SUNNIEST, HOTTEST DAY of the year, sip a mojito or lemonade in the shade while your mattress gets a suntan. This simple cleaning routine and the amazing power of sunshine will freshen your mattress and kill off the dust mite intruders who think your bed is a perfect all-you-can-eat buffet. Tea tree, cinnamon, and eucalyptus essential oils have proven the most effective against dust mites, but you can use other essential oils if you prefer.

MAKES ENOUGH FOR 1 MATTRESS AIRING

Vacuum with upholstery and crevice attachments

Hydrogen peroxide

Liquid castile soap

Bug-Be-Gone Dust Mite Spray (recipe follows)

+ Strip the bed of all sheets, mattress protectors, etc. Run everything through the washing machine on the hot setting to kill any dust mites.

+ Thoroughly vacuum the mattress with an upholstery attachment and crevice attachment, paying particular attention to seam lines, buttons on quilting, and any areas that might tend to stay darker and moister than the rest of the mattress.

+ Tackle any stains on the mattress. Pour hydrogen peroxide into a small spray bottle and lightly mist any areas of staining. (Hydrogen peroxide is fine for most fabrics, but do a small test in an inconspicuous place if you are concerned about bleaching.) Blot away stains gently with a rag.

+ If the hydrogen peroxide doesn't take a stain out, you can try a diluted solution of castile soap and water. Just be very careful not to soak your mattress. Spot clean until the stain either fades or proves itself thoroughly unwilling to leave despite your best efforts.

+ Now mist the hydrogen peroxide all over the mattress, paying particular attention to the seams and less open areas. Don't saturate the mattress—just mist.

✦ Let the mattress dry thoroughly, for at least 1 hour.

✦ Haul the mattress outside, someplace clean where it will be in full sun for several hours—2 at a minimum, but 6 is better. If it's too much work to get the mattress outside or you live in an apartment, condo, or other place where a mattress on the lawn would be frowned upon, just open every window in your bedroom and prop the mattress up against a wall or the bed frame to maximize airflow. While the mattress is off the frame, you might as well vacuum under the bed. Why not, right?

✦ Return the mattress to its normal location. Lightly mist the entire mattress with Bug-Be-Gone Dust Mite Spray, being particularly thorough anywhere on the mattress that will tend to stay dark and moist. Let the mattress dry completely.

✦ Make your bed with fresh sheets and enjoy your clean, well-aired, and refreshed mattress!

bug-be-gone dust mite spray

2 tablespoons vodka

1 teaspoon tea tree essential oil

1 teaspoon cinnamon essential oil

1 teaspoon eucalyptus essential oil

✦ To mix up a batch of the spray, in an 8-ounce spray bottle, mix the vodka and essential oils. Fill the rest of the bottle with water.

✦ Lid and shake gently to combine.

concrete patio cleaner

IN SUMMER, LIFE MOVES OUTSIDE. Interior cleanups are put off until cooler weather rolls around and everything from cooking to playing happens under the open sky. In Seattle, October to April is reliably one long, continuous drizzle. All that damp and gray does a number on our outdoor living spaces as mold, mildew, and fungi colonize patios, porches, and balconies. When the sun finally starts to shine, the outdoor extensions of our homes need a little TLC before we fire up the barbecue, pour the cold beer, and relax.

This caustic concrete cleaner will clean your patio of grease, dirt, and mildew. Try not to let it run into your plants—what's good for busting grime will make your plants unhappy.

MAKES ABOUT 1 GALLON

1 gallon very hot water

1½ cups washing soda

½ cup powdered oxygen bleach

2 tablespoons liquid castile soap

✦ Before you begin, put on rubber gloves. In a big bucket (I like to use a 2-gallon mop bucket), combine the water, washing soda, and oxygen bleach and stir well. Add in the soap and give it another good stir. Use immediately.

To use:

✦ Dip a scrub brush or stiff-bristled push broom into the cleaner as often as needed. Scrub the concrete one section at a time. When the concrete is well scrubbed, rinse it with fresh water.

stink stopper toilet spray

THERE'S A PRETTY HILARIOUS COMMERCIAL PRODUCT that promises to trap the—*ahem*—crappy odor of a certain bodily bathroom function under the toilet bowl water. When I heard about this product I had to try to create a DIY version (because poop spray is what I do for fun), and I succeeded beyond my wildest dreams.

What can I say? If you want the world to think your shit doesn't stink (literally!), this is the DIY project for you. This spray isn't an air freshener. You spray it on the toilet water before you sit down. The spray creates a fine film on the surface of the water that keeps the stink of poo trapped.

I use sweet orange essential oil in this spray because it's cheap compared to other essential oils. The spray takes a good amount of essential oil and sweet orange doesn't break the bank. You can mix the formula up with whatever essential oils you like—just keep the total around one tablespoon essential oil per half cup water.

MAKES 5 FLUID OUNCES

+ In a 6-ounce spray bottle, add all the ingredients. Lid tightly and shake to combine. The spray will last for at least 3 months, though the essential oil scent may fade over time.

To use:

+ Shake the spray well before each use. Spray the surface of the toilet bowl water 2 to 3 times before sitting down to use the bathroom.

½ cup water

1 tablespoon sweet orange essential oil

1 teaspoon grapeseed oil

1 teaspoon rubbing alcohol

1 teaspoon vegetable glycerin

Personal Care

surfer hair salt spray

WANT THAT TOUSLED BEACH-HAIR LOOK WITHOUT tousling your wallet for
commercial salt sprays? This DIY spray will enhance your hair's natural
wave and add body to fine hair. I don't recommended this as an everyday
styling aid, because, even though it's far gentler than commercial versions,
any salt spray is drying to the hair if used long-term. But hey, in summer,
sometimes you just need beach hair. I understand.

MAKES ¼ CUP

+ In a 2-ounce spray bottle, add the Epsom salts, sea salt, Vitamin E,
vegetable glycerin, and essential oils. Fill the bottle with warm water,
close the lid tightly, and shake to combine. The spray will last for at
least 3 months, though the essential oil scent may fade over time.

To use:

+ Shake the spray well, then spray it onto lightly damp hair, focusing
on the middle and ends. Use your fingers to gently scrunch your hair
for more texture, then allow hair to air-dry. You can also use this spray
on dry hair for a milder effect. Just brush first, then finish with the salt
spray and gently work your fingers through your hair, breaking it up
into chunky pieces and scrunching the ends.

1 teaspoon Epsom salts

¼ teaspoon fine sea salt

3 drops vitamin E oil

1 drop vegetable glycerin

10 drops lemon essential oil

6 drops orange essential oil

6 drops bergamot
essential oil

gardener's hard-core hand scrub

AS AN AVID GARDENER, I GET these lines of dirt on the edges of my index finger and thumb that stick like a tattoo no matter how many times I wash my hands. I've bonded with my father-in-law, an auto mechanic, over the frustration of perma-dirt. After all, just because you like to get your hands dirty, doesn't necessarily mean you want them to stay dirty. I developed this hand scrub specifically to combat perma-dirt. The essential oils are optional but add a nice, clean, woodsy smell that is gender-neutral and very refreshing. Lemon or orange would also be great if you don't have sensitive skin.

MAKES 1½ CUPS

+ In a medium bowl, combine the coconut oil, castile soap, and sugar.

+ Let the mixture cool, then stir vigorously with a spoon. This will "whip" the oil for a pourable but creamy texture.

+ Stir in the essential oils, then scrape the hand scrub into a clean pint-size jar or other container. The hand scrub will last at least 6 months, though the essential oil scent may fade over time. If the scrub begins to separate, just re-whip it with another good stir.

To use:

+ Wet your hands with warm water, then spoon a generous dollop of hand scrub into your palms. Scrub away, paying particular attention to the sides of the fingers and crease lines where dirt likes to stick. Rinse with warm water.

¼ cup coconut oil, melted

¼ cup liquid castile soap

1 cup sugar

10 drops rosemary
    essential oil

10 drops peppermint
    essential oil

5 drops tea tree essential oil

oil-based moisturizer for any skin and any season

A TRUE LOTION IS A LIGHT, stable emulsion of water and oils that absorbs quickly into the skin. Sounds simple enough, right? Actually . . . no. There are two issues when it comes to lotion. First, oil and water don't like to mix, so a special emulsifier has to be added to make a true lotion stable. Second, all emulsified lotions require a preservative to be safely kept at room temperature for any length of time. From a bacterium's perspective, an emulsified lotion of water and oil isn't much different from an emulsified mayonnaise of lemon juice and oil. You wouldn't leave mayonnaise in your bathroom for a month and then rub it all over your skin, and homemade lotion is no different.

Luckily, there's a solution for folks who want to DIY their moisturizer without investing in specialty ingredients and preservatives. Just skip water-and-oil emulsion lotions altogether and use pure oils and oil blends for all your skin-hydration needs. Vegetable oils and butters are shelf-stable for months at a time without preservatives, and the right weight of oil will rub in cleanly, leaving your skin smooth but not greasy.

The trick to a great oil-only moisturizer is to match the oils you use to your skin's need for hydration and the season. Naturally dry skin in cold winter areas may benefit from a heavy-duty cream of thick, whipped Shea butter. Skin with only a light need for moisture might be best served by a few drops of apricot kernel oil.

MAKES ABOUT ½ CUP

½ cup moisturizing oil

20 to 30 drops essential oil

+ Select a moisturizing oil based on your skin's moisture needs, climate, and preference, using the chart on the opposite page. Blend one or more oils to get the weight you want. If you are using a solid body butter, like coconut, cocoa, or shea butter, consider whipping the butter in a stand mixer for a lighter, easier to apply texture.

+ Select one or more essential oils. Use the chart on the opposite page to determine what is best for your skin type.

+ In a small bowl with a whisk, mix the essential oils into the moisturizing oil(s) well. Transfer the moisturizer to a small mason jar or container with a tight-fitting lid. The moisturizer will keep for at least 3 months, or longer if kept refrigerated.

To use:

+ Smooth the moisturizer onto skin as needed, and rub until the oil is fully absorbed into the skin.

MOISTURIZING OILS

Light to heavy

Sunflower oil

Apricot kernel oil

Rosehip seed oil

Macadamia nut oil

Grapeseed oil

Sweet almond oil

Olive oil

Light sesame oil

Avocado oil

Castor oil

Jojoba oil

Coconut oil

Shea butter

Cocoa butter

ESSENTIAL OIL COMBINATIONS BY SKIN-TYPE	
EVERY SKIN	Lavender, geranium, rose, and ylang ylang
DRY SKIN	Jasmine, chamomile, rosewood, and myrrh
OILY SKIN	Bergamot, patchouli, orange, and rosemary
ACNE-PRONE SKIN	Cedarwood, tea tree, lemon, and frankincense
MATURE SKIN	Carrot seed, rose hip seed, clary sage, and neroli

comfrey and aloe skin-soothing gel

IN THIS SKIN-NURTURING SPRAY, THE POWERFUL healing herb comfrey is combined with aloe and cooling essential oils. There is, in my humble opinion, nothing better for skin that's spent a bit too much time out in the summer sun.

Comfrey is so useful for skin care because it contains allantoin, a compound that helps skin regenerate, soften, and recover from damage. In my neck of the woods, comfrey is a common and aggressive weed. To get the roots used to make the comfrey gel in this skin soother I literally walk across the street and dig. Familiarize yourself with this underappreciated medicinal herb and you may start to see it everywhere too. If you live someplace where comfrey isn't available wild, you can substitute one ounce of dried comfrey root, available online.

Aloe is also an amazing soother, helping to moisturize and cool sun-damaged skin. For this formula, you can use fresh, finely pureed aloe pulp or commercially available aloe gel. If you buy your aloe gel, try to get as high a proportion of aloe as possible, 98 percent or better.

MAKES ABOUT 2 OUNCES

For the comfrey gel:

4 ounces fresh comfrey root, scrubbed and finely chopped

3 cups water

2 tablespoons aloe vera gel

5 drops vitamin E oil

10 drops lavender essential oil

10 drops peppermint essential oil

+ To make the comfrey gel, in a medium saucepan, combine the comfrey root and the water. Over medium-low heat, bring the mixture to a bare simmer and maintain it for 30 minutes. Remove the pan from the heat, cover, and let the gel cool completely, about 2 hours.

+ When the gel has cooled, strain it through a very fine-mesh strainer. It will be highly mucilaginous (goopy). Using a spatula, push as much of the gel through the strainer as possible without getting any root bits in the finished gel.

+ You should have about 2 cups of comfrey gel when you are done. Use what you need for the skin-soothing gel immediately, then freeze the remainder in an ice cube tray for future batches, up to 1 year. Label the ice cubes clearly so everyone knows they aren't edible.

+ To make the skin soother, mix 2 tablespoons of the comfrey gel with the aloe vera gel. Add in the vitamin E and essential oils. Depending on the thickness and texture of the gel, you may be able to use a spray bottle to apply it. If the gel is too thick, a small pump-bottle will work better. Kept refrigerated, the skin soother will last for 2 to 4 weeks, though the essential oil scent may fade over time.

To use:

+ Spray the skin soother directly onto sunburned or otherwise damaged skin. Or pump a small amount onto your fingertips and smooth the gel over skin.

NOTE: Two words of warning. Any time you wildcraft (harvest medicinals or edibles from the wild) you must be absolutely, 100 percent sure of your plant identification. If you are uncertain, find an experienced herbalist who can show you what to look for before embarking on the wonderful adventure of wildcrafting.

Also, comfrey is not for internal use. There are compounds in comfrey that can cause liver failure if ingested in large doses. If you have any concerns about limited, external use of comfrey decoctions, talk to a qualified herbalist or doctor before making this gel.

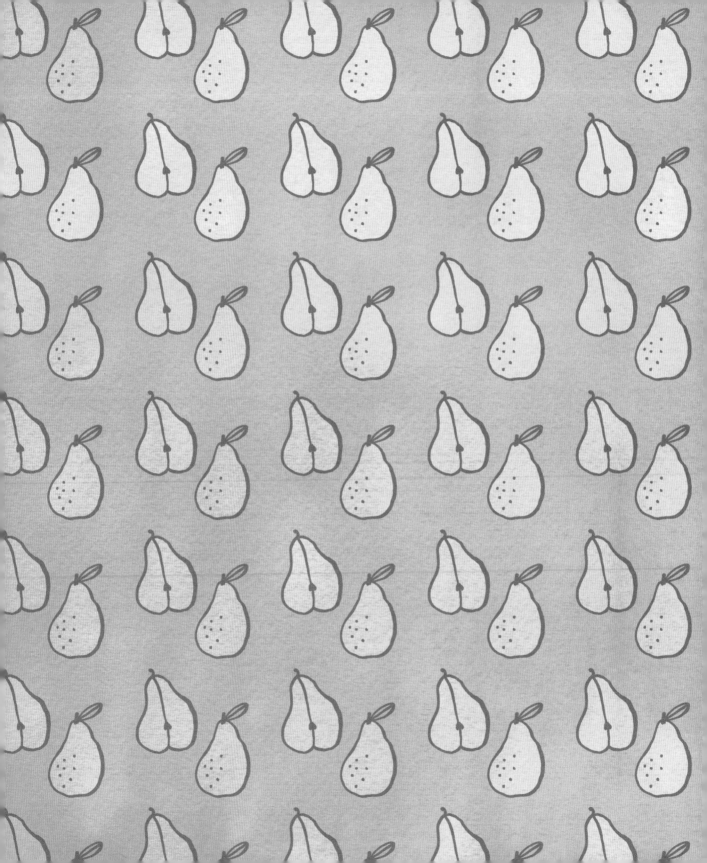

Cooking

THOUGHTS ON THE SEASON OF STALWARTS

A miraculous thing happens about when the kids head back to school. As if the pitter-patter of little rain boots and the slosh of great heaving school buses has some deeper power, the hurried fruits of summer collapse into exhaustion, and fall, sweet fall, steps up with cool-season crops you can count on. Brassicas and roots and storage squashes and alliums and hardy greens hit their stride and hot foods again appeal to hungry bellies.

I am always fairly relieved at this time of year. There is something about the slowing down of autumn and the return to a more balanced indoor-outdoor routine that I find comforting.

In the garden and in the kitchen, fall is my favorite season. Spring is slow to produce, buttoned up and shy like a virgin. Summer is lusty, throwing her fecundity around in a stream of zucchini, beans, peaches, cherry tomatoes, cucumbers, and melons that never seem to stop.

But fall, steadfast fall, is the wife. She is the backbone, the workhorse. Fall isn't flashy, but she is beautiful, clad in the multi-hued greens of kales and cabbages and bejeweled with beets and purple-blushed rutabagas and dusky-blue plums.

In the garden, if you have planned right, and if you have shown loyalty to her over the past months despite the overwhelming temptations of summer, fall will be waiting in the wings, ready with hardy greens, lovely, long-lasting roots, tenaciously sweet winter squashes, and crisp brassicas at the exact moment when you think, *Hey, you know? It kind of feels like fall now.*

While summer parties, fall quietly gets the garden house in order. We do what we can to capture the delirious magic of slutty summer in a jar, but a family will not thrive on peach jam alone. And so the pale, broad shoulders of fall will carry our meals along with chard and apples and brussels sprouts for as long as we can hold back the frigid, sleepy crone of winter.

Neither maiden nor temptress, stalwart fall meets us where we are and holds her gifts steady through the long, low months of the year. This is when roots and greens reign. Fall stewards kale into small trees, and nurtures beets and kohlrabi to a globe-like perfection that rival even the rotundity of a summer peach. I dare not push this thinly veiled analogy onto parsnips. Suffice it to say, it's true about frost-kissed being sweeter.

curried butternut squash soup with caramelized apples and cider cream

LIKE SO MANY WONDERFUL FOODS, WINTER squash soup is more an idea than a hard-and-fast recipe. I like curry and the gorgeous addition of sweet, caramelized apples as a garnish, so that's what I'm sharing here. But when the air of the evenings turns crisp, when the leaves throw on their red-and-gold capes and whirl themselves like dervishes on the wind, there is time for more than a few pots of smooth, comforting squash soup. So try this version, then play around: add sage leaves and serve with a few crunchy Parmesan croutons. Or build a rich, decedent soup by adding strong splashes of heavy cream and brandy. Branch out from butternut and try out some lesser-known heirloom winter squashes that are more available today. Sweet Meat, Sugar Hubbard, Kabocha, and Banana Squash all make excellent soup.

MAKES 6 TO 8 SERVINGS

+ Move an oven rack to the center position and preheat the oven to 400 degrees F.

+ Cut the butternut squash in half lengthwise and scrape the seed cavity clean. Place the squash on a sheet pan, cut side up, and brush with about 1 tablespoon of the butter. Sprinkle the squash evenly with the curry powder and season with salt and pepper to taste.

+ Roast the squash until tender, 50 minutes to 1 hour. A butter knife should pierce the thickest part of the flesh without resistance.

+ While the squash is roasting, in a large, heavy stockpot set over medium heat, heat the remaining 2 tablespoons of butter. Add the onion and ginger and cook, stirring occasionally, until the onion is translucent, 5 to 6 minutes. Remove the pot from the heat and set aside.

+ When the squash is tender, set aside until just cool enough to handle, then scrape the squash meat from the skin with a big spoon. Add the squash meat to the onions and ginger in the pot. Compost the cooked skin.

4 pounds (about 2 medium) butternut squash

3 tablespoons butter, melted, divided

1 tablespoon curry powder

Kosher salt and freshly ground black pepper

1 large yellow onion, chopped

2 tablespoons minced fresh ginger

4 cups chicken or vegetable broth

1 tablespoon apple cider vinegar

For the garnishes:

¼ cup sour cream

1 tablespoon maple syrup

1 tablespoon apple cider vinegar

(continued)

1 large tart baking apple,
    such as Granny Smith

1 tablespoon unsalted butter

1 teaspoon curry powder

1 teaspoon lightly packed
    light brown sugar

Kosher salt and freshly
    ground black pepper

✦ Mash the squash in the pot with a potato masher, sturdy whisk, or fork. Add the broth, stir well, and return the pot to medium heat. Bring the soup a simmer, reduce the heat to maintain a gentle simmer, and cook, covered, for about 30 minutes.

✦ Prepare the garnishes while the soup is simmering. They aren't hard additions, but they make a simple butternut puree soup seem quite elegant. First, in a small bowl, mix the sour cream, maple syrup, and apple cider vinegar together until combined. Cover and refrigerate until serving.

✦ Peel, core, and dice the apple into uniform ¼-inch cubes. In a sauté pan set over medium-high heat, melt the butter. When the butter foams, add the diced apples and curry powder and cook, stirring often, until the apple pieces caramelize, about 3 minutes. Add the brown sugar and continue to cook until the sugar melts and coats the apples, another minute or so. Season with a tiny pinch of kosher salt and a few turns of freshly ground black pepper. Remove the pan from the heat and set aside.

✦ When the soup is done cooking, use an immersion blender to puree it to a smooth, creamy consistency, or transfer the soup to a blender and very carefully puree in batches before returning to a clean pot. (If using a blender, vent the lid by removing the center pour cap, place a clean kitchen towel over the lid of the blender, and hold the towel-covered lid down firmly while pureeing.)

✦ Stir in the apple cider vinegar, and adjust seasonings to taste with salt, pepper, or additional vinegar, as desired. If the puree is too thick, add in additional broth or water to adjust. The soup should be about the consistency of heavy cream.

✦ Ladle soup into wide, shallow bowls. Mound a generous spoonful of the caramelized apples in the center of the bowl and drizzle a bit of the cider cream around the soup. Serve immediately.

fresh fig salad with arugula, blue cheese, and bacon

I LIVE IN AN AREA THAT's marginal for growing really great figs, and the main crop of these heavy drops of sweetness don't reliably ripen, if they ripen at all, until fall. I love fresh figs, and it's worth it to me to baby my fig trees with sheltered, sunny locations, because biting into a perfect fig, right off the tree and still warm from the autumn sun, is about the most luscious experience one can have with a fruit without getting weird.

In this salad, the sweetness of fresh ripe figs is enhanced with other powerful flavors: arugula, which is peppery without being bitter in the cooler seasons; creamy blue cheese; and lardons of smoky bacon.

MAKES 4 SERVINGS AS A LIGHT MEAL

+ In a heavy skillet over medium heat, cook the bacon, stirring occasionally, until the bacon renders its fat and crisps. Remove the bacon lardons from the skillet with a slotted spoon and set them aside on a paper towel or perfectly clean lint-free rag to drain.

+ Add 2 tablespoons of the rendered bacon fat to a large bowl. Add the oil, vinegar, mustard, and honey to the bacon fat and whisk together to make a dressing. Add the arugula and toss to combine.

+ Divide the dressed arugula among 4 plates. Top the arugula with the figs, cheese, and bacon lardons. Serve immediately.

6 ounces thick-cut bacon, cut crosswise into strips about ½-inch wide

2 tablespoons extra-virgin olive oil

2 tablespoons red wine vinegar

1 teaspoon Dijon mustard

1 tablespoon honey

4 cups fresh arugula

12 fresh, sweet figs, halved

2 ounces firm-creamy blue cheese, such as Danish Blue, Maytag Blue, or Gorgonzola, crumbled

kamut salad with roasted delicata squash and dried cherries

KAMUT IS A GRAIN WITH A great marketing angle: one common origin story is that this ancient wheat was discovered in the tombs of Egyptian pharaohs. What we do know is that Kamut is a registered trademark for a selected variety of large, high-protein wheat called Khorasan that has been grown in the fertile crescent for millennia. It's got a nutty flavor and chewy texture that I love—it's one of my favorite grains. Soak your kamut overnight for quicker cooking.

This particular salad is one of those things that came about, as much good food does, when I was staring at my open refrigerator, hoping that the act of staring would somehow produce ready-to-eat food. I had some leftover Kamut pilaf and roasted squash—so one quick vinaigrette and a few dried cherries from the pantry later, I had dinner. I like delicata squash in this dish, because it doesn't require peeling—the skin is thin and quite edible; just give it a good scrub.

MAKES 4 TO 6 SERVINGS AS A LIGHT MEAL, OR 8 TO 12 SERVINGS AS A SIDE

+ To make the dressing, in a very small saucepan over medium-low heat, add the oil, garlic, and sage and cook until the sage and garlic begin to gently bubble.

+ Meanwhile, in a small bowl, combine the vinegar, mustard, and maple syrup. When the garlic begins to change color slightly, pour the hot oil into the vinegar mixture. Season with salt and pepper to taste. Whisk to emulsify, then set aside. The dressing can be made up to 3 days ahead.

+ Rinse and soak the Kamut for several hours or overnight. Drain the soaked Kamut, then bring it to a gentle simmer in a large pot full of lightly salted water. Cover and simmer the Kamut until the grain is tender and plump, 30 to 75 minutes. Cooking time will depend on the soaking time, variety, and age of the grain. Drain the Kamut well,

(continued)

For the dressing:

¼ cup extra-virgin olive oil

2 cloves garlic, finely minced

1 sprig fresh sage, finely minced

3 tablespoons apple cider vinegar

2 teaspoons Dijon mustard

2 teaspoons maple syrup

Kosher salt and freshly ground pepper

1½ cups Kamut, farro, or other heirloom whole wheat berry

2 pounds (about 2 medium)
delicata squash

2 tablespoons extra-virgin
olive oil

Kosher salt and freshly
ground black pepper

½ cup dried cherries

½ cup chopped pecans

1 bunch flat-leaf parsley,
chopped

1 bunch green onions,
chopped

spread it out, and allow it to cool to room temperature. You should have about 3½ to 4 cups of cooked Kamut. The Kamut may be prepared up to 3 days ahead and kept tightly covered and refrigerated until the salad is assembled.

✦ While the Kamut is simmering, roast the squash. Move an oven rack to the center position and preheat the oven to 450 degrees F. Line a sheet pan with parchment paper.

✦ Trim off the stem and blossom end of the squash, then halve it lengthwise. Scoop out the seeds, then slice crosswise into ½-inch-thick C-shaped pieces. Toss the squash with the oil, then sprinkle generously with salt and several grinds of black pepper. Lay the squash slices out on the sheet pan in a single layer. Roast until tender and lightly caramelized, 25 to 30 minutes, giving the squash a stir about halfway through cooking. You should have about 3 to 4 cups of roasted delicata. The squash may be prepared up to 2 days ahead and kept well wrapped and refrigerated.

✦ To assemble the salad, in a large bowl, combine the cooked Kamut, roasted squash, cherries, pecans, parsley, green onions, and the dressing. Toss everything together and serve at room temperature.

crispy roasted brussels sprouts with lemon

POOR BRUSSELS SPROUTS. THEY'RE IN THE running with lima beans and liver for the "most unloved food" award. It's a pity, because sprouts really can be scrumptious. When cold-tolerant crops like brussels sprouts are exposed to frost, the vegetable pumps sugar into its cells to create a kind of natural anti-freeze. If you eat brussels sprouts in season, grown in an area where the temperatures dip down into the low thirties or high twenties, and blast them with high heat until they get crispy and caramelized, they are really delicious. Try this super simple dish of roasted brussels sprouts and see if you agree.

MAKES 4 SERVINGS AS A SIDE

+ Preheat the oven to 475 degrees F.

+ Cut the sprouts in half lengthwise and place them in a medium bowl, then add the oil, salt, pepper to taste, and the lemon zest. Toss together, making sure all the sprouts are well coated.

+ Transfer the sprouts to a heavy sheet pan. Spend a minute arranging the sprouts so that they are in one layer, cut side down. Roast the sprouts until deeply caramelized and golden brown and tender throughout, 15 to 18 minutes.

+ Remove the sprouts from the oven and, while the pan is still hot, drizzle the lemon juice over the sprouts. Stir together right on the pan and serve immediately.

1 pound brussels sprouts, trimmed

3 tablespoons extra-virgin olive oil

2 teaspoons kosher salt

Freshly ground black pepper

1 tablespoon lemon zest

2 tablespoons freshly squeezed lemon juice

NOTE: When zesting citrus, the goal is uniform, bright-yellow pieces of peel with no bitter white pith attached. Use a Microplane grater to easily zest lemons, limes, oranges, and more. The rasp-like design of the Microplane creates fine, fragrant zest and leaves all the pith behind. Just make sure to give the grater a good tap on a cutting board periodically to dislodge all the zest that tends to stick to the back of the grater.

swiss chard gratin

SWISS CHARD IS MUCH EASIER TO get a culinary handle on if you think of these glossy, crinkly leaves as two vegetables masquerading as one. The leaf is a tender, fast-cooking green used like spinach; the wide, fibrous center stem has more in common with celery. It's good slow-cooked, braised, simmered with cream, or stir-fried until crisp-tender. Regardless of the final dish, the first step in any chard recipe is to separate these conjoined vegetables so you can cook each of them to their best advantage.

MAKES 4 SERVINGS

2 large bunches (about 2 pounds) Swiss chard

2 tablespoons extra-virgin olive oil

½ large onion, finely chopped

4 cloves garlic, minced

½ cup well-drained canned tomatoes, chopped

2 tablespoons apple cider vinegar

1 teaspoon anchovy paste or finely minced anchovy canned in oil

Kosher salt and freshly ground black pepper

½ cup panko or coarse dry bread crumbs

2 ounces Parmesan or sharp white cheddar cheese, grated

2 tablespoons unsalted butter, softened

✦ Trim the Swiss chard of any browned bits or yellowing on the leaves, then pull the leaves away from the center stems. Wash the leaves and the ribs separately, then set each to dry on a clean kitchen towel. Finely slice the stems crosswise into ¼-inch wide pieces. Roughly chop the leaves.

✦ In a large nonreactive, ovenproof sauté pan over medium-high heat, heat the oil. Add the onion, garlic, and sliced chard stems and cook, stirring occasionally, until the chard is just tender, about 10 minutes.

✦ Reduce the heat to medium, then stir in the tomatoes, vinegar, anchovy paste, and salt and pepper to taste. Stir together well, then pile the chopped chard leaves over the top, cover the pan, and allow the leaves to steam until tender, 5 to 8 minutes.

✦ While the chard leaves are steaming, move an oven rack to the highest position and preheat the broiler.

✦ In a small bowl, mix together the panko, Parmesan, and butter. Add a pinch of salt and a few grinds of black pepper to taste.

✦ Uncover the pan and stir in the steamed chard until everything is nicely distributed. Everything in the pan should be tender by this point. Continue to cook a few minutes longer if necessary.

✦ Sprinkle the panko mixture thinly and evenly over the chard mixture, then pop the pan under the broiler and broil the topping until golden and crispy, 1 to 2 minutes. Serve immediately.

red cabbage with cambazola

CAMBAZOLA IS THE CHEESE THAT HAPPENS when super creamy French Camembert falls in love with tangy Italian Gorgonzola and they make a baby. Both the French and the Italians are pretty specific (not to say rigid) about such fromage frottage, so it's perhaps unsurprising that a German company makes and markets Cambazola. I'd say that makes it perfectly legit to pair this cheese with my adaptation of a German classic: braised red cabbage.

This dish is an ideal side for roasted or braised pork, or for simple bratwurst. Try it with the Pork Porterhouse with Apples, Sage, and Dijon-Bourbon Pan Sauce (page 281) or, if you want to go full-on Teutonic for a special occasion like Octoberfest, consider rounding out your meal with the German dumpling noodles called spaetzle and a stein of beer.

MAKES 4 TO 6 SERVINGS

8 ounces Cambazola, at room temperature

2 tablespoons unsalted butter

1 small red onion, halved and thinly sliced

1 medium (about 2½ pounds) red cabbage, cored and thinly sliced

1 Granny Smith apple, peeled, cored, and sliced

1½ teaspoons kosher salt

½ teaspoon freshly ground black pepper

½ cup water

¼ cup balsamic vinegar

¼ cup red wine

+ Trim the rind from the Cambazola. You should be left with about 6 ounce of Cambazola. Set aside.

+ Heat a very large nonreactive, ovenproof skillet over medium heat. Add the butter, and when it foams, add the onion. Sauté until the onion is translucent and starting to brown, about 5 minutes. Add the cabbage, apple, salt, and pepper and stir to combine.

+ Add the water, vinegar, and wine and cover the pan. Cook, stirring occasionally, until the cabbage softens, about 12 minutes. Remove the lid and cook uncovered, stirring frequently, until the cabbage is tender and the vinegar and wine have reduced to a syrup that clings to the cabbage, about 5 more minutes. Adjust the seasoning with salt and pepper to taste. Remove the skillet from the heat.

+ Move an oven rack to the top position and preheat the broiler. Break off dollops of Cambazola and drop them onto the hot braised cabbage. Transfer the skillet to the oven and broil until the Cambazola is beginning to melt and brown on top, about 2 minutes. Serve immediately, directly from the skillet.

simple crispy chicken with roasted lemon pan sauce

THE KEYS TO ACHIEVING SHATTERINGLY CRISP, delicious skin on a roast chicken are very dry skin, very high oven temperature, a preheated cast-iron skillet, and not trussing. I'm convinced that trussing—or, as I think of it, light poultry bondage—came about because of some Victorian-era holdover about the impropriety of food looking obscene. And it's true—an untrussed bird does splay its legs in a decidedly unladylike way. But that spread-eagle position allows more skin to get delectably crispy, and allows the thigh meat to roast more quickly and evenly.

Roasting a chicken at very high temperatures is a technique originally popularized by Barbara Kafka. Chicken eaters everywhere owe her a debt of gratitude. This technique works best if your oven is quite clean, or you may find your kitchen a bit smokier than you'd like.

MAKES 4 TO 6 SERVINGS

✦ Remove the giblets and neck from the chicken and reserve them for another use. Leave the chicken on a rack or clean kitchen towel set over a sheet pan or plate. Let the chicken come to room temperature for 1 hour—this makes a big difference in the even cooking of the bird.

✦ While the chicken is coming to room temperature, move an oven rack to the center-low position and preheat the oven to 500 degrees F.

✦ Pat the chicken very dry with a clean lint-free towel. The drier your bird, the crispier the skin, so don't skip this step. Heavily salt the chicken, inside and out.

✦ Stuff the thyme, sage, and garlic in the chicken cavity, and tuck the wing tips behind the chicken's back.

✦ Preheat a large cast-iron skillet over high heat. You want the skillet very hot, so let it preheat for 3 or 4 minutes, or until a few drops of water tossed on the skilled dance and evaporate immediately.

1 (4- to 5-pound) whole chicken

1 to 2 tablespoons kosher salt

A few sprigs fresh thyme and sage

A few cloves garlic

1 large lemon, quartered

1 rounded tablespoon all-purpose flour

1 cup chicken broth

Freshly ground black pepper

(continued)

+ Place the chicken breast-side up in the skillet, positioned so that, when you put the skillet in the oven, the legs and cavity of the chicken face the back of the oven. Let the chicken sear (don't move it!) for 2 minutes, then tuck the quartered lemon around the edges of the pan and immediately transfer the skillet to the preheated oven. Make sure the cavity of the chicken faces the back of the oven.

+ Roast the chicken for 10 to 11 minutes per pound. A 5-pound bird should take about 50 minutes. When the chicken is done, it will have a crisp, crackling, golden-brown skin and an instant-read thermometer inserted into the thickest part of the thigh will read 165 degrees F. Try not to peek and let all the hot air out of your oven.

+ When the chicken is fully cooked, transfer the skillet from the oven to the stovetop. Use a pair of tongs or a fork to tip the bird up so that all the juices that have pooled in the cavity run into the skillet. Pull the herbs from the chicken's cavity and add them to the skillet with the chicken juices and the roasted lemons. Set the chicken aside on a rack or plate in a warm spot to rest for 10 minutes while you make the pan sauce.

+ Turn the burner on medium-high heat and whisk the juices in the skillet so that they dissolve any caramelized chicken drippings. Add the flour to the drippings and whisk to a lump-free slurry. Add the chicken broth, whisk together, and bring to a simmer to thicken the pan sauce. Season with salt and pepper to taste, and, if you like a more lemony flavor, mash up the lemons into the sauce.

+ When the pan sauce tastes the way you like, strain it through a fine-mesh sieve and serve it alongside the roasted chicken.

NOTE: The chicken will be even better if you pre-salt it. If you manage to plan ahead enough, just salt the chicken inside and out very generously a day or two before cooking it and leave it uncovered in the refrigerator until cooking. This guarantees nice dry skin too. If you forget (I typically do), salting as described in the recipe makes for a perfectly scrumptious bird too.

pork porterhouse with apples, sage, and dijon-bourbon pan sauce

THE PORK PORTERHOUSE IS A BONE-IN, "T-Bone" cut equivalent that gives the lucky diner a section of both the pork loin and the pork tenderloin. For my money, it's one of the best cuts of meat on the planet, and one I am thrilled to indulge in occasionally. The trick with pork is not to overcook it—luckily, the days of shoe-leather pork are far behind us, and a trace of pink at the center of this chop is nothing to run screaming from. The pork porterhouse is a fast-cooking, tender cut well suited to this easy skillet preparation. I like to pair this with Red Cabbage with Cambazola (page 278) and spaetzle or mashed potatoes for a complete meal.

MAKES 4 SERVINGS

✦ To make the sauce, in a medium bowl, whisk the broth, bourbon, apple juice, mustard, maple syrup, and vinegar together. Set aside.

✦ In a very large cast-iron skillet over medium-high heat, heat 1 tablespoon of the lard until it shimmers. Add the onion and cook, stirring frequently, until it begins to brown, about 5 minutes. Add the apples and sage and continue to cook until the apples begin to brown and the onions are soft, about 5 more minutes.

✦ Scrape all the onions, apples, and sage into the bowl with the sauce ingredients and set aside while you cook the pork. If your skillet isn't well seasoned, some of the onions or apples might stick—if necessary, give the skillet a quick scrub, then return it to medium-high heat.

✦ Pat the pork chops very dry with a lint free towel and season generously with salt and pepper. Add the remaining 1 tablespoon lard to the skillet, and when it shimmers, add the pork chops to the pan. It's important that the pork chops not be crowded—each chop needs its own space; if necessary, cook the pork chops in batches. Sear the pork chops on the first side without moving them until they are deeply golden brown, about 4 minutes.

For the sauce:

½ cup chicken broth

¼ cup bourbon

¼ cup apple juice

2 tablespoons Dijon mustard

1 tablespoon maple syrup

1 tablespoon apple cider vinegar

2 tablespoons lard or vegetable oil, divided, plus more if needed

1 large yellow onion, cored and sliced into ¼-inch-thick slices

2 medium cooking apples, such as Granny Smith, cored and sliced ¼-inch thick

(continued)

Several sprigs fresh sage

4 (10-ounce) bone-in
   pork chops, at room
   temperature

Kosher salt and freshly
   ground black pepper

+ Flip the pork chops and sear on the second side for another 3 to 5 minutes. If the chops are quite thick, loosely set a lid on the skillet. This will allow steam to escape but trap a bit of heat around the chops, helping them to cook through more evenly.

+ When the chops are deeply caramelized on both sides and a thermometer inserted into the thickest part of the chop registers 145 to 150 degrees F, transfer the chops to a serving platter and let them rest for 5 minutes while you make the pan sauce.

+ With the skillet still over medium-high heat, quickly add the onions, apples, and sauce components to the hot skillet. The sauce will bubble up. Stir and cook the sauce until it thickens slightly and all the onions and apples are heated through, 2 to 3 minutes. Pour the pan sauce over the chops. Serve immediately.

roasted pears with caramel

ROASTED FRUIT? ABSOLUTELY! EVERYONE SHOULD HAVE a go-to dessert that's seasonally appropriate, inexpensive, takes about five minutes to throw together, and presents like it's something really fancy. This is one of those desserts. A simple mix of brown sugar, butter, and rum metamorphose in the roasting pan into the most delicious caramel ever. Bosc pears roast to tenderness without becoming mushy, but any firm pear will do. Serve these pears simply with their own caramel. Or add a scoop of vanilla ice cream, a slice of cake (see page 224), or a dollop of whipped cream.

MAKES 4 GENEROUS SERVINGS, OR MORE AS A TOPPING FOR ICE CREAM OR CAKE

✦ Move an oven rack to the center position and preheat the oven to 400 degrees F.

✦ Dot the butter around the bottom of a 9-by-13-inch baking dish. Sprinkle the butter with the brown sugar, ginger, and a small pinch of salt, then drizzle the rum and vanilla over. Mix everything together if it looks like the ginger, vanilla, or rum isn't evenly distributed.

✦ Arrange the pear halves, cut side down, in a single layer in the dish. Roast the pears until they are tender and a natural caramel has formed in the bottom of the pan, 30 to 40 minutes, stirring once halfway through roasting. (Don't worry if the caramel looks thin right out of the oven; it will thicken as it cools.)

✦ Let the pears cool for several minutes in the pan before transferring them to serving bowls. Top the pears with ice cream or whipped cream, and spoon the caramel sauce over the top. Serve warm.

4 tablespoons unsalted butter

½ cup lightly packed light brown sugar

¼ teaspoon ground ginger

2 tablespoons dark rum

1 teaspoon vanilla extract

Kosher salt

4 Bosc pears, peeled, cored, and halved

Vanilla ice cream or whipped cream, for serving (optional)

Preserving

vanilla-ginger-bourbon pear preserves

I LOVE GINGER WITH PEARS. I love bourbon with pears. I love vanilla with pears. Faced with a pile of pears and a decision-making disorder, I rolled the dice that all my favorites would play well together. I think they do, and this preserve has become one of my favorite sweets dolloped onto a bowl of Thick and Creamy Yogurt (page 132).

MAKES 5 HALF-PINT JARS

+ If this is your first time water-bath canning, please review the basics on page 25.

+ Prepare a water-bath canner, 5 half-pint jars, and their lids.

+ In a large, heavy, nonreactive wide pot, add the pears, sugars, ginger, bourbon, lemon juice and zest, vanilla bean, and salt. Bring the mixture to a boil over high heat, stirring frequently, until the preserves thicken and reduce, about 15 minutes.

+ When the preserves reach the gelling temperature (220 degrees F at sea level) and sheet when dropped from a spoon, reduce the heat to low and pick out the vanilla bean with a spoon or tongs.

+ Work quickly to ladle the preserves into the prepared hot jars, leaving ¼-inch headspace. Remove any air bubbles, wipe the jar rims, and set the jar lids according to the manufacturer's directions.

+ Carefully lower the filled jars into the simmering water-bath canner. When the water has returned to a boil, cover the kettle, and set a timer for 10 minutes. When jars have processed for 10 minutes, remove the canner from the heat and allow the jars to cool in the water for 5 minutes, then use a jar lifter to transfer the jars onto a clean kitchen towel to cool and set their seals.

(continued)

PROCESSING AT A GLANCE
Method: Water-bath canning
Headspace: ¼ inch
Processing time: 10 minutes in a boiling water-bath canner; adjust for altitude

5 pounds firm-ripe pears, peeled, cored, and roughly chopped (about 8 cups)

1 cup lightly packed light brown sugar

¾ cup granulated sugar

¼ cup chopped candied ginger

¼ cup bourbon

¼ cup freshly squeezed lemon juice

1 teaspoon lemon zest

1 whole vanilla bean, split lengthwise

Pinch of kosher salt

✦ Leave the jars alone until they have fully cooled—at least 8 but no more than 24 hours—then check the seals. Any jar that hasn't sealed should be refrigerated and used within 2 weeks. Jars with solid seals may be washed, labeled, and stored in a cool, dark place where they will keep for about 1 year.

NOTE: You can rinse the used vanilla bean, pat it dry, and add it to a bowl of sugar for a lovely vanilla-infused sugar.

coriander pickled beets

THE ORANGE AND CORIANDER ADD A nice spicy warmth to these pickled beets. They are great as a side-of-plate pickle and add lots of flavor to salads. In winter, try them as a topping on a simple green salad tossed with a citrus vinaigrette, crumbled goat cheese, and a few orange slices. They're also excellent in a salad with frisee, walnuts, and a fried egg.

MAKES 6 PINT JARS

+ If this is your first time water-bath canning, please review the basics on page 25.

+ Prepare a water-bath canner, 6 pint-size jars, and their lids.

+ Scrub the beets and trim any stem or skinny taproot. In a large pot, cover the beets with water and bring to a simmer over medium-high heat. Cook until the beets are just tender, about 25 minutes, depending on the size of the beets. Drain the beets and set aside until cool enough to handle. Rub off the skins of the beets with a clean kitchen rag (warning: it'll turn pink, so don't use an heirloom tea towel) or paper towels. Slice the beets into quarters or eighths, so that each section is a bite-size wedge.

+ In another large pot, combine the onion, garlic, vinegar, water, sugar, orange zest, coriander, mustard seeds, salt, peppercorns, chili flakes, ginger, and cloves. Stir well and bring the mixture to a simmer over medium-high heat. Maintain a gentle simmer for 5 minutes, then add the beets and simmer until the beets are hot throughout, about 15 minutes.

+ Working quickly, ladle the beets, onions, and liquid evenly into the prepared hot jars, leaving ½-inch headspace. Remove any air bubbles, adjust the headspace, wipe the jar rims, and set the jar lids according to the manufacturer's directions.

(continued)

PROCESSING AT A GLANCE

Method: Water-bath canning

Headspace: ½ inch

Processing time: 30 minutes in a boiling water-bath canner; adjust for altitude

---

4 pounds beets without greens

2 cups finely sliced red onion

2 cloves garlic, minced

3 cups apple cider vinegar

1 cup water

¾ cup sugar

2 tablespoons finely minced orange zest

2 tablespoons whole coriander seeds

1 tablespoon mustard seeds

1 tablespoon fine sea salt

½ teaspoon black peppercorns

½ teaspoon red chili flakes

¼ teaspoon ground ginger

2 whole cloves

✦ Carefully lower the filled jars into the simmering water-bath canner. When the water has returned to a boil, cover the kettle, and set a timer for 30 minutes. When the jars have processed for 30 minutes, remove the canner from the heat and allow the jars to cool in the water for 5 minutes, then use a jar lifter to transfer the jars onto a clean kitchen towel to cool and set their seals.

✦ Leave the jars alone until they have fully cooled—at least 8 but no more than 24 hours—then check the seals. Any jar that hasn't sealed should be refrigerated and used within 2 months. Jars with solid seals may be washed, labeled, and stored in a cool, dark place where they will keep for about 1 year.

fig preserves with thyme and balsamic vinegar

I'M A BIG FAN OF "FAKE FANCY" MEALS. By this I mean something that seems involved but really isn't. These fig preserves lend themselves beautifully to the creation of fake fancy meals. Take a simple bone-in chicken breast and slice a pocket into the meat. Stuff that pocket with a bit of these fig preserves and a spoonful of goat cheese or brie. Now bake the chicken. Voilà! Fake fancy stuffed roasted chicken. Or, mix these fig preserves with a bit of decent red wine and simmer. Now you've got a fake fancy fig wine glaze for pork, duck, beef, or venison. Only you will know how easy it was.

MAKES 4 HALF-PINT JARS

+ If this is your first time water-bath canning, please review the basics on page 25.

+ Trim any tough stems from the figs, then cut or tear the figs in half and place them in a large bowl. Add the vinegar, sugar, thyme, and pepper and stir to combine. Cover the bowl and refrigerate overnight.

+ The next day, prepare a water-bath canner, 4 half-pint jars, and their lids.

+ The figs should be surrounded by a dark syrup. Scrape the full contents of the bowl into a heavy saucepan and bring the figs to a simmer over medium heat. Stir frequently but gently to keep the figs from scorching without breaking up. Add the lemon juice, taste the preserves, and adjust the flavor with a bit more sugar or lemon juice, if needed.

+ Continue simmering, and when the preserves thicken slightly and look glossy, after about 15 minutes, turn the heat to low and ladle the figs into the prepared hot jars, leaving ¼-inch headspace. Remove any air bubbles, adjust the headspace, wipe the jar rims, and set the jar lids according to the manufacturer's directions. Turn off the heat.

PROCESSING AT A GLANCE
Method: Water-bath canning
Headspace: ¼ inch
Processing time: 10 minutes in a boiling water-bath canner; adjust for altitude

2 pounds fresh figs

¾ cup mild balsamic vinegar

½ cup lightly packed light brown sugar

1 teaspoon dried thyme

Pinch of freshly ground black pepper

2 tablespoons freshly squeezed lemon juice

(continued)

+ Carefully lower the filled jars into the simmering water-bath canner. When the water has returned to a boil, cover the kettle, and set a timer for 10 minutes. When the jars have processed for 10 minutes, remove the canner from the heat and allow the jars to cool in the water for 5 minutes, then use a jar lifter to transfer the jars onto a clean kitchen towel to cool and set their seals.

+ Leave the jars alone until they have fully cooled—at least 8 but no more than 24 hours—then check the seals. Any jar that hasn't sealed should be refrigerated and used within 2 weeks. Jars with solid seals may be washed, labeled, and stored in a cool, dark place where they will keep for about 1 year.

expanding the pantry with meats

Let's get right to the meat of the matter, so to speak. Man cannot live on jam and pickles alone, so if you eat meat, you might consider the advantages of learning to can it.

Pressure canning meat can seem a bit dodgy, both from a technical and a culinary perspective. Those tins of canned "roast beef" and "chicken breast" sold at the store don't exactly beg to be eaten, do they?

If you've never pressure canned your own meat, I'll just have to ask that you trust me on this: having shelf-stable, ready-to-heat meats in the pantry is the height of homemade omnivore convenience. Forget to take the meat out of the freezer to thaw? No problem. Haven't been to the market in three weeks? Your pantry has you covered. Need a fast grab-and-go lunch to take into the office? Done.

And, when made with a bit of care, pressure-canned meats are delicious, in the same way that a well-made stew or braise is delicious. The trick is selecting the right cut of meat for the jar. All pressure-canned meats are cooked at 240 degrees F or higher in a pressure canner for seventy-five minutes (for pints) or ninety minutes (for quarts). Seafood gets cooked even longer.

Not every cut of meat can stand up to that kind of intense cooking without turning tough and leathery. My attempts to pressure can chicken breast, for example, have never produced a product with a texture I was excited to eat. Some cuts of meat, on the other hand, actually require long cooking times to be at their best. These tend to be the inexpensive braising cuts like pork shoulder and beef chuck roast, and these cuts are what I focus on canning.

From a technical perspective, canning meat is extremely straightforward. I think it's easier than making jam or salsa. You do need the right equipment—a pressure canner with an accurate gauge—but the actual steps are easy as can be. (See Essential Equipment on page 32 for information on pressure-canning equipment.)

You can raw-pack or hot-pack meats. I've done both and generally prefer to raw pack because the product turns out more moist and it's a simpler process, but I will pre-sear meat to build flavor when the recipe benefits from it, as with the Short Ribs in Red Wine (page 301).

As a rule of thumb, a pound of meat will fill a pint jar and two pounds will fill a quart jar. When raw-packing, I find five pounds of prepared meat fills six pint jars. Buy a bit more than you need to account for extra fat that you'll trim off. Meat can be processed with just a bit of salt for the most versatility, or you can add spices or flavorful sauces to provide fast foundations for later meals.

heat-and-eat pork shoulder

WHEN I BUY PORK FROM A local farmer in the fall, I'll spend several hours trimming and pressure canning the pork shoulder. Sometimes I'll add different spices so that, after processing, I have several "flavors" (see page 299) of canned pork ready to go in my pantry. This takes a little pressure off my deep freezer, and at this time of year, it's overstuffed from a bountiful harvest and needs all the help it can get.

MAKES 6 PINT OR 3 QUART JARS

✦ If this is your first time pressure canning, please review the basics on page 32.

✦ Prepare a pressure canner, 6 widemouthed pint-size jars or 3 widemouthed quart-size jars, and their lids.

✦ Trim all excess fat from the pork, and cut the pork into large 1- to 2-inch cubes. In a large bowl, mix the pork with the salt.

✦ Use a slotted spoon or very clean hands to divide the meat cubes evenly between the scrupulously clean jars, leaving 1-inch headspace. You can pack them in quite firmly and finagle a bit to get an extra piece or two in the jar, because meat will shrink down as it cooks, but make sure you leave the full 1-inch headspace.

✦ Dampen a clean lint-free towel with hot water and a bit of vinegar (this helps cut through any grease on the jar), wipe the jar rims thoroughly, and set the lids and bands according to the manufacturer's directions.

(continued)

PROCESSING AT A GLANCE

Method: Pressure canning

Headspace: 1 inch

Processing time:
75 minutes for pint jars and 90 minutes for quart jars at 11 PSI; adjust for altitude

---

5½ pounds boneless, trimmed pork shoulder

2 tablespoons kosher salt

Distilled white vinegar

< Pictured: Ingredients for Pork and Mango in Caribbean Spices (page 300)

+ Double-check the water level in the pressure canner and adjust as necessary. Carefully lower the filled jars into the pressure canner. Fasten the canner lid securely, increase the heat to high, wait for a full stream of steam to vent from the vent pipe or petcock, and fully exhaust the canner for 10 minutes. After exhausting the canner, set a counterweight or weighted gauge on the vent pipe or close the petcock to bring the canner up to pressure. Follow the manufacturer's directions for regulating heat to maintain the correct pressure throughout the processing time.

+ Process pint jars for 75 minutes or quart jars for 90 minutes, then turn off the heat and allow the canner to naturally cool and completely depressurize.

+ After the canner has fully depressurized, open the pressure canner according to the manufacturer's directions, being careful of escaping steam. (I like to allow the jars to cool for 30 minutes in the canner after removing the weight from the vent pipe but before opening and unloading—I've found this cuts down on siphoning and leads to more reliable seals.)

+ Lift the jars straight up from the canner with a jar lifter and set them down on a clean kitchen towel to cool and set their seals. Let the jars cool undisturbed for at least 12 hours and up to 24. Any jar that hasn't sealed should be refrigerated and used within a few days. Jars with solid seals may be washed, labeled, and stored in a cool, dark place where they will keep for about 1 year.

pork shoulder variations

PORK CHILI VERDE

✦ Trim all excess fat from the pork, and cut the pork into large 1- to 2-inch cubes. Transfer to a large bowl.

✦ Preheat the broiler and broil the green chilies until the skins are blackened, turning several times to get a nice uniform char on all sides, 10 to 15 minutes. Transfer the broiled chilies to a small bowl, cover with plastic wrap, and set aside to allow the chilies to steam.

✦ Broil the tomatillos until browned in places, turning a few times to get caramelization on all sides, about 10 minutes. Do not blacken. Chop the tomatillos and set aside.

✦ In a wide saucepan over medium-high heat, heat the bacon fat. Add the onion and garlic and cook, stirring often, until the onions are golden. Add the cumin, oregano, salt, and coriander and stir the spices into the fat. Cook just until fragrant, about 1 minute. Add the vinegar, lime juice, and tomatillos. Stir together well, then add the tomatillo mixture to the pork.

4½ pounds boneless, trimmed pork shoulder

2 pounds fresh mild green chili peppers (Anaheim or poblano—add a few jalapeño or serrano for extra heat)

8 ounces tomatillos (about 10), husks removed

1 tablespoon bacon fat, lard, or extra-virgin olive oil

1 large yellow onion, chopped

8 large cloves garlic, chopped

1 tablespoon ground cumin

1 tablespoon dried oregano

1 tablespoon kosher salt

1 teaspoon ground coriander

2 tablespoons apple cider vinegar

2 tablespoons freshly squeezed lime juice

✦ Remove the green chilies from the bowl, pull off the stems (most of the seed cavity will come off with the stems), and flatten out the flesh of the chilies. Scrape the blackened skin and any remaining seeds from the flesh of the chilies. Roughly chop the chilies (you should have about 2 cups), then add them to the pork. Stir well.

✦ Divide the pork and sauce evenly between the clean jars, leaving 1-inch headspace. Proceed as directed on page 297. Process pint jars for 75 minutes or quart jars for 90 minutes.

(continued)

4½ pounds boneless, trimmed pork shoulder

3 large ripe mangoes, diced (about 4 cups)

6 cloves garlic, minced

½ cup apple cider vinegar

3 tablespoons lightly packed light brown sugar

1 tablespoon kosher salt

½ teaspoon allspice

½ teaspoon chipotle pepper powder

½ teaspoon freshly ground black pepper

½ teaspoon dried thyme

½ teaspoon ground ginger

⅛ teaspoon ground cloves

PORK AND MANGO IN CARIBBEAN SPICES

✦ Trim all excess fat from the pork, and cut the pork into large 1- to 2-inch cubes. Transfer to a large bowl. Add the remaining ingredients and stir together thoroughly.

✦ Divide the pork and sauce evenly between the clean jars, leaving 1-inch headspace. Proceed as directed on page 297. Process pint jars for 75 minutes and quart jars for 90 minutes.

5½ pounds boneless, trimmed pork shoulder

4 cloves garlic, minced

½ cup lightly packed light brown sugar

2 tablespoons smoked sweet paprika

1 tablespoon kosher salt

1 tablespoon mild chili powder

2 teaspoon ground cumin

1 to 2 teaspoons chipotle powder

1 teaspoon freshly ground black pepper

BARBECUE SPICED PORK

✦ Trim all excess fat from the pork, and cut the pork into large 1- to 2-inch cubes. Transfer to a large bowl. Add the remaining ingredients and stir together thoroughly.

✦ Divide the pork and sauce evenly between the clean jars, leaving 1-inch headspace. Proceed as directed on page 297. Process pint jars for 75 minutes and quart jars for 90 minutes.

short ribs in red wine

BEEF SHORT RIBS ARE AN INCREDIBLY rich cut that can stand up to the intensity of pressure canning. They are surrounded by a rich red wine broth in this recipe, which is a lot like beef bourguignon in a jar. If you like beef stew, I think you'll love this recipe.

MAKES 5 PINT OR 2 QUART JARS

+ If this is your first time pressure canning, please review the basics on page 32.

+ Prepare the pressure canner, 5 widemouthed pint-size jars or 2 widemouthed quart-size jars, and their lids.

+ Trim any excess fat from the short ribs and cut them into pieces that will comfortably fit in the jars. I like large strips about 2 by 3 inches. Pat the ribs dry and season generously with salt and pepper.

+ Heat a large, wide nonreactive pan over high heat. Add the lard, and when it shimmers, add enough rib pieces to fill the pan without crowding, cooking in batches as needed. Sear the meat until it is caramelized on all sides.

+ Pour off any excess fat from the pan, then reduce the heat to medium and add the onion, garlic, wine, broth, tomato paste, bay leaves, thyme and rosemary, scraping to dissolve any brown bits at the bottom of the pan. Bring the sauce to a simmer. Maintain a gentle simmer and cook until the sauce is reduced by half, about 30 minutes. Strain the sauce through a fine-mesh sieve and keep hot.

+ Pack the prepared jars with the short ribs, leaving 1-inch headspace. Fill the jars with the red wine sauce, leaving 1-inch headspace. Remove any air bubbles and adjust the headspace.

(continued)

PROCESSING AT A GLANCE

Method: Pressure canning

Headspace: 1 inch

Processing time:
75 minutes for pint jars or 90 minutes for quart jars at 11 PSI; adjust for altitude

---

5 pounds boneless thick-cut beef short ribs, very well chilled

Kosher salt and freshly ground black pepper

2 tablespoons lard, bacon fat, or mild-flavored vegetable oil

1 medium yellow onion, finely sliced

2 cloves garlic, minced

1 (750-milliliter) bottle dry red wine

4 cups beef broth

1 tablespoon tomato paste

2 bay leaves

5 sprigs fresh thyme

1 sprig fresh rosemary

Distilled white vinegar

✦ Dampen a clean lint-free towel with hot water and a bit of vinegar (this helps cut through any grease on the jar), wipe the jar rims thoroughly, and set the lids and bands according to the manufacturer's directions.

✦ Double-check the water level in the pressure canner and adjust as necessary. Carefully load the filled jars into the pressure canner. Fasten the canner lid securely, increase the heat to high, wait for a full stream of steam to vent from the vent pipe or petcock, and fully exhaust the canner for 10 minutes. After exhausting the canner, set a counterweight or weighted gauge on the vent pipe or close the petcock to bring the canner up to pressure. Follow the manufacturer's directions for regulating heat to maintain the correct pressure throughout the processing time.

✦ Process pint jars for 75 minutes or quart jars 90 minutes, then turn off the heat and allow the canner to naturally cool and completely depressurize.

✦ After the canner has fully depressurized, open the pressure canner according to the manufacturer's directions, being careful of escaping steam. (I like to allow my jars to cool for 30 minutes or so in the canner after removing the weight from the vent pipe but before opening and unloading—I've found this cuts down on siphoning and leads to more reliable seals.)

✦ Lift the jars straight up from the canner with a jar lifter and set them down on a clean kitchen towel to cool and set their seals. Let the jars cool undisturbed for at least 12 hours and up to 24. Any jar that hasn't sealed should be refrigerated and used within a few days. Jars with solid seals may be washed, labeled, and stored in a cool, dark place where they will keep for about 1 year.

smoky hot pepper sauce

FELLOW BLOGGER SARAH RUNS A GREAT website devoted to traditional fermentation called Attack of the Killer Pickles. Her Killer Hot Sauce is one of my favorites. She adds dried tomatoes and chipotle peppers to her mix of fresh peppers and spices, and this adds a little smoky-sweetness and body to the sauce that I really like. This sauce was inspired by a desire to bring together my favorite aspects of Sarah's hot sauce and Sriracha, the popular Thai hot chili sauce I can't live without. My favorite fast meal is a plate of fried eggs topped—almost frosted—with this hot sauce.

MAKES ABOUT 1 QUART JAR

+ If this is your first time fermenting vegetables, please review the basics on page 41. Prepare 1 widemouth quart-size jar, its lids, and a fermenting weight.

+ In a small bowl, soak the sundried tomatoes and chipotles in ½ cup warm water. Set aside to allow them to rehydrate for 30 minutes.

+ Trim all the peppers of their stems but leave the green stem caps in place. (This adds a nice earthy flavor.) Add them to the bowl of a food processor fitted with a metal blade. Add the rehydrated tomatoes and chipotles plus any soaking liquid, the garlic, sugar, and salt and process until the mixture is finely chopped to a paste, scraping down the bowl as necessary.

+ Scrape the chopped peppers into a scrupulously clean quart jar. With a clean spoon, press the ingredients down to release some of the juices. Do your best to press the solid ingredients under the liquid and weight the ferment.

(continued)

½ cup chopped sundried tomatoes

3 dried chipotle peppers, stemmed, seeded, and chopped

1 pound red Fresno peppers

½ pound red jalapeño peppers (for medium hot sauce) or red serrano peppers (for spicier hot sauce) (optional)

1 to 2 cayenne, Thai chili, or other super hot pepper (optional, for a very spicy sauce)

12 cloves garlic

2 tablespoons sugar

2 teaspoons fine sea salt

½ cup distilled white vinegar

½ cup water

✦ Loosely seal the jars with standard 2-piece lids, leaving the ring just fingertip tight, as you would for canning, to allow the gases of the fermentation process to escape. Leave the pepper puree at cool room temperature out of direct sunlight for 2 to 4 days. Check the ferment daily. Look for bubbles and other signs of fermentation, and burp the lid to release any pent-up carbon dioxide in the jar.

✦ Taste the ferment daily and when the mixture tastes good to you, transfer it and all the juices from the fermentation jar to a blender. Add the vinegar and water and puree until the pepper sauce is smooth. If necessary, puree the sauce in batches. If you like a very smooth sauce, strain through a fine-mesh sieve.

✦ Adjust the seasoning as desired with a bit more vinegar or sugar, then bottle and refrigerate. The sauce keeps for at least 4 months in the refrigerator.

sauerkraut with apples and caraway

IF YOU COULD COUNT ALL THE grandmas from Germany to Korea and every place in between, you'd have a good approximation of the number of ways you can ferment cabbage. From sauerkraut to kimchi, cabbage just takes to fermenting well. I love this version of a traditional caraway-studded kraut, given a little twist with juicy apples. I eat this raw as a salad, or I warm it slightly and serve it alongside sausages.

MAKES ABOUT ½ GALLON

+ If this is your first time fermenting vegetables, please review the basics on page 41.

+ Prepare 1 half-gallon or 2 quart-size jars, their lids, and a fermenting weight.

+ Peel off a few clean large outer leaves of cabbage and reserve. Quarter, core, and finely shred the remaining cabbage. You should have about 4 pounds cabbage after shredding. Add the cabbage to a very large nonreactive bowl. Add the salt and 1 tablespoon of the caraway seeds, or a bit more if you really like caraway.

+ Make sure your hands are squeaky clean and squeeze, pound, and massage the salt into the cabbage. You don't have to be gentle with this; if you have any pent-up frustrations from your day, take them out on the cabbage. Lightly cover the cabbage with a clean lint-free towel and set aside for 30 minutes.

+ After about 30 minutes, the cabbage should be sitting in a small pool of liquid. This is exactly what you want. Peel, quarter, core, and finely slice the apples. Add the apples to the cabbage and gently toss together to distribute the apple.

1 large head green cabbage (about 4½ pounds)

3 tablespoons fine sea salt

1 to 2 tablespoons caraway seeds

2 large firm cooking apples, such as Granny Smith

(continued)

✦ Pack the cabbage mixture into the prepared jar firmly. If you are using 2 jars, divide both the cabbage and liquid evenly between the jars. Use your clean fist or a tamper like a cocktail muddler to press down on the cabbage and compress it, but be careful not to tamp so hard you shatter the jar (I've done that, and it really harshes your fermentation groove). The liquid should rise up even with or above the level of the shredded cabbage.

✦ Make sure all the shredded cabbage is tucked down under the liquid, then add 1 or 2 of the reserved leaves to the top of the ferment, trimming if necessary to get it to just fit the jar. The cabbage leaf will hold down little pieces that would rise up to the surface of the ferment.

✦ Weight the ferment well so that everything, including the top cabbage leaf, is under the brine. Cover the jar lightly and ferment for at least 3 days at cool room temperature, out of direct sunlight. Vent the lid as necessary to prevent pressure from building up in the jar, and skim off any white scum that develops on the brine.

✦ Opinions vary greatly as to how long sauerkraut should ferment. I've enjoyed fresh, crispy, tangy sauerkraut at 3 to 4 days, and still enjoyed it 1 month later when it softens and takes on a sharper tang but also the greater complexity of age. Taste frequently throughout the fermentation and when the sauerkraut tastes good to you, remove the weight, lid the kraut, and move it to the refrigerator, where it will keep for at least 6 months.

Home Care

liquid laundry detergent

I RESISTED DIY LAUNDRY DETERGENT for a long time. I'm not sure why, but I just couldn't quite believe that anything but the full power of industry was strong enough to get my kid's clothing clean. As it turns out, DIY laundry detergent is every bit as capable of getting out the dirt as the commercial stuff, and it's far, far less expensive.

As I write this in late 2014, the cost to make a batch of this soap is $3.32, including $1.21 for the essential oils, which are optional. That's about 3 cents per load. National brands typically cost from 18 to 30 cents per load, so the long-term savings on DIY detergent can really add up. This is also a quick project that doesn't need to be done very often—even if you do five loads of laundry a week, a batch of this detergent will last about six months. This low-suds formula is suitable for top- or front-loading washing machines.

MAKES ABOUT 3 GALLONS

✦ In a large saucepan over medium heat, bring 8 cups of the water to a bare simmer. Meanwhile, grate the soap with a box grater or in a food processor fitted with the grating blade. It will look a bit like shredded cheese.

✦ Sprinkle the grated soap into the barely simmering water and whisk the soap until it melts. Add the borax and washing soda and whisk until all the components are dissolved and no grittiness remains on the bottom of the pot. You may whisk up a head of foam while doing this—don't worry, it will settle back into the detergent in time.

✦ Add the remaining 2 gallons water to a large, clean bucket (I use a 5-gallon bucket fitted with a twist-off lid). Pour the warm soap mixture into the bucket and stir to combine. At this point the detergent will have a texture like thin dish soap.

✦ Add the essential oils and give the detergent one final good stir, then set it aside to cool and cure for 24 hours.

2½ gallons cool water, divided

1 bar Fels-Naptha soap (see note)

1 cup borax

1 cup washing soda

20 drops sweet orange essential oil

20 drops lemongrass essential oil

20 drops tea tree essential oil

(continued)

+ After 24 hours, the detergent will have thickened considerably and will have a firm gel-like texture. This is normal. If the mixture looks like bits of gel floating in thinner liquid, that's fine too.

+ Using an immersion blender, blend the soap gel. Make sure to blend all the way down to the bottom of the bucket to puree all of the gel. It might take a few minutes, but the gel will emulsify into a creamy white, easily pourable liquid that will dissolve and clean beautifully.

+ For easy use, transfer about 4 cups of this detergent to a 1-quart mason jar fitted with a flip-top, plastic pour lid, and refill from the bucket of detergent as necessary.

To use:

+ As a stain pretreatment, rub a little bit of the detergent directly on the stain.

+ As a laundry detergent, add ⅓ cup of the detergent to your washing machine according to the manufacturer's directions.

NOTE: Fels Naptha is a low-sudsing, laundry-specific bar soap. If desired, you can use a different bar soap in this recipe, but the texture of the final product will vary with different soap formulations. Look for a soap that's low-sudsing to keep this detergent appropriate for modern high-efficiency washing machines.

If, over time, your detergent begins to re-gel, just shake it up or reblend as necessary to get that pourable, creamy texture back. (Or don't—the detergent will work perfectly fine if it's clumpy and gelled, and will never re-gel as firmly as after that initial cure.)

nontoxic laundry softener

I'M A LITTLE EMBARRASSED TO INCLUDE something as simple as this recipe in a book, but the plethora of laundry softeners available at every megamart, drugstore, and supermarket has forced my hand. Liquid fabric softener and dryer sheets are some of the biggest offenders when it comes to icky chemicals in our home. Both work by depositing a thin layer of lubricating chemicals on the fabric of clothing. These lubricants are packaged with artificial fragrances and preservatives, and all that stuff goes right against your skin when you wear your clothing.

You know what works just as well to smooth natural fabric fibers and reduce static cling? Plain ol' vinegar. Vinegar added to the rinse cycle softens clothing and helps to remove any residual detergent from clothing. It also helps prevent build up of soap scum and scale in your laundry machine.

MAKES 1 GALLON

+ Open the bottle of vinegar. If you want a scented laundry softener, add the essential oils of your choice to the vinegar right in the bottle. Lid the bottle and shake to combine. The laundry softener will last indefinitely, though the essential oil scent may fade over time.

1 gallon distilled white vinegar

1 to 2 tablespoons essential oil (optional)

To use:

+ If you've added essential oils to your vinegar, shake the vinegar bottle well to distribute the oils before each use. Add ¼ to ½ cup of the laundry softener to the fabric softener or rinse cycle compartment of your washing machine. If your machine does not have a fabric softener or rinse cycle compartment (top loaders frequently don't) just add the fabric softener to the machine when the rinse cycle begins. Scale the amount of softener you use to the size of your laundry load.

air freshener

IF YOU WERE TO MAKE A list of the household care products most likely to foul up your indoor air quality and poison your home with chemical pollutants, anything specifically designed to *linger in the air* would top that list. Those scent-releasing plug-in candles? Terrible. Spray air fresheners? Horrible. Fabric "refreshers"? I'm not sure what's so refreshing about products that contain chemicals linked to developmental and reproductive disorders, but okay.

A good basic cleaning routine should keep your home smelling inoffensive, but when you want to bring a specific scent to your home, turn to essential oils.

MAKES ABOUT ½ CUP

6 tablespoons water

2 tablespoons vodka

30 to 60 drops essential oils
(see page 89 for some of
my favorite blends)

+ In a 4- to 8-ounce spray bottle, combine the water, vodka, and essential oils. Lid tightly and shake to combine. The freshener will last indefinitely, though the essential oil scent may fade over time.

To use:

+ Shake the spray bottle well, then spray the freshener into the air, around furniture, or on rugs. Don't saturate fabrics, just mist.

Personal Care

almost-traditional castile soap

CASTILE IS A REGION IN SPAIN, and traditionally castile bar soap is made with 100 percent olive oil. An all–olive oil soap is an exercise in patience: the soap takes a long time to cure but gets better with age. Modern castile soaps are often blended with other vegetable-based oils to create a slightly more balanced, economical, and faster-to-cure bar of soap with better lather than you get with 100 percent versions.

Let this soap set for 48 hours after pouring, and cure for at least 4 weeks after cutting—8 to 12 weeks is better. I like using herbal scents here, like thyme or rosemary.

MAKES ABOUT 1½ POUNDS AFTER CURING

9 ounces cold water

3.3 ounces pure granular lye

16.8 ounces olive oil

6 ounces coconut oil

1.2 ounces sweet almond oil

1 to 2 teaspoons essential oils (optional)

+ Before you begin, read the basic steps of soap making and all safety information and notes on page 92. Empty your sink if necessary, get on your protective gear (eye goggles, gloves, long sleeves, etc.), and make sure kids, pets, and other trip hazards are out of your workspace. Prepare a 2-pound soap mold.

+ In a heat-resistant pitcher, add the water. Set the pitcher in the sink. In a small stainless steel bowl, precisely measure the lye. Carefully add the lye to the water. *(Never add water to lye!)* The water will become cloudy and will get quite hot. It may even "smoke" a bit—this is normal. Do not breathe the fumes from this reaction. Stir with an old plastic or stainless steel spoon, or disposable wooden chopsticks, to fully dissolve the lye, then let the lye solution sit to cool while you melt the oils.

+ In a large stainless steel pot over medium heat, carefully add the oils. Warm them slowly together, stirring occasionally until just melted. Remove the oil mixture from the heat and set aside to cool.

+ When the lye and the oils are both around 100 degrees F—anything from about 90 to 105 degrees F is fine, but the lye and the oil should be within about 10 degrees F of each other—set the pot in the sink and carefully pour the lye solution into the oil. *(Never add the oil to the lye!)*

✦ Stir the mixture gently with an immersion blender (not turned on) to help bring the oils and lye together, then turn the immersion blender on the lowest speed. Blend the soap thoroughly, moving the blender around the pot, until the mixture thickens and achieves trace, 15 to 25 minutes. This soap will take a bit longer to reach trace than a soap with a higher percentage of hard fats.

✦ Add any essential oils as desired, blend to fully incorporate, then pour and scrape the soap into the prepared mold. Cover the soap with a layer of plastic wrap, then insulate or chill soap as desired, to achieve a fully gelled or a no-gel soap.

✦ Leave your protective gear on and clean your soap-making equipment and work area very well. Finish cleanup by lightly wiping down anything that may have come in contact with lye with undiluted vinegar.

✦ After 48 hours, check the soap. Put on a pair of disposable gloves and give the soap a gentle press to see if it easily pulls away from the edges of the mold. If the soap is firm, turn the soap out of the mold. If not, give the soap another 12 to 24 hours to cure in the mold before turning out.

✦ If necessary, slice the soap into bars. Set the soap in a cool, out-of-the-way place on a wire rack. Cover it loosely with a lint-free cloth, and turn the soap periodically. Cure for at least 4 weeks before using, and longer if possible.

To use:

✦ Use at the sink or in the shower for cleaning of hands or body.

refreshing peppermint foot scrub

Fall

WHEN YOUR FEET HAVE GIVEN THEIR all over a long day, give a little back with this hard-core invigorating scrub. Sugar and Epsom salts buff off rough skin, natural oils hydrate, and peppermint and eucalyptus add a soothing, cooling feeling, while tea tree lends a bit of natural antifungal protection to your feet.

MAKES ABOUT 2 CUPS

1 cup sugar

1 cup Epsom salts

¼ cup coconut oil, melted

¼ cup sweet almond oil

20 drops peppermint
essential oil

10 drops tea tree essential oil

10 drops eucalyptus
essential oil

✦ In a medium bowl, add the sugar, Epsom salts, coconut oil, and sweet almond oil, and stir to combine. The texture should be firm but scoopable. If the scrub seems a bit too thin or oily, you can add a little more sugar or Epsom salts. If it's too thick, add another tablespoon of sweet almond oil.

✦ Stir in the essential oils, or other essential oils of your choice, and transfer the scrub to a widemouthed airtight jar, like a 1-liter wire-bail glass storage jar. The scrub will last for at least 6 months, though the essential oil scent may fade over time.

To use:

✦ In the bath or shower, scoop about ¼ cup of the scrub into your hands or a washcloth and rub firmly all over your feet, elbows, knees, or other areas of dry skin. Avoid delicate facial and décolletage skin with this exfoliant scrub. After scrubbing away dry skin, rinse well with warm water. Exercise caution anytime you use an oil-containing product in the bath or shower—no slipping, please!

styling wax for him or her

HAIR-STYLING WAX IS AN EASY PERSONAL CARE DIY. Guys are generally more familiar with styling wax then woman, but this styling aid is great for short-haired folks of any gender. I wear my hair pretty short for a woman, and this is just right for creating some nice chunkiness without adding much weight to hair or losing movement. Use whatever essential oils you like, or try my "his" and "hers" essential oil blends for classically masculine and feminine scents.

MAKES ABOUT 2 OUNCES

+ Melt the beeswax, oil, and shea butter in a double boiler, or in a microwave at medium power, until the beeswax is just melted. Allow the mixture to cool slightly, then add the essential oil blend of your choice, or other essential oils, and stir to combine. Pour the liquid wax into a widemouthed 2-ounce tin and allow it to cool completely. The wax will last for at least 6 months, though the essential oil scent may fade over time.

To use:

+ Rub a very small amount of the wax between your fingertips to soften, then apply to dry hair. Work from the back of the head forward, smooth the wax along the underside of the hair to boost volume, twist hair strands together for chunkiness, or rub over hair lightly for a tousled look.

¾ ounce beeswax

¾ ounce coconut oil

½ ounce shea butter

Additions for him:

12 drops fir essential oil

8 drops sweet orange essential oil

8 drops bergamot essential oil

3 drops clove essential oil

Additions for her:

10 drops ylang-ylang essential oil

8 drops sweet orange essential oil

3 drops bergamot essential oil

muscle-soothing eucalyptus bath soak

EPSOM SALTS ARE ONE OF THOSE old lady folk remedies that really work. Think of them like Chicken Soup for Your Muscles. Epsom salts are pure magnesium sulfate, and soaking in an Epsom salt bath has been clinically shown to increase both magnesium and sulfate levels in the body.

I use this bath soak regularly to soothe tired muscles, reduce surface inflammation from bumps and bruises, and relax away soreness. This blend is particularly useful after a hard workout, hike, or long day in the garden. Two cups of Epsom salts in a standard-size tub provides the right dilution for the benefits of magnesium sulfate absorption through the skin. If you have a big soaking tub, you might want to double the amount of the soak you use. Thankfully, Epsom salts are inexpensive, so it's easy to be generous with this bath soak.

I like the refreshing addition of eucalyptus here—I find it encourages deep breathing and a kind of spa-therapy vibe in the tub, but use whatever essential oils or blend you love.

MAKES ENOUGH FOR 1 SOAK

+ In a medium bowl, blend all the ingredients together. Add the bath soak directly to a hot bath, or store it in an airtight container for later use. The bath soak will last indefinitely, though the essential oil scent may fade over time.

1 cup Epsom salts

½ cup baking soda

20 drops eucalyptus essential oil

To use:

+ Add the bath soak to hot water and soak for 15 to 30 minutes.

Winter

Cooking

THOUGHTS ON COMFORT FOOD

When the weather turns cold, something in me cries out for fat. Rich cuts of meat; long, slow braises; and vegetables bathed in heavy cream offer a happy insulation through the gray chill of winter.

Some foods seem to be almost universally welcoming, soothing, and (dare I say it?) comforting. These are dishes that invoke the feelings of a hearth and a roaring fire, there to tell us that we are safe at home and among friends and family after a hard day of plowing the fields or the cubicle rows. There's something visceral about these comfort foods. They have the same sort of gut appeal that a crackling, warm fire in the hearth possesses. Perhaps this is because so many of these foods come from that same slow, patient place as the fire itself.

These are the stews and roasts that we can picture, turning over the logs on a wrought-iron spit or hanging over the flames in an ancient cauldron, emitting aromas of caramelizing juices and warm, just slightly exotic spices.

The soups, stews, and braises of this time of year warm the body, while lengthy cooking methods help warm the home. Even though most of us have long since abandoned actual cooking hearths in favor of ovens and ranges, there is something deep in our cultural evolution that makes a simmering pot of something rich and savory appealing during the deep cold.

These kinds of meals are eminently practical too—they may take several hours to cook, but for nearly all of this time they fend for themselves. Meals that cook slow always reheat well too and are usually better after a night in the refrigerator. The food we simmer and braise and stew is, with hardly an exception, cheap food. It is the tough and the overlooked and the humble that we coax to glorious succulence through time and a bit of love.

You cannot rush slow cooking. You must let the meat, or the vegetables, or the soup relax into tenderness. If you poke and prod and hurry a braise along, your poor meal is apt to get all tense and dry and nervous. Far better to embrace the slowness of the season and let dinner come along in its own time.

onion soup gratiné

I NEVER MAKE THIS SOUP FROM scratch. It's an assembly thing—pull out the caramelized onions, crack open the home-canned beef broth, fiddle with the flavor, top with toasted baguette and lots of cheese, et voilà! Having the onions ready to go in half-pint jars makes this an easy recipe to scale up in quantity too. If you want to go start-to-finish on this soup some lazy winter Sunday, just make Caramelized Onions (page 354), measure out four cups, and proceed from there.

MAKES 6 SERVINGS

✦ In a large, heavy stockpot set over medium heat, melt the butter. When the butter foams, add the flour and stir to make a paste. When no lumps remain, whisk in 1 cup of the beef broth and stir until the paste is fully incorporated. Add the remaining 5 cups beef broth, onions, thyme, and bay leaf and bring the soup to a bare simmer. Add the sherry and maintain a bare simmer for 15 minutes to allow the flavors to meld.

✦ Meanwhile, move an oven rack to the highest position and preheat the broiler. Lay the baguette slices on a sheet pan, and broil until uniformly brown and toasty, about 3 minutes. Flip the slices over and broil the other sides, 2 to 3 minutes more. Set the baguette slices aside, but leave the broiler on—you'll need it for the final step in assembling the soup.

✦ Season the soup with salt and pepper to taste, and—if the soup needs a bit of brightening—a few drops of red wine vinegar.

✦ Set 6 ovenproof bowls on a sturdy sheet pan. Divide the soup among the bowls, then float 2 toasted baguette slices in each bowl. Divide the cheeses equally between the bowls, then carefully slide the sheet pan under the broiler. Broil until the cheese is melted, bubbly, and browning. Serve the soup immediately.

2 tablespoons unsalted butter

2 tablespoons all-purpose flour

6 cups rich beef broth

4 cups Caramelized Onions (page 354)

2 sprigs fresh thyme

1 bay leaf

½ cup dry sherry

Baguette, cut into 12 slices

Kosher salt and freshly ground black pepper

Red wine vinegar (optional)

8 ounces grated Gruyère cheese

2 ounces grated Parmesan cheese

warm french lentils with celeriac and hazelnuts

WHEN I WAS A KID, MY parents used to make a totally delicious side dish called Hot German Potato Salad. It was a mass of boiled potatoes smothered in a tangy, creamy dressing and studded through with lots of bacon and celery. For some reason, it was always served with a teardrop-shaped sausage called Polish kielbasa that was made by a company in Chicago. This was before the fat-free craze hit, obviously.

Despite the total lack of pork products in this lentil dish, there's something about it that reminds me of that Hot German Potato Salad. The lentils have a similar warm, filling starchiness and the celery root adds the right earthiness. So, as strange as it is to say about lentils, this recipe takes me back to my childhood. No geographically tenuous sausage required.

MAKES 4 SERVINGS

1 cup French lentils (Green Le Puy or Black Beluga lentils)

2 tablespoons unsalted butter

1 large celery root (about 1½ pounds), trimmed and cut into ½-inch dice

1 shallot, thinly sliced

2 tablespoons extra-virgin olive oil

2 tablespoons red wine vinegar

1 tablespoon freshly squeezed lemon juice

2 teaspoons Dijon mustard

1 large bunch fresh parsley, leaves and tender stems chopped, plus more for garnish

½ cup chopped hazelnuts

+ Bring a large pot of heavily salted water to a boil over high heat. Add the lentils, then reduce the heat to maintain a gentle simmer and simmer the lentils until tender, 30 to 40 minutes. Drain the lentils very well and set them aside.

+ Meanwhile, in a large skillet over medium heat, melt the butter. When the butter foams, add the celeriac and cook, stirring occasionally, until the celeriac is soft and caramelized, about 20 minutes. When the celeriac is nearly cooked through, add the shallot to the pan and continue cooking until both the shallot and celeriac are tender.

+ Reduce the heat to low, add the lentils to the skillet and stir to combine. In a small bowl, whisk together the oil, vinegar, lemon juice, and mustard. Add the vinaigrette to the skillet and stir to combine. Add the parsley and hazelnuts and stir just to incorporate, then scrape the lentils into a serving dish and top with additional parsley.

indian creamed spinach

MY AT-HOME COOKING OFTEN INCORPORATES THE flavors and spices I love from Indian cuisine, but I wouldn't call it authentic. This is my take on Indian Saag—highly spiced, rich, and creamy. Pair the spinach with basmati rice and lentils or yogurt-marinated salmon.

MAKES 4 SERVINGS AS A SIDE

2 pounds spinach, trimmed, or a blend of spinach and other tender greens, such as chard, mustard, arugula, or tender kale

2 tablespoons extra-virgin olive oil

1 large onion, finely chopped

4 cloves garlic, minced

1 tablespoon minced fresh ginger

1 tablespoon mustard seeds

1 teaspoon ground cumin

1 teaspoon kosher salt

½ teaspoon ground fenugreek

½ teaspoon ground turmeric

⅛ teaspoon ground cardamom

1 cup drained chopped canned tomatoes

½ cup heavy cream

Zest of 1 lemon

✦ Add about 1 inch of water to a big, wide pot and bring to a boil over medium heat. Add the spinach, cover, and steam until the greens are tender, 3 to 4 minutes. Transfer the spinach to a colander and squeeze out as much liquid as possible. Coarsely chop the spinach. (You should have about 2 cups of cooked spinach.) Set aside.

✦ In a large skillet over medium-high heat, heat the oil. When the oil shimmers, add the onion and cook, stirring frequently, until it browns and softens, about 5 minutes.

✦ Add the garlic, ginger, mustard seeds, cumin, salt, fenugreek, turmeric, and cardamom to the skillet and cook, stirring, until the spices are toasty and fragrant, about 30 seconds. Add the tomatoes, cream, and lemon zest and stir well. Bring the sauce to a simmer, add the spinach, and lower the heat to maintain a bare simmer. Stirring frequently, cook until the sauce thickens and the flavors meld, about 15 minutes. Serve immediately.

green cabbage with slab bacon, pasta, and mustard cream

THIS SIMPLE SAUTÉ IS A GREAT recipe for using up leftover cooked pasta. It comes together in minutes from pantry staples but tastes like the ultimate comfort food. I like a short, curled, forkable pasta in this application, like fusilli, gemelli, or cavatelli. Penne is fine too.

MAKES 4 SERVINGS

+ In a large pot of boiling salted water, cook the pasta to al dente, then drain well.

+ In a very large skillet over medium heat, cook the bacon, stirring occasionally, until the bacon renders its fat and crisps, about 7 minutes. When the bacon is nicely browned, add the garlic and cook until fragrant, about 2 minutes. Add the cabbage and cook, stirring occasionally, until the cabbage is browned in places and just tender, about 5 minutes.

+ Add the cream, water, and mustard to the skillet and sprinkle the nutmeg over the cabbage. Stir well to incorporate the mustard. Add the pasta and cook, stirring frequently, until the pasta is heated through and tender and the sauce has reduced to coat the pasta and cabbage, 5 to 7 minutes. Season with salt and pepper to taste and serve immediately.

NOTE: Use a Microplane to grate a fine dusting of nutmeg from a whole nutmeg for the freshest flavor.

4 cups pasta

6 ounces slab or thick-cut bacon, cut into lardons

2 cloves garlic, minced

1 small head green cabbage (about 2 pounds), cored and finely shredded

¼ cup heavy cream

¼ cup water

2 tablespoons mild whole grain mustard

Pinch of freshly grated nutmeg (see note)

Kosher salt and freshly ground black pepper

braised pork cheeks with plum jam and star anise

THE CHEEK GETS MY VOTE FOR most overlooked meat cut. From pork, beef, or even lamb, the cheek makes an incredible braising cut. These odd little pucks of muscle are transformed into pure succulence when slow cooked. If your local butcher doesn't offer pork cheek, cubed pork shoulder is a good substitute.

Braises like this are very flexible and do well with fruity jams. Beef, venison, lamb, and other red meats pair nicely with the dark berries (blackberries, huckleberries, etc.); chicken and pork do well with stone fruits and apples. Play around with using some of your own homemade jam in savory applications like this. Serve this dish with something starchy to soak up the delicious braising liquid.

MAKES 4 SERVINGS

+ Move an oven rack to the center position and preheat the oven to 325 degrees F.

+ Pat the pork cheeks dry and season generously with salt and pepper. In a large cast-iron skillet with a lid or a Dutch oven set over medium-high heat, heat the oil. When the oil shimmers, add the pork cheeks and sear on each side until deeply golden brown, 2 to 3 minutes. If all the cheeks don't fit without crowding, sear in batches. Set aside.

+ Add additional oil to the pan if necessary and add the onion and garlic. Scrape up any brown bits from the pork stuck to the bottom of the pan and mix them in with the onions. Cook until the onions are beginning to brown, 3 to 5 minutes. Add the broth and soy sauce to the skillet and stir to deglaze. Add the jam to the skillet. Use a vegetable peeler to zest 4 or 5 long strips of orange peel (no pith) and drop the peel into the skillet, then cut the orange in half and squeeze in the juice. Add the star anise pods, stir well to combine, and bring the sauce to a simmer.

(continued)

2 pounds pork cheeks (8 to 12 cheeks)

Kosher salt and freshly ground black pepper

2 tablespoons extra-virgin olive oil, plus more for as needed

1 large onion, peeled, cored and thinly sliced

4 garlic cloves, minced

1 cup chicken broth

¼ cup soy sauce

½ cup plum jam, jelly, or preserves

1 large orange

4 star anise pods

+ Add the pork cheeks back to the skillet. Bring the liquid up to a gentle simmer, then cover the skillet and transfer the braise to the oven. Cook until the pork cheeks are very tender, about 2 hours.

+ Transfer the pork cheeks to a serving bowl and set aside someplace warm. Return the skillet to medium heat (careful, your pan is hot) and bring the braising liquid to a simmer. Reduce the liquid by half, about 5 minutes. Adjust the seasoning with salt and pepper as needed, then strain the liquid through a fine-mesh sieve into the serving bowl with the pork.

moroccan-spiced lamb shoulder chops braised with quince

QUINCE IS A ONCE COMMON BUT now rare fruit that deserves more love. It's related to pear and apple, but is fairly inedible when raw. Take a deep whiff of quince and you'll see what all the fuss is about—it has an amazing spicy-floral quality. Quince's dense raw texture is transformed by long, gentle cooking. This makes it an excellent companion to braised meats. It's also one of the latest-ripening non-citrus fruits around, which makes it a darling of seasonal eaters. Look for quince in late fall and winter in well-stocked supermarkets or specialty stores. Or, do what I did—plant a quince tree in your backyard. Lamb shoulder chops are a delicious braising cut and, when rubbed with an exotic Moroccan-influenced spice blend, pair perfectly with the quince.

MAKES 4 SERVINGS

For the spice rub:

1 tablespoon kosher salt

1 teaspoon ground cumin

1 teaspoon ground ginger

½ teaspoon ground cardamom

½ teaspoon freshly ground black pepper

½ teaspoon ground cinnamon

½ teaspoon smoked paprika

Pinch of ground cloves

Pinch of saffron (optional)

+ To make the spice rub, in a small bowl, combine the salt, cumin, ginger, cardamom, pepper, cinnamon, paprika, cloves, and saffron, if using.

+ Rub the lamb generously with the spice rub. If you have time, set the chops on a tray, cover, and refrigerate for 8 to 24 hours. (If you don't, the lamb will still be delicious.)

+ Move an oven rack to the center position and preheat the oven to 300 degrees F.

+ In a large cast-iron skillet with a lid or a Dutch oven set over medium-high heat, heat the oil. When the oil shimmers, add the lamb and sear on each side until deeply golden brown, 3 to 4 minutes. If the chops do not fit without crowding, sear the chops in batches. Set aside.

(continued)

For the braise:

4 (10-ounce) bone-in lamb
shoulder (blade) chops

2 tablespoons extra-virgin
olive oil, plus more as
needed

1 large onion, thinly sliced

4 cloves garlic, minced

1 cup chopped canned
tomatoes

2 wedges (½ lemon)
Salt-Preserved Meyer
Lemons (page 347),
seeded and chopped
(optional)

1 to 2 cups chicken broth

2 large quince
(about 1 pound)

2 tablespoons honey

Mashed potatoes, couscous,
or rice, for serving

¼ cup chopped almonds,
for garnish

¼ cup chopped fresh cilantro,
for garnish

✦ Add additional oil to the skillet if necessary, then add the onion, garlic, chopped tomatoes, and preserved lemon, if using. Scrape up any brown bits from the lamb that stuck to the bottom of the pan, and mix them in with the onion. Cook until the onions soften, 3 to 5 minutes. Add 1 cup of the broth to the skillet and stir to deglaze.

✦ Reduce the heat to medium-low and return the lamb to the skillet. Peel, core, and slice the quince into ½-inch slices, dropping them into the skillet as you go and tucking them in around the lamb. Drizzle the honey over the contents and, if necessary, add extra broth to bring the liquid about halfway up the side of the lambchops. Bring the liquid to a gentle simmer, then cover the skillet and transfer it to the oven.

✦ Cook until the quince and lamb are very tender and the lamb is pulling away from the bone, about 2 hours. Serve the lamb and a generous spoon of sauce, onions, and quince in shallow bowls with mashed potatoes, couscous, or rice. Garnished each bowl with chopped almonds and cilantro.

olive oil–rosemary cake with lemony glaze

SOME COMBINATIONS ARE SO CLASSIC THEY are nearly impossible to tire of: chocolate and peanut butter, tomato and basil, Fey and Poehler. So it is with rosemary and lemon—a flavor combo so great it works magic on everything from roast chicken to refreshing summer drinks to this cake. The herbal punch of rosemary perfumes this moist olive oil cake and the lemony glaze adds a lovely sweet-tart contrast. I think there is nothing better on a cold winter's day than a slice of this cake and a piping hot mug of Earl Grey tea.

MAKES 8 TO 12 SERVINGS

✦ Grease and flour a deep 9-inch round cake pan (see note). Move an oven rack to the center position and preheat the oven to 350 degrees F.

✦ In a medium bowl, whisk together the eggs, sugar, oil, milk, and lemon juice until well blended. In a large bowl, stir together the flour, cornmeal, baking soda, baking powder, and salt.

✦ Make a well in the center of the flour mixture, then pour the wet ingredients into the well and fold together until the batter is just blended.

✦ Fold in the rosemary and lemon zest, then scrape the batter into the prepared cake pan. Bake the cake until the top and sides are golden brown and a skewer inserted into the center of the cake comes out clean, 55 to 65 minutes.

✦ Set the pan on a rack for 10 to 15 minutes to cool, then remove the cake from the pan and allow it to cool completely, top-side up, on the rack.

(continued)

3 large eggs, lightly beaten

1¾ cups sugar

1 cup good quality extra-virgin olive oil

¾ cup whole milk

½ cup freshly squeezed lemon juice

2 cups all-purpose flour, sifted

2 tablespoons fine cornmeal

¾ teaspoon baking soda

½ teaspoon baking powder

½ teaspoon fine sea salt

1 tablespoon finely minced fresh rosemary, or more to taste

2 teaspoons lemon zest

For the glaze:

1½ cups powdered sugar

2 to 3 tablespoons freshly squeezed lemon juice

1 teaspoon lemon zest

✦ When the cake is completely cool, prepare the glaze. In a small bowl, stir together the powdered sugar, 2 tablespoons lemon juice, and the lemon zest until no lumps of sugar remain. If the glaze is too thick, add in a bit more lemon juice, a teaspoon at a time, until it is pourable.

✦ Place the cake and cooling rack on top of a sheet pan to catch drips, then pour the glaze onto the center of the cake. The natural dome of the cake will help the glaze spread out over the surface. Quickly but gently use a flat or offset spatula to evenly spread the glaze toward the edges of the cake. Allow the glaze to drip down the sides of the cake. Some will drip off the cake (that's okay—that's why you have a sheet pan under it).

✦ Let the glaze set for at least 30 minutes, then serve.

NOTE: The batter for this cake will fully utilize a 2½-inch deep, 9-inch round pan. If you do not own a deep cake pan, consider baking this cake in a 10-inch pan, or splitting the batter between 2 (8-inch) round cake pans. Adjust baking time as needed.

Preserving

persimmon-apple chutney

FOR AN EASY HOLIDAY APPETIZER, top a small round of brie with a generous dollop of this chutney, then bake the brie until it's melty. This chutney is also excellent served with pork, chicken, and soft cheeses of all kinds.

For this preserve you want to use crisp, non-astringent, Fuyu-type persimmons that are sweet while still firm. The astringent types, like Hachiya, are not suitable for this recipe.

MAKES 5 PINT JARS

+ If this is your first time water-bath canning, please review the basics on page 25.

+ Prepare a water-bath canner, 5 pint-size jars, and their lids.

+ Combine all the ingredients in a large, wide nonreactive pot over medium heat. Bring the chutney to a simmer and cook, stirring frequently, until the chutney is thick, about 25 minutes.

+ Ladle the chutney into the prepared hot jars, leaving ½-inch headspace. Remove any air bubbles, adjust the headspace, wipe the jar rims, and set the jar lids and bands according to manufacturer's directions.

+ Carefully lower the filled jars into the simmering water-bath canner. When the water has returned to a boil, cover the kettle, and set a timer for 10 minutes. When the jars have processed for 10 minutes, remove the canner from the heat and allow the jars to cool in the water for 5 minutes, then use a jar lifter to transfer the jars onto a clean kitchen towel to cool and set their seals.

+ Leave the jars alone until they have fully cooled—at least 8 but no more than 24 hours—then check the seals. Any jar that hasn't sealed should be refrigerated and used within 2 weeks. Jars with solid seals may be washed, labeled, and stored in a cool, dark place where they will keep for about 1 year.

PROCESSING AT A GLANCE

Method: Water-bath canning

Headspace: ½ inch

Processing time: 10 minutes in a boiling water-bath canner; adjust for altitude

---

3 pounds Fuyu-type persimmons, peeled, cored, and diced (about 7 cups)

1½ pounds Granny Smith apples, cored and diced (about 5 cups)

1 cup diced onion

1 lemon, scrubbed, seeded, and finely minced (peel and all!)

1 small hot pepper, such as serrano, seeded and finely chopped

1 clove garlic, minced

1 tablespoon minced fresh ginger

1 cup raisins

2 cups apple cider vinegar

½ cup granulated sugar

½ cup lightly packed light brown sugar

2 tablespoons mustard seeds

2 teaspoons curry powder

2 teaspoons kosher salt

½ teaspoon ground cinnamon

cranberry-pear-walnut conserve

THIS SWEET-TART CONSERVE IS SO MUCH better than the wiggly cranberry sauce with the ripples from the tin, so please don't limit it to Thanksgiving. I love this conserve with roast or sautéed chicken or pork, or as a component of a cheese plate, paired with a nice sharp cheddar.

MAKES 6 HALF-PINT JARS

+ If this is your first time water-bath canning, please review the basics on page 25.

+ Prepare a water-bath canner, 6 half-pint jars, and their lids.

+ In a wide, shallow saucepan set over medium-high heat, add the cranberries, pear, orange and lemon zests, orange and lemon juices, sugars, candied ginger, and pepper to taste.

+ Stirring frequently, bring the cranberry mixture to a simmer and cook until most of the cranberries burst and the sauce thickens, about 10 minutes. Stir in the walnuts and simmer for 5 more minutes. The sauce should be thick but pourable.

+ Ladle the cranberry sauce into the prepared hot jars, leaving ¼-inch headspace. Remove any air bubbles, wipe the jar rims, and set the jar lids and bands according to the manufacturer's directions.

+ Carefully lower the filled jars into simmering water-bath canner. When the water has returned to a boil, cover the kettle, and set a timer for 10 minutes. When the jars have processed for 10 minutes, remove the canner from the heat and allow the jars to cool in the water for 5 minutes, then use a jar lifter to transfer the jars onto a clean kitchen towel to cool and set their seals.

+ Leave the jars alone until they have fully cooled—at least 8 but no more than 24 hours—then check the seals. Any jar that hasn't sealed should be refrigerated and used within 2 weeks. Jars with solid seals may be washed, labeled, and stored in a cool, dark place where they will keep for about 1 year.

PROCESSING AT A GLANCE

Method: Water-bath canning

Headspace: ¼ inch

Processing time: 10 minutes in a boiling water-bath canner; adjust for altitude

---

6 cups fresh or frozen cranberries

2 cups peeled, diced pear

Zest of 2 oranges

Zest of 1 lemon

1½ cups freshly squeezed orange juice

¼ cup freshly squeezed lemon juice

1½ cups granulated sugar

1 cup lightly packed light brown sugar

2 tablespoons chopped candied ginger

Freshly ground black pepper

1 cup finely chopped walnuts

mustard three ways

THERE ARE RECIPES OUT THERE FOR canning mustard, but I don't see the point when this culinary staple is so easy to whip up in small batches and keeps for at least six months in the refrigerator. I prefer to make homemade mustard in very small quantities—a cup or two at a time—so that I can play with flavors. Here are a few of my favorites.

MAKES ABOUT 1 PINT

+ In a small bowl or jar, combine all the ingredients for the mustard of choice. Cover the bowl and let it sit at room temperature for 1 to 2 days, until the mustard seeds have absorbed almost all the liquid.

+ Decide how smooth you want your mustard. For chunky whole grain mustard, just leave the mixture as is. For a smoother mustard, use an immersion blender, blender, or mini food processor to puree the mixture to your desired texture. Add 1 to 2 tablespoons of water, if needed, to thin the mustard. For a perfectly smooth texture, like commercial Dijon, you can push the mustard through a fine-mesh sieve after pureeing.

+ Transfer the mustard to a small mason jar, lid tightly, and store in the refrigerator. This mustard is best if you give the flavors a few weeks to meld and mellow, but you can eat it right away if you like. The mustard keep for at least 6 months.

BASIC DIJON-STYLE MUSTARD

½ cup dry white wine

½ cup white wine vinegar

½ cup mustard seeds

2 tablespoons finely diced shallot or onion

1 teaspoon kosher salt

Pinch of cayenne pepper

WHOLE GRAIN PORTER MUSTARD

½ cup dark, sweet beer, such as porter

½ cup malt vinegar

½ cup mustard seeds (a mix of yellow and brown are nice)

1 clove garlic, minced

1 tablespoon lightly packed light brown sugar

1 teaspoon kosher salt

APPLE-MAPLE MUSTARD

½ cup apple cider vinegar

½ cup apple juice

½ cup mustard seeds

1 teaspoon kosher salt

1 tablespoon maple syrup

< Pictured clockwise from top: Whole Grain Porter, Basic Dijon-Style, Apple-Maple

spiced ginger carrots

CARROTS ARE GOOD FOR YOU, fermented foods are good for you, ginger is good for you, and turmeric-rich spices like curry are good for you. Therefore, it's possible this jar of spiced, naturally pickled ginger carrots is the healthiest food ever. But that's not why I make these carrots and spoon big heaping piles onto my plate. It's not why I add sparkly little shreds of these carrots to sandwiches, salads, or bean dishes, or mix them with thick yogurt for an easy dip. Nope, it's the flavor that keeps me coming back for more.

MAKES ABOUT 1 QUART JAR

✦ If this is your first time fermenting vegetables, please review the basics on page 41.

✦ In a medium bowl, stir together the carrots, cilantro, ginger, garlic, lime zest and juice, and salt. Set aside.

✦ In a small, dry cast-iron skillet over medium heat, toast the fennel seeds, mustard seeds, peppercorns, and coriander, shaking the skillet occasionally, until the spices are fragrant, 1 to 2 minutes. Do not let the spices burn. Scrape the spice blend into a mortar and grind with a pestle until the seeds are powdery. (Alternatively, pulse the spices in a spice grinder until coarsely ground.) Add the ground spices, curry, and cumin to the carrot mixture and mix together thoroughly.

✦ Pack the carrot mixture into a scrupulously clean widemouthed quart-size jar. Tamp the carrots down very firmly until the juices of the carrots rise up level with the carrot shreds themselves. Add the water, or a bit more or less as necessary, to bring the level of the liquid up over the shredded carrots. Weigh down the carrot shreds so they stay submerged.

2 pounds carrots, trimmed, peeled, and shredded (about 4 cups)

1 bunch fresh cilantro, trimmed and chopped

1 (4-inch) knob fresh ginger, peeled and shredded

1 teaspoon minced garlic

Zest and juice of 1 lime

1 tablespoon plus 1 teaspoon fine sea salt

1 teaspoon fennel seeds

1 teaspoon mustard seeds

1 teaspoon whole black peppercorns

½ teaspoon coriander seeds

½ teaspoon ground curry

½ teaspoon ground cumin

About ½ cup water

(continued)

+ Loosely seal the jar with a standard 2-piece lid, leaving the ring just fingertip tight, as you would for canning, to allow the gases of the fermentation process to escape. Leave the carrots at cool room temperature out of direct sun for 3 to 4 days. Check the ferment daily. Look for bubbles and other signs of fermentation, burp the lid to release any pent-up carbon dioxide in the jar, and taste the development of the carrots periodically with a clean spoon.

+ When you like the tang of the carrots, or after 4 days, transfer the carrots to the refrigerator, where they will keep for at least 4 months.

salt-preserved meyer lemons

THIS MIGHT BE THE MOST VERSATILE condiment in my refrigerator. Salt-preserved Meyer lemons are salty and tart but not sharp in the same way fresh lemons are. I toss them into braises, sauces, and dressings; mince them into pilafs; and generally rely on them as an easy all-purpose seasoning.

MAKES 2 QUART JARS

+ If this is your first time fermenting vegetables, please review the basics on page 41.

+ Prepare 2 widemouth quart-size jars, their lids, and a fermenting weight.

+ Cut 3 pounds of the lemons into quarters lengthwise. Reserve the remaining lemons for juice. In a large nonreactive bowl, toss the lemon quarters with the salt so that the lemons are lightly but uniformly coated.

+ Divide the lemons between 2 scrupulously clean widemouthed quart-size jars. Let the jars sit, covered, at room temperature for about 1 hour so that the salt can draw some of the juice from the lemons. After some juice is released, pack the lemons into the jar by pressing down firmly. You can use a spoon or your very clean fist, if the jar opening is large enough. The jar should fill halfway or more with lemon juice.

+ Juice the remaining 1 pound lemons, and add the extra juice to the jars. This should bring the juice level above the lemons, and to within about an inch of the top of each jar. Weigh down the lemons so they stay submerged.

(continued)

4 pounds organic Meyer lemons, scrubbed, divided

¼ cup kosher salt

+ Loosely seal the jar with a standard 2-piece lid, leaving the ring just fingertip tight, as you would for canning, to allow the gases of the fermentation process to escape. Leave the lemons at cool room temperature out of direct sunlight for 4 to 7 days. After 4 to 5 days, the lemon rinds should begin to take on a glossy translucency. When the rinds look translucent all the way through, or after 14 days, transfer the jar to the refrigerator. Let the lemons cure for another week in the refrigerator before using.

+ After 1 week in the refrigerator, the lemons can be used, but they will continue to mellow and the flavor will improve with longer aging. They will keep in the refrigerator for at least 6 months.

pressure-canned beans

IF YOU HAVE A PRESSURE CANNER, I highly recommend canning your own dry beans. This might seem a bit silly—after all, beans will keep perfectly well in their dry state for years, so why would you need to can them? In a word: convenience. What I've found is that an already-cooked, ready-to-go jar of garbanzo or black beans in my pantry makes me about nine hundred times more likely to actually use these beans for fast, affordable, and easy dinners. I get all the convenience of store-bought canned beans, but at the much lower dry-bean price, and without any of the concern about what aluminum cans might be leaching into my staple legumes.

MAKES 7 PINT OR ABOUT 3 QUART JARS

PROCESSING AT A GLANCE

Method: Pressure canning

Headspace: 1 inch

Processing time: 75 minutes for pints or 90 minutes for quarts at 11 PSI; adjust for altitude

---

2½ pounds dried beans, such as black, garbanzo, or kidney beans

3½ teaspoons fine sea salt

✦ If this is your first time pressure canning, please review the basics on page 32.

✦ Place the beans in a large pot and cover generously with fresh, cool water. Soak overnight. After at least 12 hours, and up to 18, drain the beans and discard the soaking liquid.

✦ Prepare the pressure canner, 7 widemouthed pint-size jars, and their lids.

✦ Return the beans to the large pot and cover with fresh water. Bring the beans to a gentle simmer over medium heat. Simmer for 30 minutes, or until just tender but firm.

✦ Ladle the beans into the prepared hot jars, filling three-quarters full, then top off with the hot cooking liquid to 1-inch headspace. Remove any air bubbles, adjust the headspace, wipe the jar rims, add ½ teaspoon salt to each pint jar, and set jar lids according to the manufacturer's directions.

✦ Double-check the water level in the pressure canner and adjust as necessary. Carefully lower the filled jars into the pressure canner.

Fasten the canner lid securely, increase the heat to high, wait for a full stream of steam to vent from the vent pipe or petcock, and fully exhaust the canner for 10 minutes. After exhausting the canner, set a counterweight or weighted gauge on the vent pipe or close the petcock to bring the canner up to pressure. Follow the manufacturer's directions for regulating heat to maintain the correct pressure throughout the processing time.

+ Process the pint jars for 75 minutes or quart jars for 90 minutes, then turn off the heat and allow the canner to naturally cool and completely depressurize.

+ After the canner has fully depressurized, open the pressure canner according to the manufacturer's directions, being careful of escaping steam. (I like to allow my jars to cool for 30 minutes in the canner after removing the weight from the vent pipe but before opening and unloading—I've found this cuts down on siphoning and leads to more reliable seals.)

+ Lift the jars straight up from the canner with a jar lifter and set them down on a clean kitchen towel to cool and set their seals. Let the jars cool undisturbed for at least 12 hours and up to 24. Check the seals and transfer any unsealed jars to the refrigerator for use within a few days. Remove the rings, wash jars to remove any processing residue, and store the sealed jars in a cool, dark place where they will keep for about 1 year.

NOTE: Try the pressure-canned bean variations on the following pages.

pressure-canned bean variations

2½ pounds small white beans, such as navy

1 quart tomato juice

½ cup minced onion

3 cloves garlic, minced

½ cup sugar

2 tablespoons Worcestershire sauce

2 tablespoons apple cider vinegar

1 tablespoon kosher salt

Pinch of mustard powder

BRITISH-STYLE BEANS

✦ Soak and prepare the beans as described on page 350. While beans are simmering, in a large nonreactive pot, combine the tomato juice, onion, garlic, sugar, Worcestershire sauce, vinegar, salt, and mustard powder and bring the mixture to a simmer.

✦ Drain the beans and fill the hot jars three-quarters full with the beans. Add the tomato sauce mixture to the jars, leaving 1-inch headspace. Proceed with canning as directed on page 350. Process pint jars for 75 minutes or quart jars for 90 minutes.

2½ pounds black beans

2 cups chicken or vegetable broth

2 cups tomato juice

½ cup minced red onion

4 cloves garlic, minced

1 tablespoon vinegar-based hot sauce, such as Cholula or Tabasco

1 tablespoon ground cumin

1 tablespoon kosher salt

1 teaspoon ground oregano

BLACK BEANS WITH CUMIN

✦ Soak and prepare the beans as described on page 350. While the beans are simmering, in a large nonreactive pot, combine the broth, tomato juice, onion, garlic, hot sauce, cumin, salt, and oregano and bring the mixture to a simmer.

✦ Drain the beans and fill the hot jars three-quarters full with the beans. Add the tomato sauce mixture to the jars, leaving 1-inch headspace. Proceed with canning as directed on page 350. Process pint jars for 75 minutes and quart jars for 90 minutes.

COWBOY BEANS WITH BACON

✤ Soak and prepare the beans as described on page 350. In a large nonreactive pot over medium heat, cook the bacon, stirring frequently, until the bacon is crisp and has rendered its fat. Use a slotted spoon to remove the bacon and set it aside. Pour out all but 1 tablespoon of the bacon fat from the pot.

✤ Add the onion, garlic, and jalapeño to the bacon fat and cook, stirring frequently, until the onion is translucent and caramelized, about 7 minutes. Add the broth, tomato juice, sugar, molasses, vinegar, Dijon, cloves, and allspice and stir well, then bring the mixture to a simmer.

✤ Drain the beans and fill the hot jars half-full with beans. Divide the bacon evenly between the jars, sprinkling it over the beans, then add more beans to fill each jar three-quarters full. Add the sauce mixture to the jars, leaving 1-inch headspace. Proceed with canning as directed on page 350. Process pint jars for 75 minutes and quart jars for 90 minutes.

2½ pounds pinto beans

½ pound thick-cut bacon, sliced ½-inch thick

1 cup minced onion

4 cloves garlic, minced

2 jalapeños, seeded and minced

2 cups chicken broth

1 cup tomato juice

¼ cup lightly packed light brown sugar

2 tablespoons dark molasses

2 tablespoons apple cider vinegar

2 tablespoons Dijon mustard

¼ teaspoon ground cloves

¼ teaspoon ground allspice

caramelized onions

TRUE SLOW-CARAMELIZED ONIONS TAKE TIME, BUT they aren't hard. The trick is to cook lightly salted sliced onions in a tall pot over moderate heat so that they release their moisture before they begin to brown. Only after the onions throw off their moisture and make a kind of soup do you increase the heat and start browning the onions. Because this process takes awhile, I like to make a big batch of caramelized onions in the winter when it's cold and I'm happy to stay inside. I spend several hours futzing with various kitchen projects, stirring my multitude of pots like a crazy alchemist, and come away with little golden jars of onions to use year-round.

MAKES ABOUT 7 HALF-PINT JARS

8 pounds yellow onions, cored and halved

About 4 tablespoons extra-virgin olive oil

Kosher salt

6 to 10 sprigs fresh thyme, tied in a tight bundle with kitchen string

½ cup red wine vinegar

½ cup dry red wine

½ cup sugar

Freshly ground black pepper

✦ In a food processor fitted with a narrow slicing disk, slice the onions. Try to keep each onion positioned so that it is sliced from root to stem, not from edge to edge. If all the slices look like half circles, you're slicing the wrong way. (You can also slice the onions by hand, if you have an extra 17 hours to kill.)

✦ Coat the bottom of a large, tall stockpot with the oil. As the food processor fills up, dump the sliced onions into the stockpot. Sprinkle each onion layer with a bit of salt as you add it, and toss the onions a bit as you go.

✦ When all the onions are sliced, put the stockpot over medium-low heat and cook, covered, until the onions start to release moisture. Periodically lift the lid and stir the onions to ensure they do not brown or stick. After about 1 hour, the onions should have deflated and reduced by about a third.

✦ When the level of moisture in the pot is about equal with the top of the onions, remove the lid and add the thyme to the pot. Use a spoon to push it into the mass of onions. Leave the pot uncovered and allow the onions to slowly reduce and caramelize. This can take several hours. Adjust the heat as needed and stir periodically so the onions do not burn but continue to darken. The entire mass of onions should slowly and uniformly take on color, getting progressively darker as they reduce.

✦ When the onions are reduced by half or more, are no longer soupy, and have taken on a light-golden color, add the vinegar, red wine, and sugar.

✦ Increase the heat to medium and finish caramelizing the onions. Stir often—at this stage, the onions can scorch quickly—and cook until the onions are a rich dark-caramel color and look moist but not at all liquidy.

✦ Remove the pot from the heat, fish out the bunch of thyme and discard, and adjust the seasoning with salt and pepper to taste. Ladle the caramelized onions into clean half-pint jars. Press a layer of plastic wrap down over the onions to prevent freezer burn, lid the jars, and transfer them to the refrigerator or freezer. The onions will keep for 5 days in the refrigerator and for 4 to 6 months in the freezer.

meyer lemon curd

WHEN I WAS A KID, MY mom would make me a four-layer cake with lemon-pie filling on my birthday. The first time I made lemon curd, my mind went back to that cake. It was like the lemon-pie filling had grown up, discovered mascara, and slipped into a damned sexy strapless sundress. Lemon curd is a head-turner—sweet, bright with citrus flavor, just a bit tart, smooth, and equally at home with a slice of the cake from Berries, Cake, and Cream (page 224) or as the star of a high-end French tartlet.

When Meyer lemons come into season, I make a batch or three of this curd and tuck jars in the freezer so I can enjoy my favorite lemon curd for months. If you can't track down Meyer lemons, this recipe is equally delicious (though a bit more puckery) with regular lemons. Or substitute lime juice and lime zest for lime curd. You really can't go wrong.

MAKES ABOUT 7 HALF-PINT JARS

1 cup plus 2 tablespoons (2¼ sticks) butter, at room temperature

3 cups sugar

1 tablespoon grated Meyer lemon zest

6 large eggs

6 large egg yolks

2 cups freshly squeezed Meyer lemon juice

+ Prepare 7 clean, dry half-pint jars and set them near your work space.

+ In the bowl of a food processor fitted with the metal blade, pulse the butter, sugar, and lemon zest until combined. Scrape down the bowl.

+ Run the blade for about 1 minute to fully mix the butter and sugar, then add in the whole eggs and egg yolks while the food processor is running. Blend until creamy, pale yellow, and a bit frothy, about 1 minute. Scrape down the bowl to ensure the mixture is fully blended.

+ Transfer the egg mixture to a large, heavy-bottomed, nonreactive saucepan. Add the lemon juice to the saucepan and stir. The mixture may look a bit curdled at this stage, but it will be fine as it heats up.

+ Turn the heat to low and cook the curd mixture until it is smooth and thickens, stirring constantly. When the mixture reaches 170 degrees F and becomes thick enough to coat the back of a spoon, remove the pan from the heat.

+ Strain the curd through a fine-mesh sieve, then ladle it into the pre-pared half-pint jars. Cut small squares of plastic wrap or waxed paper and press them down onto the curd to prevent a skin from forming. Lid the jars and transfer them to the refrigerator. The curd will thicken as it cools. For long term storage, transfer the cooled jars to the freezer.

+ The curd will keep for 2 weeks in the refrigerator or up to 6 months in the freezer.

Home Care

petite mason jar beeswax candles

THESE CANDLES ARE SO PINTEREST-PERFECT ADORABLE they'd almost be
irritating if they weren't so functional too. Beeswax burns long—expect
twelve-plus hours out of each of these petite candles—so they are helpful to
have on hand for winter storm power outages. They also smell great naturally, won't release any weird chemicals into your home when you burn
them, and make absolutely delightful last-minute holiday gifts.

MAKES 12 MINI CANDLES

+ If necessary, chop the beeswax into rough chunks and melt it in a
double boiler set over medium heat until just liquid. Beeswax takes a
long time to melt, so be patient. Don't rush the melting—you don't
want to scorch the wax.

+ If necessary, prime the wick and set the wick tabs. To do this, cut
12 wicks, each about 1 inch longer than the mason jar is tall. Set out a
sheet of parchment or waxed paper, then dip the wick into the melting
beeswax several times. Lay the dipped wick onto the parchment and,
when the wick is just cool enough to handle, pull it tight and straight
then allow it set completely. Repeat with each wick, then feed the
primed wicks through the wick tabs and crimp the tabs tightly at the
very bottom of the wick. You don't want the wick to stick out below
the wick tab; if it does, trim it. If you are using pre-primed wicks that
are already tabbed, just smooth the wick perfectly straight. It can help
to roll it between your palms to soften the wax.

+ When all your wicks are set and tabbed and the beeswax has melted,
begin ladling or pouring the melted wax into each jar. Go slow and
steady, filling each jar about one-third of the way. Arrange each wick
so the wick tab is perfectly centered at the bottom of the jar and the
wick is straight. Use a skewer or a chopstick to press the wick tab down
into the cooling wax.

(continued)

2½ pounds clean beeswax or
beeswax pastilles

#2 square braided cotton
wick and 12 square wick
tabs or 12 pre-waxed
#2 square cotton wicks
with tabs

24 thin bamboo skewers

Scotch tape

12 (4-ounce) mason jars

✦ Rest two bamboo skewers across the edges of the jar, one on each side of the wick, to hold the wick steady and centered. Press the bamboo skewers into the wick and tape them together snuggly. Adjust the wick as needed to keep it nice and centered, then slowly fill the jars with wax to within about ¼ inch of the lip of the jar. Allow the candles to cool completely without touching.

✦ Depending on how quickly the candles cool, you may end up with a dip in the surface of the candle near the wick. This doesn't impact your candle's usefulness at all, but if it bothers you aesthetically, just top up the candle with a bit more melted beeswax.

notes on beeswax candle-making

If you have your own hive, or know someone who does, you may be able to get inexpensive raw-state beeswax. Cleaning beeswax is simple: just chop it up and put in it a big pot with at least as much water as you have wax. Set everything over medium heat, and bring the temperature up until the wax melts. Give it the occasional stir and prod to help any trapped grit or propolis out of the wax.

Take the pot off the heat and let everything cool. The clean wax will float to the surface and harden while any dirt and contaminants sink to the bottom. Remove the clean wax block from the surface, scrape any contaminants from the bottom of the wax, and let the block of wax dry. Occasionally, a few rounds of melting and cooling are necessary to get perfectly clean wax. Already cleaned beeswax can be purchased online—I like the pastilles, which melt quickly and evenly without chopping.

The trickiest part of candle making is figuring out what wick to use with what candle. If your wick is too small, it won't melt the wax effectively. If it's too large, it will burn too hot and can overheat the mason jar. Different waxes burn differently, confounding the issue (i.e., a soy wax candle of one size and a beeswax candle of the same size do not necessarily need the same size wick). I found through numerous trials that a #2 square cotton wick is just right for a 4-ounce mason jar beeswax candle, but if you chose a different size container or a different type of wax, your wick size will probably be different.

Wick tabs are those little metal things you see at the very bottom of commercial candles. They keep the wick nice and centered. You can make container candles without wick tabs, but for the small extra cost, they really do simplify candle making. If you are gung-ho about the thriftiness, you can reuse appropriate size wick tabs too.

citrus vinegar concentrate

NOTHING COULD BE SIMPLER THAN THIS cleaning vinegar boosted with essential citrus oils. You can use leftover peels from grapefruit, orange, lemon, mandarin, or a combo—whatever you have. The citrus peels infuse plain distilled white vinegar with their delightful scent and cleaning power. Throw in some fresh herbage, like rosemary, lemon verbena, sage, or mint, and you've got a yummy-smelling citrus cleaner boosted with the power of d-Limonene, a powerful grease cutter.

MAKES A VARIABLE AMOUNT

Citrus peels

A few sprigs rosemary or other fragrant garden herb

Distilled white vinegar

+ Fill a big, airtight jar (I use a half-gallon mason jar) halfway with citrus peels, then add the rosemary. Exact measurements aren't that important. Fill the jar with vinegar, tightly lid, then store the mixture somewhere out of the way for at least 2 weeks and up to several months. You can add more peels to the jar over time if you need to. Just make sure that there's enough vinegar in the jar to fully cover all the peels.

+ When the vinegar has taken on a golden color and a strong citrus scent, strain the cleaner through a sieve lined with a coffee filter or a piece of clean loose-weave cloth. Discard or compost the citrus rinds and herbs, and store the citrus vinegar in a glass jar. This cleaner will last for at least a year, though the citrus scent may fade over time.

To use:

+ Add ½ cup concentrate to a 32-ounce spray bottle, then fill the bottle with water for an all-purpose acidic cleaner for cutting through mineral and hard-water deposits. Or, spray undiluted on greasy areas like kitchen vent filters and stovetops. The citrus oil in this cleaner is an excellent grease cutter.

NOTE: Because this is an acidic cleaner, don't use it on delicate stone like marble or anything else that needs a pH-neutral cleaner.

diy oven cleaner that really works

BACK BEFORE I GAVE ANY THOUGHT to the dangers of many common household cleaners, I loved oven cleaner. Oh, sure, it made me cough and my lungs hurt when I sprayed it on the oven, and it stank, and when some got on my hands (because I totally ignored the part about putting on gloves) there was an ominous burning feeling. But I was lazy and I didn't clean my oven or my stovetop very often, so by the time I couldn't ignore the burnt-on grease any longer, nothing but oven cleaner would cut through the mess.

When I got wise to the dangers of products like oven cleaner, I tried many natural alternatives, most of which involved baking soda and scrubbing and *scrubbing* and SCRUBBING. Now, a paste of baking soda is a great option for routine cleanups of your oven, but if it gets to the burnt-on grime stage, you need something more powerful. That's where this cleaner comes in.

Washing soda is a powerful alkaline cleaner. I use it when I need something to really bust through grease, like in my laundry detergent and in this oven cleaner. It's powerful stuff, so wear gloves and be careful with it, but unlike spray-on commercial oven cleaners, you won't be subjected to a barrage of noxious fumes.

MAKES ENOUGH TO CLEAN ONE 30-INCH OVEN

✦ Put on a pair of disposable gloves. In a small bowl, combine the washing soda, baking soda, and soap. Add 1 cup of the hot water and use an immersion blender to mix the cleaner into a thick, smooth paste. Add more water as needed to achieve a paste about the texture of pancake batter. Once you add the hot water, work quickly—as the paste cools, it will gel and become harder to apply. Use immediately.

6 tablespoons washing soda

6 tablespoons baking soda

3 tablespoons liquid castile soap

1 to 2 cups very hot water

Distilled white vinegar, for wiping the oven

(continued)

To use:

✦   Make sure your oven is completely cool. Remove the racks and any other removable parts from the oven. Wipe out any loose or carbonized grime. Scoop the warm, just-mixed oven cleaner into your gloved hand and spread a thin, uniform layer all over the inside walls and door of the oven. Let the oven cleaner sit for at least 4 hours or overnight.

✦   Wipe out any big chunks of the oven cleaner. Dip a scouring pad in water and scrub any particularly tough areas of burned-on grease. Fill a spray bottle with distilled vinegar. Working one section of the oven at a time, spray a wall with the vinegar and wipe down the residue. If needed, use a toothbrush to scrub the corners and crevices. Repeat until the entire oven has been sprayed and wiped. Finish by wiping the oven dry.

Personal Care

slippery shaving soap

THIS IS A CREAMY SHAVING SOAP for men or women. The lightweight kaolin clay increases the "slip" of this soap so razors glide over it smoothly, and the avocado and castor oil contribute a thick, moisturizing, and protective lather.

MAKES ABOUT 1½ POUNDS, AFTER CURING

9 ounces cold water

3.4 ounces pure granular lye

8 ounces coconut oil

7 ounces lard

7 ounces olive oil

1 ounce castor oil

1 ounce avocado oil

2 tablespoons kaolin clay

1 to 2 tablespoons essential oils (optional)

✦ Before you begin, read the basic steps of soap making and all safety information and notes on page 92. Empty your sink if necessary, get on your protective gear (eye goggles, gloves, long sleeves, etc.), and make sure kids, pets, and other trip hazards are out of your work space. Prepare a 2-pound soap mold.

✦ In a heat-resistant pitcher, add the water. Set the pitcher in the sink. In a small stainless steel bowl, precisely measure the lye. Carefully add the lye to the water. *(Never add water to lye!)* The water will become cloudy and will get quite hot. It may even "smoke" a bit—this is normal. Do not breathe the fumes from this reaction. Stir with an old plastic or stainless steel spoon, or disposable wooden chopsticks, to fully dissolve the lye, then let the lye solution sit to cool while you melt the oils.

✦ In a large stainless steel pot over medium heat, carefully add the lard and oils. Warm them slowly together, stirring occasionally until just melted. Add the kaolin clay and whisk to combine. Remove the mixture from the heat and set aside to cool.

✦ When the lye and the oils are both around 110 degrees F—anything from about 90 to about 120 degrees F is fine, but the lye and the oil should be within about 15 degrees of each other—set the pot in the sink and carefully pour the lye solution into the oil. *(Never add the oil to the lye!)*

✦ Stir the mixture gently with an immersion blender (not turned on) to help bring the oils and lye together, then turn the immersion blender on the lowest speed. Blend the soap thoroughly, moving the blender around the pot, until the mixture thickens and achieves trace, 12 to 20 minutes.

✦ Add any essential oils as desired, blend to fully incorporate, then pour and scrape the soap into the prepared mold. Cover the soap with a layer of plastic wrap, then insulate or chill soap as desired to achieve a fully gelled or a no-gel soap.

✦ Leave your protective gear on and clean your soap-making equipment and work area very well. Finish cleanup by lightly wiping down anything that may have come in contact with lye with undiluted vinegar.

✦ After 24 hours, check the soap. Put on a pair of disposable gloves and give the soap a gentle press to see if it easily pulls away from the edges of the mold. If the soap is firm, turn the soap out of the mold. If not, give the soap another 12 to 24 hours to cure in the mold before turning out.

✦ If necessary, slice the soap into bars. Set the soap in a cool, out-of-the-way place on a wire rack. Cover it loosely with a lint-free cloth and turn the soap periodically. Cure for 4 weeks before using.

To use:

✦ Rub into a rich lather with your hands or a shaving brush, then apply to body or face and shave.

oat and milk skin-soothing bath soak

THIS IS THE ULTIMATE BATH SOAK for when your skin needs to relax as
much as you do. The milk powder in this blend contains protein and lactic
acid, which help to gently exfoliate and firm the skin. The oat flour soothes
inflamed and irritated skin, while the baking soda relieves itchiness.

Bergamot, lavender, and lemon—what I call the "Tea, Earl Grey, Hot"
essential oil blend—is soothing and calming for most skin types. It's just lovely
in this application, but other essential oils can be substituted as desired. If you
prefer to make this bath soak in larger quantities, scale up as needed.

MAKES ENOUGH FOR 1 SOAK

+   In a medium bowl, blend all the ingredients together. Add the bath
soak directly to a hot bath, or store it in an airtight container for later
use. The bath soak will last for at least 6 months, though the essential
oil scent may fade over time.

To use:

+   Add the bath soak to a hot bath and soak for 15 to 30 minutes.

¼ cup powdered milk

¼ cup baking soda

¼ cup oat flour

15 drops lavender
essential oil

8 drops bergamot
essential oil

4 drops lemon essential oil

fizzy bath bombs

THESE BATH BOMBS REQUIRE A BIT more work than your basic bath salts, but they are just so fun! Basically, you're doing a chemistry experiment in the name of spa day. How could anyone not like that combo? These make great gifts, and kids love them.

MAKES ABOUT EIGHT ½-CUP BATH BOMBS

+ In a large bowl, mix together the baking soda, cornstarch, citric acid, and Epsom salts. In a small bowl, mix 2 tablespoons of the water with the food coloring and essential oils, if using.

+ With one hand, stir the dry mixture constantly with a whisk. With the other hand, drizzle in the wet mixture a drop at a time until it just holds together if you squeeze a bit in one hand. If the mixture doesn't hold together at all, drizzle more drops of water, one or two at a time. If you start to see fizzing, that means there is too much water in one area and you should stir that area quickly to distribute the moisture.

+ Pack the mixture into molds very firmly, then smooth the surface of each bath bomb. Carefully unmold the bath bombs onto a sheet pan or other flat, dry surface. If any of the bath bombs break during unmolding, just scoop up the crumbs and repack them in the mold.

+ Let the bath bombs dry for about 24 hours, until fully dry. Package them as desired for gifts or use for your own personal spa day. Kept away from moisture, the bath bombs will last for at least 6 months, though the essential oil scent may fade over time.

To use:

+ Fill a tub with hot water and drop in 1 or 2 bath bombs. Enjoy the fizzing-geyser experience.

(continued)

2 cups baking soda

1½ cups cornstarch

1 cup citric acid

½ cup Epsom salts

2 to 4 tablespoons water

Food color (optional)

20 drops essential oil (optional)

notes on fizzy bath bombs

Dry, a bath bomb is yummy-smelling but rather boring. But when a bath bomb hits the water, the alkaline baking soda and the acidic citric acid react to create a frothing, bubbling, foaming volcano of fun. Use this recipe as a template and customize away. Just keep in mind a few tricks to making great bath bombs.

Getting the dry mixture wet enough to be moldable without activating the acid-base reaction doesn't take much water! Stir constantly as you sprinkle the water over the baking soda mixture.

Mix the food coloring into your water before sprinkling—liquid food colorings often contain enough liquid to activate the acid-base reaction if you try to color your bath bombs after already achieving the right texture.

Bath bombs work best when you can pack them tightly, so use a stiff plastic or metal mold, like a muffin tin, that won't deform when you press the mixture in.

These gift are the best when you match the color and fragrance. I like a purple color with lavender essential oil and a pale yellow-green color with lemongrass essential oil.

pucker up lip-soothing balm

A GOOD LIP BALM WILL HAVE a beeswax to oil ratio of between 1:3 to 1:5. So, for every gram of beeswax, you'll want three to five grams of oil. If you prefer a firmer lip balm, are using purely liquid oils, or live in a hot environment, you'll want to err of the side of less oil to beeswax. If you like a softer texture, are using oils that are solid at room temperature (like coconut oil), or live someplace that never gets too hot, you can use a bit more oil to beeswax.

Within the general 1:3 to 1:5 ratio, you can play around with the oils you use. I like a firm balm that isn't sticky, so I make my lip balms at about 1:3 and blend several different oils and butters. If you don't keep a variety of body care oils on hand, you can make a perfectly respectable lip balm using one part beeswax to three parts olive oil and dropping in any skin-friendly essential oils you like. While you can use measuring spoons to portion out the ingredients for this balm, your results will be more accurate if you measure by weight. I set my kitchen scale to grams for this purpose.

MAKES ABOUT 45 GRAMS, ENOUGH TO FILL TWO ¾- TO 1-OUNCE LIP BALM TINS OR ABOUT 10 STANDARD-SIZE LIP-BALM TUBES

+ In a small double boiler, or in the microwave set at medium-low power, melt the beeswax, shea butter, and coconut oil together. Add the castor and sweet almond oils, vitamin E, and essential oils to the melted beeswax mixture and stir to combine.

+ While the balm is still warm and liquid, pour it into a small, shallow tins or clean lip balm tubes. The balm will last for at least 6 months, though the essential oil scent may fade over time.

To use:

+ Rub lightly over dry or chapped lips as often as needed.

10 grams beeswax

5 grams shea butter

5 grams coconut oil

10 grams food-grade castor oil

10 grams sweet almond oil

10 drops vitamin E oil

7 drops peppermint essential oil

3 drops lemon essential oil

3 drops bergamot essential oil

Acknowledgments

To Mom and Dad, for putting up with eighteen years of food experiments, and to Bella and Oliver, for putting up with a year of recipe testing.

To Theresa Loe, for being my eagle eye when everything seemed blurry.

To Sarah Forrest, Lauren Gardiner, Lisa Simpson, and Kristen Ward, for keeping me sane-ish through this process and providing me with loads of wine for "recipe testing." To Colin and Johanna Coolbaugh, for your incredible patience despite four Cards Against Humanity expansion sets.

To the team at Sasquatch Books, without whom a haphazard stack of recipes and ramblings could never have grown up to become a real book. Susan Roxborough, Em Gale, Michelle Hope Anderson, Charity Burggraaf, and Anna Goldstein, thank you all for your skill and caring professionalism.

To the regular readers of my blog, *Northwest Edible Life*, who are the reason I was offered the opportunity to write a book, and the reason I accepted. I just hope this work makes you proud.

Extra special thanks to my recipe testers. When I asked for help, you guys were there. Your generosity with time and ingredients helped shape and improve this book more than you know. To Alan Post, Amaret Johnson, Amber Karr, Amber Shehan, Anne Figge, Beth Cummings, Beth Price, Betsy True, Blair Wardwell, Caitlin Lawrence, Carol Simpson, Caroline Minkowski, Caroline Mitchell Carrico, Cassie Rauk, Chrissy Mullender, Colleen and Mark Richardson, Coree and Adam Howard, Cory Knight, Crystal Jeffrey, Crystal Warsop, Cyndia Smith, Cynthia Scheiderer, David Hughes, Deanna Camp, Deanna Zipp, Diana Rose, Edith Jensen,

Eileen Conner, Emily Slofstra, Erin McCain-Anderson, Evey Frerotte, Grace Judson, Gwenn Weiss, Heather Laidlaw Kraft, Jacquelyn Speare, Janet Newman Sclar, Janet Parks, Jeffiner Fornuff, Jennie Norman, Jenny Hagglund, Jesamine Gilmour, Jessica Margarito, Joanna Lepore, John and Julie Schmidlkofer, Julie Shipman, K. Coghlan, Kari Urberg Carlson, Karyn Brudnicki, Kat Satnik, Kathleen Love, Kathy Dennis, Kelly O'Keefe, Klark and Kristi Dahlman, Lanette Lepper, Lenny Demoranville, Lévis Thériault, Linda Lee, Liz Larson, Maiya Martin Burbank, Margaret Curtis, Margaret Johnston, Marian Martin, Mary Glod, McCain-Anderson, Merrie James-Bell, Michael Sanders, Michelle Morrell, Mimi Waltke, Miranda Jackson, Nicki Albrecht, Nicole and Thor Stoddard, Nicole Matisse and Dwight Duke, O'Bryan and Daniel Worley, Pam Schaw, Paul Haak, Paula Bock, Rebecca Linde, Renate Kroll, Rhiannon Laurie, Rhonda Hancock, Sally E. Trulson, Sara Kidd, Sara Schroeter, Shannon Thomsen, Sheila K. Gray, Staci Sirois, Stuart Whitby, Sue Butler, Sue Denham, Susanne Wiggins, Suzanne Joneson, Tiffany Coleman, Tori, Casey, Teiya, Traci Stenson Hildner, Trisha, Victoria Patience, Vivian Bliss, Wendy Buss, Wendy Coffman, Wendy Posson, Wynne Kelch, and several others who prefer not to be named publicly, this book would not have been possible without you. My most sincere gratitude.

To Nick, always, for building a hands-on life with me.

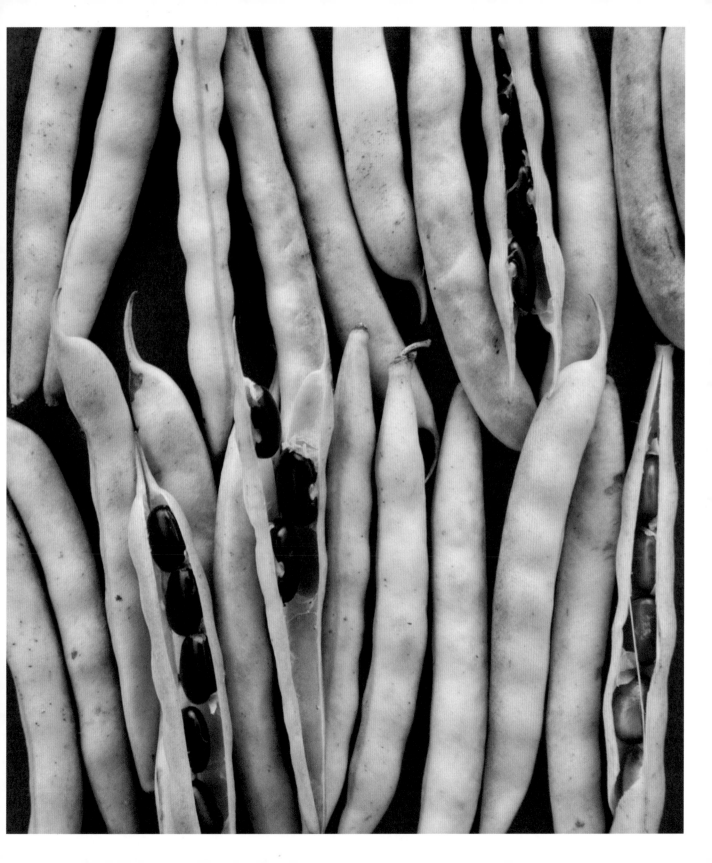

Index

Note: Photographs are indicated by *italics*.

The Hands-On Home

Conversions

VOLUME

UNITED STATES	METRIC	IMPERIAL
¼ tsp.	1.25 ml	
½ tsp.	2.5 ml	
1 tsp.	5 ml	
½ Tbsp.	7.5 ml	
1 Tbsp.	15 ml	
⅛ c.	30 ml	1 fl. oz.
¼ c.	60 ml	2 fl. oz.
⅓ c.	80 ml	2.5 fl. oz.
½ c.	125 ml	4 fl. oz.
1 c.	250 ml	8 fl. oz.
2 c. (1 pt.)	500 ml	16 fl. oz.
1 qt.	1 l	32 fl. oz.

LENGTH

UNITED STATES	METRIC
⅛ in.	3 mm
¼ in.	6 mm
½ in.	1.25 cm
1 in.	2.5 cm
1 ft.	30 cm

WEIGHT

AVOIRDUPOIS	METRIC
¼ oz.	7 g
½ oz.	15 g
1 oz.	30 g
2 oz.	60 g
3 oz.	90 g
4 oz.	115 g
5 oz.	150 g
6 oz.	175 g
7 oz.	200 g
8 oz. (½ lb.)	225 g
9 oz.	250 g
10 oz.	300 g
11 oz.	325 g
12 oz.	350 g
13 oz.	375 g
14 oz.	400 g
15 oz.	425 g
16 oz. (1 lb.)	450 g
1 ½ lb.	750 g
2 lb.	900 g
2¼ lb.	1 kg
3 lb.	1.4 kg
4 lb.	1.8 kg

TEMPERATURE

OVEN MARK	FAHRENHEIT	CELSIUS	GAS
Very cool	250–275	130–140	½–1
Cool	300	150	2
Warm	325	165	3
Moderate	350	175	4
Moderately hot	375	190	5
	400	200	6
Hot	425	220	7
	450	230	8
Very Hot	475	245	9

About the Author

ERICA STRAUSS is the founder of *Northwest Edible Life*, one of the most popular and well-respected edible-gardening and urban-homesteading blogs in the country. From her one-third acre near Seattle, Washington, Erica grows mountains of vegetables and fruit, keeps chickens and ducks, and writes about her approach to hands-on productive homekeeping.

Erica has written for numerous national magazines, including *Urban Farm*, *Chickens*, and *Hobby Farms*. One of her most popular blog posts was selected for inclusion in the prestigious *Best Food Writing 2013*.

Erica and her family were featured in *Backyard Roots: Lessons on Living Local From 35 Urban Farmers*, a book of photoessays showcasing notable West Coast urban homesteaders, and on the award-winning national PBS television show *Growing A Greener World*.